PROJECT IMPACT REPORTS

CHATTANOOGA

MISSION INCREASE
CHATTANOOGA

rethinking the development of people

979-8-2878-7490-2

Dialogues In Action
69 Nansen Summit
Lake Oswego, OR 97035
503.329.4816
dialoguesinaction.com

CONTENTS

INTRODUCTION TO THE PROJECT

The aim of Project Impact is to develop in nonprofits the ability to do credible self-studies of their impact. As such, this is a capacity-building project.[1] The reports in this compendium are written by the nonprofit teams and represent the findings from their data collection and analysis.

This project follows the traditions of participatory evaluation. In a participatory evaluation approach, those who are doing the work also become the evaluators of the effects of the work. This requires capacity-building for the teams, for a self-study form of evaluation requires the development of skills, theoretical understanding, practice in the techniques, and attention to fidelity of implementation in order to ensure the proper level of rigor.

The development of evaluation capacity takes time and iteration. It requires both instruction and practice – training in some of the leading techniques of research accompanied by ongoing applications and practice.

1 This project is primarily focused on developing the ability of staff teams to implements self-studies about the effects of their programs. It is not designed to provide an experimental or quasi-experimental version of impact evaluation. Instead, it is an effort to upgrade the existing capability of each organization and give them to tools to gather data on the attributed impact both qualitatively and quantitatively from the subjects they serve.

This project recognizes the power of partnership, the enrichment of cross-pollination of ideas among like-minded organizations, the durable impact of a learning community, and the potential inspiration for a sector when exemplars are developed and elevated.

Project Impact takes teams of leaders from nonprofits through a process of discovery about the power of evaluation. The idea is to develop the ability to see and communicate the effects of the programs on the people they are designed to serve. There are three primary movements to the project: (1) Intended impact, (2) Inquiry, and (3) Implication.

Project Design

The project begins with a focus on the work of identifying and clarifying the intended impact of each of the participating programs. Once the ideas have been developed and indicators identified, the teams then design a questionnaire to collect data about quantitative measures and a qualitative interview protocol to collect qualitative data. These data are analyzed. Themes are identified and then translated into findings. From the findings, the teams develop program responses and communiques of their impact.

The fundamental elements of the Project Impact follow an arc of evaluation design:

Part 1 - Intended Impact

This project begins with the identification and clarification of what effects are intended through the work of each of the projects. Each team develops an articulation of intended impact to include the components necessary for evaluation design.

A. Main Ideas of Impact

Each team identifies and crafts ideas of impact to frame the intention of direct impact for the program. In some cases, these ideas are mapped in relation to the secondary and tertiary impacts of the program to gain clarity about the fundamental notions of desired effect as a direct consequence of the program or service rendered.

B. "What We Mean"

From these primary ideas, the teams then develop a brief explication of the meaning of their ideas of impact. This translates ideas that are occasionally technical and into messages accessible to all.

C. Quantitative Indicators

Teams then identify Quantitative indicators for each of the ideas. The aim is to generate five or six of the most critical indicators for each idea, paying attention to the data power, proxy power, and communication power of each of the key ideas. As well, the intent in this step is to identify a range of cognitive, affective, and behavioral indicators that can be measured through metrics.

D. Qualitative Indicators

Teams also identify qualitative indicators in this stage. These indicators are articulations of the structural and qualitative elements of growth and development that signal progress toward key ideas of impact. The qualitative indicators become the basis for the protocol construction to inform the in-depth interviews in the inquiry phase.

E. Principles of Change

Recognizing that an underlying logic exists for each program, the teams articulate the rationale for their intervention. This step connects what they do (action) to what will result from what they do (outcome). Each team builds a set of principles that explain why the do what they do in the way they do it. In so doing, the underlying philosophy of logic is exposed and can then be examined through the data from the evaluation.

This section of the project leads each team to develop a clear theory of change, including the outcomes, indicators, and principles embedded in the particular approach that is implemented by each team.

Part 2 - Inquiry

In the inquiry stage of the project, each team designs and implements a strategy for data gathering. These take two forms: a questionnaire to collect quantitative data and an in-depth interview to gather qualitative data.

A. Quantitative Data and Analysis

For each of the quantitative indicators, teams construct items for a questionnaire. Since these projects are not intended to provide experimental or quasi-experimental inquiry, the attribution of effect is built into the questionnaire items. The questionnaire is deployed, in most cases, to the entire population of recipients the program reaches. Data are analyzed mostly using measures of central tendency. The teams then design displays of the data and narrative for their report.

B. Qualitative Data and Analysis

The development of a qualitative design encompasses a number of steps, including the following:

1. Protocol Design. Each team designs an in-depth interview protocol that uses the *Heart Triangle*™

method of question design. These produces a protocol of about nine sequences of questions (18 questions in total) to be used as a guide for seeking data about the awareness and reflection of subjects' structural shifts and developments of growth and progress.

2. **Sample.** Each team identifies a sample of subjects using a purposeful stratified technique to identify a selection representing of the population being served.
3. **Data Collection.** Interviews a convened, most lasting between 45 minutes and 1 hour in length. Data are collected via notes during the interview, and then augmented immediately following the interview to provide a substantive rendering of the interview.
4. **Data Analysis.** Team members apply a four-step model of analysis to each of the interviews. This process provides them with an accessible version of analysis and interpretation to illuminate the primary themes from each interview. While the process is accessible, working through the data from each interview four times using different lenses of analysis each time provides a rigor to the analytical process that yields insight far beyond what is overt and obvious in the data.
5. **Thematics.** Through a guided and facilitative process, the entire data corpus is then examined. Themes are mapped through meta-analysis of the emerging insights.
6. **Findings.** The teams then examine each of the themes to discover and communicate the findings. These are rendered with explanation, illustration from the raw data, and significance.

Part 3 - Implications

The intent of the project is not to leave teams simply with a report about their program's effects, but rather to use the insights from the evaluation to guide the further development of the program. This takes two forms:

A. Program Adjustments

The team then takes each of the findings from the evaluation and considers possible program adjustments informed by the discoveries of the evaluation. This keeps the evaluation relevant for program application and improvement.

B. Program Experiments

In addition, the teams work to identify potential design experiments that they might run as an implication of the insights gained through the evaluation.

In this stage, the teams also begin to develop a report of the evaluation findings as well as other possible communiques of their discoveries to staff, stakeholders, funders, and other members of the community.

The Reports

The reports from the organizations in this cohort are included in the following compendium. These include highlights from the three movements of Project Impact. For each participating organization, there is an explication of the primary findings from the evaluation accompanied by the programmatic responses of strategy and design. Since each organization has unique strategy and ethos, each report exhibits unique character and personality. Each report also includes both "prove" findings (evidence of impacts being achieved) and "improve" findings (areas for attention and further development). These reports are windows into the effects of the work of these organizations in the lives of the people they serve.

LIVING FREE

Cara Woodall

Organization and Program Overview

Introduction to Organization

Living Free exists to facilitate hope, faith and freedom by connecting and equipping people with solutions for better living. Living Free's Biblically-based small groups provide a safe place where group members face their life-controlling issues and find lasting hope through Jesus. By connecting the Word of God, the Spirit of God and the people of God, Living Free is able to restore hope, empower people and create community.

Program Description

Churches, recovery and counseling centers, jails and community organizations across the globe use Living Free curriculum in small group settings to help participants learn to overcome life-controlling issues. Living Free groups provide the participants a safe place to face their challenges and find lasting hope through Jesus. The small groups typically meet once a week and are led by a facilitator who helps the group study God's Word. Living Free curriculum is available for a wide range of topics including, but not limited to anger, depression, forgiveness, addiction, family restoration, parenting, grief, and peacemaking. The group members find encouragement, accountability, connection and Biblical truths that provide relevant solutions for their struggles.

Intended Impacts

Living Free participants cope with life's challenges with positive Godly choices. Living Free participants are free from addictions and destructive coping mechanisms. They utilize the Word of God, Spirit of God and people of God to face and resolve life's challenges.

Living Free participants grow in spiritual maturity. Living Free participants strengthen their relationship with God, experience peace and confidence found in their identity in Christ, and exhibit Christ-like character and values.

Living Free participants build and maintain healthy relationships. Living Free participants overcome generational challenges to strengthen and maintain healthy relationships with family, friends and co-workers.

Living Free participants lead productive lives. Living Free participants maintain employment, achieve financial stability and actively serve others in their community.

Evaluation Methodology

The aim of our evaluation was to determine the type and quality of impact Living Free is having on the participants of Living Free small groups. To understand this, we explored two broad evaluation questions:

1. What type and quality of impact are we having on Living Free small group members?
2. What aspects of our program are causing this impact?

Over the course of the project, we (a) developed and refined our ideas of intended impact and indicators, (b) designed and implemented a mixed methods outcome evaluation using both qualitative and quantitative means to collect and analyze data, (c) identified themes and findings, and (d) considered the implications to those findings for program improvement and innovation.

This project began by identifying and clarifying the intended impact of Living Free. Once the ideas of impact had been developed, we used the Heart Triangle™ model to identify qualitative and quantitative indicators of impact on the mental, behavioral, and emotional changes in our participants. We used these indicators to design a qualitative interview protocol and a quantitative questionnaire to evaluate progress toward achieving our intended impact.

Qualitative Data Collection and Analysis

For the qualitative portion of the evaluation, we designed an in-depth interview protocol to gather data about the structural, qualitative changes resulting from our program. We contacted our Living Free Representatives and small group facilitators who helped recruit Living Free small group participants for interviews. Due to time constraints, we employed a convenience sampling approach, interviewing all available and willing participants. Our sample size was 19 participants. While this approach limited our ability to ensure representation across different demographic or participation-level categories, it allowed us to gather rich data from engaged program participants within our evaluation timeline.

Cara Woodall conducted our interviews, holding one-on-one sessions that lasted from 45 minutes to two hours. She gathered interview data through handwritten notes and a voice-to-text transcription application.

We then analyzed the data inductively using a modified version of thematic analysis. The data was analyzed to identify themes within each interview, then common themes were developed from all of the interviews collectively. We identified the overarching and inter-interview themes that emerged from the full scope of our data analysis to illuminate the collective insights and discoveries. We mapped these themes visually and examined the dynamics among the themes, causes and catalysts of the themes, new or surprising insights related to the themes, and relationships between the themes that were revealed in the data. We then identified the most significant and meaningful discoveries and presented them as findings.

Quantitative Data Collection and Analysis

For the quantitative portion of the evaluation, we designed a questionnaire to collect data on our quantitative indicators of impact. We administered this instrument to 70 Living Free small group participants and received 37 responses, a 53% response rate. The data were analyzed primarily using measures of central tendency. We identified key insights, patterns, and gaps within the data and incorporated these discoveries into the related findings. The most significant insights from the quantitative data are described in the following narrative.

Limitations

Living Free partners with churches, recovery and counseling centers, jails and various organizations across the country and around the world to share our curriculum with individuals struggling with various life-controlling issues. Since the staff at Living Free does not directly facilitate the small group sessions, we relied on the small group facilitators across the country to reach out and contact the Living Free graduates to seek their participation in the data collection process. Due to time and staffing limitations, the participants included in the study were limited to the USA. Future research will include participants from outside the USA. Future evaluations would benefit from stratified sampling to ensure diverse voices across age groups, length of participation, and other relevant characteristics. Also, the sample size was restricted due to time constraints and will be increased in follow-up data collection.

Findings

Finding 1. Crisis as Divine Catalyst - Rock Bottom Becomes Sacred Ground.

The data reveals that participants consistently experience their lowest moments as turning points for spiritual transformation. Whether facing prison, the death of loved ones, cancer, or severe trauma, these crises become the fertile ground for encountering God in profound ways. This isn't merely about hitting bottom - it's about recognizing these moments as divine appointments for radical life change. Throughout our interviews, we discovered that participants view their darkest hours retrospectively as necessary catalysts that opened them to God's transformative power. The universality of this pattern across diverse backgrounds and crisis types suggests that Living Free provides a framework for reinterpreting life's most devastating moments as opportunities for spiritual breakthrough.

Key Themes from Qualitative Interviews

- Participants identify specific crisis moments (addiction, incarceration, illness, loss) as the starting point of their spiritual transformation journey.
- Rock-bottom experiences create an openness to God that wasn't present during more stable life periods.
- Crisis events are reframed from sources of shame to testimonies of God's redemptive power.
- The depth of the crisis often correlates with the profound nature of the transformation experienced.
- Participants express gratitude for their lowest moments, seeing them as necessary for their current spiritual state.

Interview Quotes

"I got arrested and was looking at 18 years in prison, and got to jail and literally woke up three days pursuing God and never wanted a drug again. And I've never had a trigger. I was a needle junkie, heroin, nothing better than me. And I woke up telling people about the Lord."

"Three and a half, three years ago, on March 7, a family that I was staying with suffered a farmhouse fire... I survived the fire, but unfortunately we lost five, five members of the family... My first instinct was to call Skip. And I told him, I don't want to hear about God... My faith in trusting God right now isn't there."

"I was arrested for DWI for the third time, and I was facing 15 years... I was just at wit's end. I didn't know what to do, what was going to happen to me... When I came out of jail, Doctor called me and says, Oh, you better come in, because you're bleeding internally... I had cancer."

Quantitative Insights and Charts

- Survey data shows a dramatic increase in hope for the future, with participants reporting "a lot" of hope jumping from only 7.89% before Living Free to 63.16% after participation (see Figure 1).
- The percentage of participants with low hope (reporting "none" or "a little") decreased substantially, from 39.48% before to 0% after Living Free participation (see Figure 2).
- Participants now confront disappointments and challenging situations with renewed strength as 95% of survey respondents reported feeling at least "quite a bit" of spiritual strength from the Holy Spirit, up from 40%, with 61% reporting "a lot".

Possible Responses

- Develop specific crisis intervention protocols that help facilitators recognize and support participants during acute crisis moments.
- Create testimony-sharing opportunities where participants can reframe their crisis stories as redemption narratives.
- Partner with crisis intervention services (jails, hospitals, shelters) to offer Living Free at critical intervention moments.
- Train facilitators in trauma-informed care to better support participants processing crisis experiences.

Figure 1:
My feeling of hope for the future before participating in Living Free

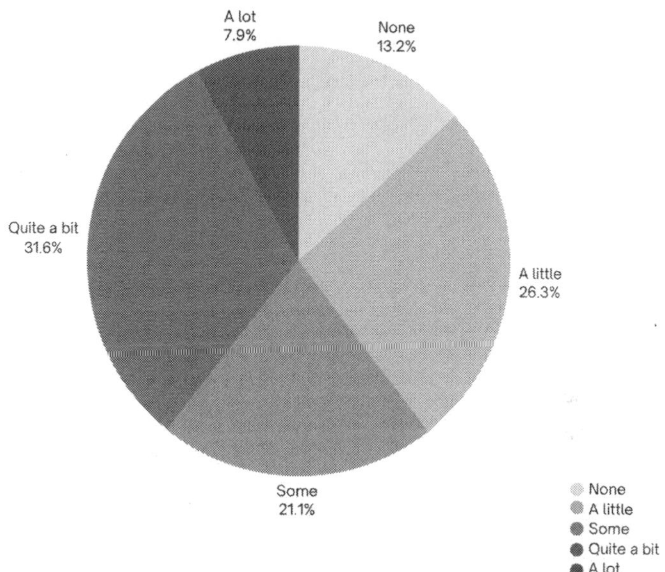

n=34

Figure 2:
My feeling of hope for the future after participating in Living Free

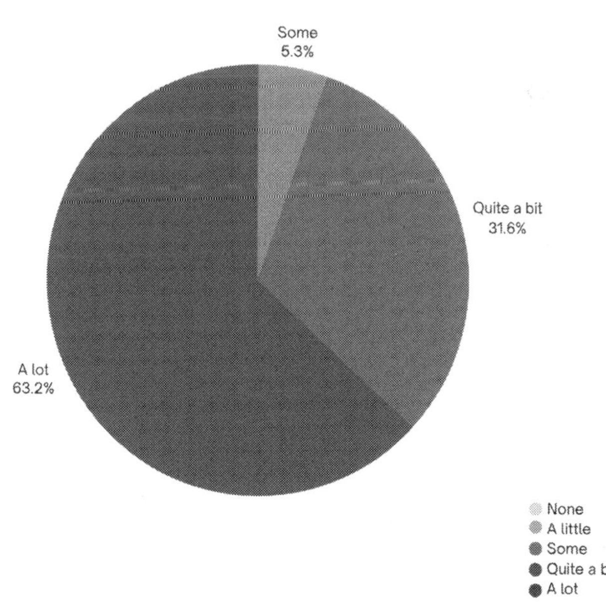

n=34

Finding 2. Identity Reconstruction Through Christ - From Labels to Liberation.

Participants undergo a fundamental identity transformation that goes far beyond behavior modification. The shift from "needle junkie" to business owner, from "relapser" to sustained sobriety, from "fake" to authentic represents a complete rewriting of self-understanding. This identity change occurs through understanding one's worth in God's eyes rather than through one's failures or achievements. The data reveals that Living Free facilitates a process where participants shed destructive labels that have defined them, often for decades, and embrace new identities rooted in their relationship with Christ. This transformation is not superficial; it represents a profound shift in how participants perceive themselves, their potential, and their role in the world.

Key Themes from Qualitative Interviews

- Participants shed long-held negative labels (addict, failure, victim, angry person) and embrace positive identities in Christ.
- Identity transformation occurs through understanding God's unconditional love and acceptance.
- A new identity becomes the foundation for sustained behavior change, rather than relying on willpower alone.
- Participants express surprise and joy at discovering who they really are beneath years of shame and labels.
- Identity shift enables participants to envision and pursue futures previously thought impossible.

Interview Quotes

> *"I used to be very fake. Now I actually desire to have relationships and care about other people... I truly believe that I do have that Heavenly Father for me... I don't feel inadequacy or lack of value anymore."*

> *"I'm a man of God that treats my family correctly... I've got three babies. I've developed a relationship with the Lord that nobody can shake or take away from me... I got a wife that's mine and a house that's mine, and boys that are mine."*

"When I would go to AA, you know, stay away from this guy. He's one angry person, and that followed me forever... Jimmy has shown me by following Christ, that person don't live here anymore... That old person doesn't live here anymore. I ain't got nothing to prove to anybody."

Quantitative Insights and Charts

- Survey data reveals tremendous growth in the participants' understanding of their worth through their identity in Christ, as 97% of the survey respondents reported feeling at least "quite a bit" of worth in Christ, an increase from only 49% before their Living Free experiences. 74% of the respondents reported they now believe they have "a lot" of worth (see Figure 3).
- Respondents are more secure in their relationship with God as 100% of the survey respondents reported feeling close to God and His presence in their life "often" or "always" as compared to only 57% prior to joining a Living Free group. Since becoming a Living Free participant, 63% reported "always" feeling near to God.

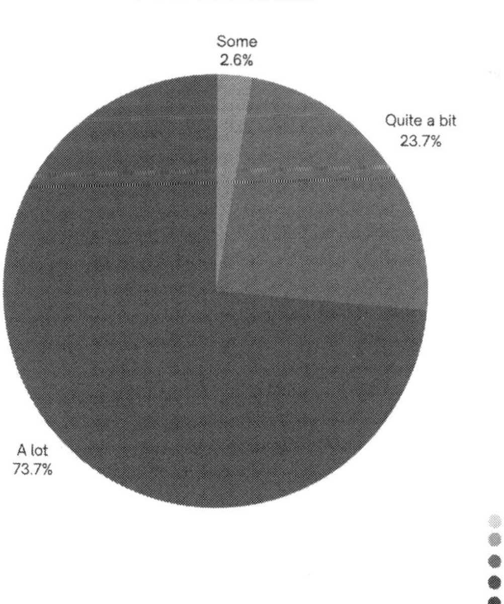

Possible Responses

- Develop curriculum modules specifically focused on identity formation and understanding worth in Christ.
- Create visual exercises or activities that help participants literally "remove" old labels and embrace new identities.
- Implement regular identity affirmation practices in groups where participants speak new truths about themselves.
- Train facilitators to recognize and address identity-based shame that keeps participants stuck in old patterns.
- The identity transformation described in our qualitative interviews represents a rich area for future quantitative measurement, particularly around participants' sense of worth in Christ and freedom from destructive labels.
- Future surveys could capture this powerful dimension of change through targeted questions about identity in Christ, self-perception shifts, and confidence in God-given worth, which would complement our strong qualitative evidence of fundamental identity reconstruction.

Finding 3. Living Free as Bridge Where Secular Programs Failed.

Multiple participants explicitly state that Living Free succeeded where AA, NA, and other secular programs failed. The Christ-centered approach provides what one participant called "the bridge to God" that was missing in other programs. This isn't about dismissing secular approaches but recognizing that for many participants, the spiritual component was the missing piece for lasting transformation. The data reveals that while secular programs may have provided tools and community, they lacked the spiritual foundation that participants needed for deep, lasting change. Living Free's integration of biblical truth with practical recovery principles creates a comprehensive approach that addresses not just behaviors but the spiritual void that often underlies life-controlling issues.

Key Themes from Qualitative Interviews

- Participants report multiple failed attempts with secular programs before finding success with Living Free.
- The explicit Christ-centered approach provides meaning and purpose that was missing in other programs.
- Biblical foundation offers absolute truth and unchanging principles versus relative recovery concepts.
- Participants find freedom, rather than just sobriety, and transformation, rather than just behavioral management.
- The combination of the Word of God, the Spirit of God, and the people of God creates comprehensive support.

Interview Quotes

"I had tried treatment and NA and, you know, the secular 12 step programs, and nothing worked. And it wasn't until I came to Christ that I became free of my addiction... when I was going through those programs, I would see people that had, oh, 30 years clean or 30 years sober, and they still just seemed to be struggling with inner turmoil."

"I had been around AA since 1974 and I was just... a constant relapser... everybody would laugh at me. I got labeled as a relapser. It just wasn't connecting... I needed the bridge, and Jesus was the bridge for me. I needed a loving father. I didn't have one as a child. It brought me to God."

"The Word of God is the only thing that works... it works every time. It's the answer to Al-Anon and AA, it's the answer. Those programs are great, but they fall short of the throne."

Quantitative Insights and Charts

- Survey data reveals that 36.84% of participants report experiencing "a lot" of change in their relationship with Christ, with an additional 31.58% reporting "quite a bit" of change, totaling 68.42% experiencing substantial spiritual transformation (see Figure 4, next page).

Figure 4:
As a result of participating in a Living Free group, how has your relationship with Christ changed?

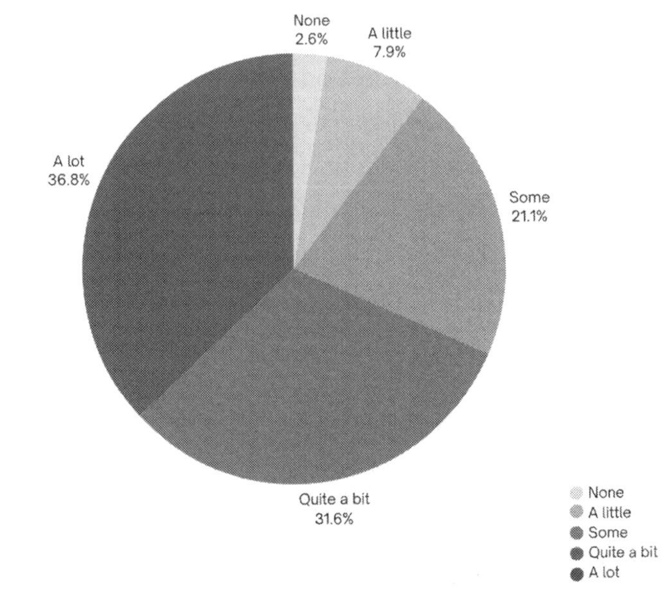

Survey Responses for *"How has your relationship with Christ changed?"*:

> *"I went from a hard hearted, hateful, and just down right mean individual to one with a heart, guided by the Holy Spirit and loving my life."*
>
> *"I find myself reaching to Him about choices I'm facing more often."*
>
> *"I cannot live my life without Him in it. He is at the forefront of my life."*
>
> *"It has brought me closer to Him and given me the confidence to rely on Him in every situation."*
>
> *"Dependent on Him for all things. I've learned to be content in all circumstances. I try to put into practice all that I have received and learned from Him, all that I've heard and seen from Him , which has resulted in peace in my life . Always thanking God for the Holy Spirit in my life to guide and be in control of my life! I thank God for Living Free that helped me grow into the person and child of God that I am!."*

Possible Responses

- Develop clear messaging about how Living Free complements or differs from secular programs without disparaging them.
- Create bridge programs for those transitioning from secular recovery programs to Living Free.
- Document and share success stories specifically highlighting the spiritual transformation aspect.

Finding 4. From Profound Isolation to Authentic Community Leadership.

A remarkable pattern emerges, where participants transition from deep isolation to becoming community builders and leaders. Throughout our interviews, we heard stories of individuals who initially wanted to be hermits but now teach in multiple counties, who had no friends at church but now know everyone, and who were once considered dangerous loners but have become trusted helpers. This transformation occurs through the safety of Living Free groups, which allow for vulnerability without judgment. The data reveals that Living Free creates a unique environment where broken people can gradually open up, build trust, and eventually become sources of support for others. This progression from isolation to leadership appears to be a natural outcome of the healing process rather than a forced expectation.

Key Themes from Qualitative Interviews

- Participants move from extreme isolation and mistrust to active community engagement and leadership.
- Safe group environments allow gradual opening up and vulnerability without fear of judgment.
- Former participants frequently become facilitators, creating a multiplication effect.
- Building authentic relationships in groups transfers to relationship building in broader life contexts.
- Leadership emerges naturally as participants gain confidence and desire to give back what they received.

Interview Quotes

"I wanted to live alone on the tundra by myself and not ever talk to another human being. But here I am... I didn't want to be building relationships, but I wanted to live alone on the tundra by myself... And then God really dropped that seed in my heart... There's probably a need in this county. Here we are."

"Before I been to the same church and still had hardly any friends there and now I'm friends with just about everybody... I didn't have any friends, and I didn't trust anyone in my church. I have opened up to her and other people in my church, and I do have friends."

"We worked over 100 addicts in recovery the last six years... we feed all the guys on Monday nights... we got too many people... we've got like, four classes on Monday nights."

Quantitative Insights and Charts

- Quantitative data shows that 57.89% of participants developed or strengthened five or more close, supportive relationships since participating in Living Free (see Figure 5).
- An additional 26.32% developed three to four relationships, demonstrating that over 84% of participants significantly expanded their supportive community connections (see Figure 5).

Possible Responses

- Create structured pathways for participants to move from group member to facilitator roles.
- Develop community-building activities within groups that foster deeper connections and promote a sense of belonging.
- Establish mentorship programs pairing isolated newcomers with those further along in their journey.
- Recognize and celebrate community leadership development as a key outcome metric.

Figure 5:
Since participating in Living Free, how many close, supportive relationships have you developed or strengthened?

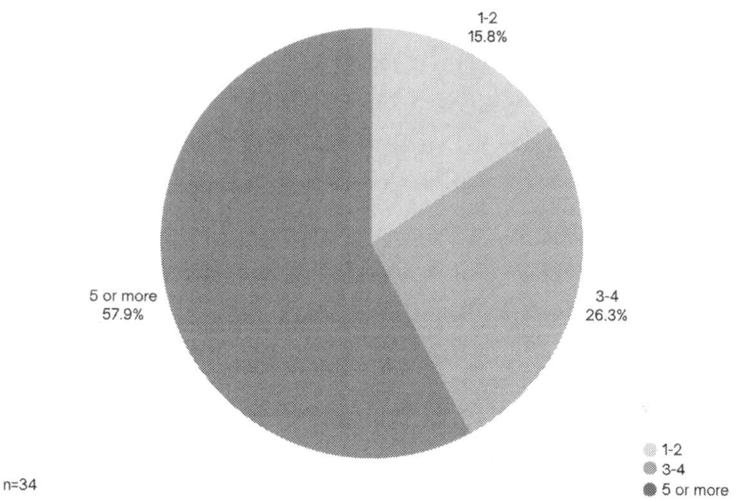

Finding 5. The Wounded Healer Dynamic - Brokenness Becomes Ministry.

Participants consistently transform their deepest wounds into their most powerful ministry tools. The data reveals a profound pattern where those who have experienced the depths of addiction, mental illness, trauma, and loss become the most effective ministers to others facing similar struggles. This finding reveals that healing happens despite ongoing struggles, through serving others while still in the process. Participants don't wait until they're "completely healed" to begin helping others; rather, their ongoing journey becomes a source of hope and authenticity for those they serve. This wounded healer dynamic creates a culture where brokenness is not hidden but transformed into a ministry asset.

Key Themes from Qualitative Interviews

- Participants use their stories of struggle and recovery as primary tools for ministering to others.
- Ongoing challenges and vulnerabilities increase rather than decrease ministry effectiveness.

- Helping others becomes a crucial component of participants' own continued healing and growth.
- Participants feel called to serve those facing the specific struggles they've experienced.
- Ministry opportunities arise naturally as participants share authentically about their journeys.

Interview Quotes

"I get to help other women who are, who are in my position I used to be in... not everyone has a story that will help these women and I do."

"Everything that I've been through, He's used that to help me reach other people... When I share in the sessions, and people listen, and they say, I just see the love of God in you... I'm so humbled that they can see it."

"The pastor told me didn't really give me a choice... I told them that I'm still on rocky ground because of what I had just gone through... They said, well, that's what people need to see."

Quantitative Insights and Charts

- Survey results show that 60.53% of participants have served in both group member and facilitator roles, demonstrating the natural progression from receiving help to providing it.
- The high percentage of participants transitioning to leadership roles (78.95% serving as facilitators either exclusively or in combination with membership) validates the wounded healer phenomenon.

Possible Responses

- Develop "wounded healer" training that helps participants understand how to share their stories effectively (see Figure 6).
- Create structured opportunities for participants to minister within appropriate boundaries (see Figure 6).

- Establish peer support programs that match participants with others facing similar challenges.
- Celebrate and normalize the concept that ongoing struggles don't disqualify one from ministry.

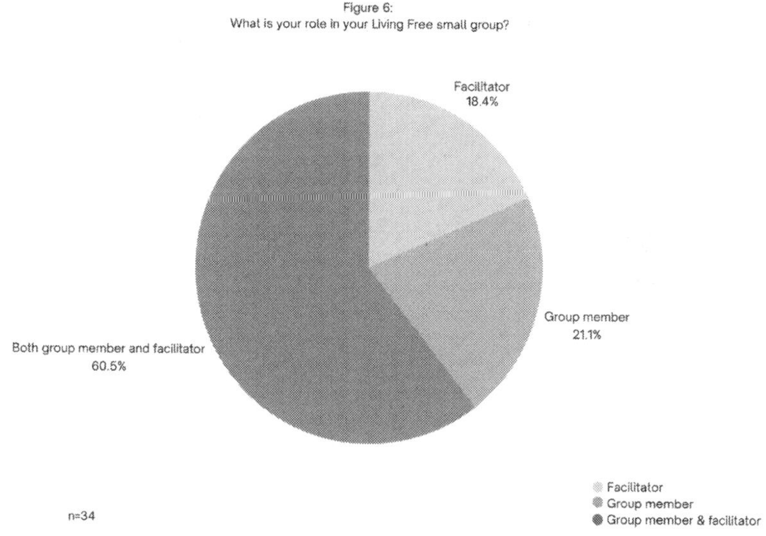

Finding 6. Long-Term Engagement Creates Sustainable Transformation.

The data shows participants engaging in Living Free groups for multiple years, taking multiple courses, and returning even after periods of absence. This long-term engagement model differs dramatically from quick-fix approaches and suggests that sustainable transformation requires patient and persistent participation over time. Unlike programs that promise rapid results, Living Free participants understand their journey as an ongoing process of growth and transformation. The data reveals engagement patterns spanning 4-5 years for many participants, with some involved for over a decade. This extended involvement allows for deep, lasting change as participants cycle through different curricula addressing various life issues, building upon previous growth while tackling new challenges.

Key Themes from Qualitative Interviews

- Participants typically engage with Living Free for multiple years rather than completing a single course.
- Long-term involvement allows for addressing multiple life issues in a systematic, layered approach.
- Participants often cycle through the same curriculum multiple times, gaining deeper insights with each experience.
- Extended engagement creates stable support systems that weather life's ongoing challenges.
- Transformation is viewed as a journey rather than a destination, encouraging continued participation.

Interview Quotes

"I stuck with Jimmy when I got out of jail in 2012... we've been there, you know, for the past 13 years, going through the booklets... I was able to stay up in that cell block... for my whole year, and I got to go over and over and over."

"I've done so many of them multiple times... However long Mary's been with living free. I started classes, then I even went to facilitator training with her... Oh my gosh, everyone that they've had... I've done the Insight group three times this year."

"I first took the class 22 years ago... I took a couple of the classes and then quit taking them for maybe five years, and they got involved in facilitating for the past 15 years."

Quantitative Insights and Charts

- Quantitative data reveals remarkable program retention, with 52.63% of participants involved for more than five years and 76.31% engaged for two or more years (see Figure 7).
- Only 13.15% of participants have been involved for less than one year, indicating that the program successfully retains participants for the extended engagement necessary for lasting transformation (see Figure 7).

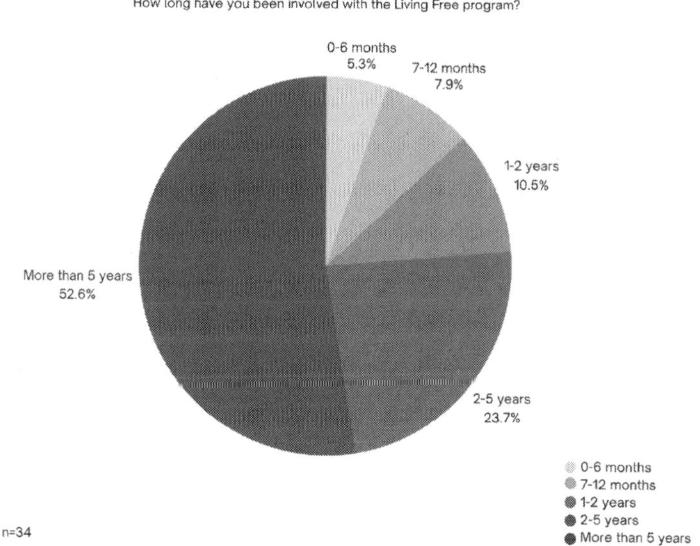

Possible Responses

- Develop "graduate" level curricula for long-term participants seeking deeper engagement.
- Create recognition systems that celebrate long-term commitment without creating hierarchy.
- Design curriculum pathways that build systematically on previous learning.
- Establish alumni networks to maintain connections with long-term participants.

Finding 7. Daily Spiritual Disciplines Anchor Lasting Change. Nearly every participant developed consistent morning routines involving prayer, Bible study, and devotions. These aren't portrayed as religious obligations but as life-giving practices that provide daily strength. The data reveals a remarkable consistency in how participants structure their spiritual practices, with many rising early (some as early as 3-4 AM) to ensure uninterrupted time with God. These daily disciplines become the foundation for maintaining transformation, providing participants with spiritual resources to face daily challenges.

The establishment of consistent spiritual practices represents a fundamental lifestyle change that supports all other areas of growth and transformation.

Key Themes from Qualitative Interviews

- Daily spiritual practices become non-negotiable routines that anchor participants' days.
- Morning devotions, prayer, and Bible reading provide strength for facing daily challenges.
- Participants develop personalized spiritual practices that fit their life circumstances and schedules.
- Consistency in spiritual disciplines correlates with sustained transformation in other areas of life.
- Spiritual practices evolve from duty to delight as participants experience the life-giving benefits of their practices.

Interview Quotes

> *"I get up, usually around 3 or 4 o'clock... I text out to the team a daily devotional video, usually 25 to 30 minutes long, a good sermon, a prayer... Every day I do at least two plans, you know, one a financial plan and one a spiritual plan."*

> *"In the morning, when I get that quiet time before I hear little footsteps running down the stairs... I can definitely just tell a whole shift in my day from when I do get some of that personal quiet time in, even if it's just a few minutes."*

> *"Well, I read the Bible every day, and I have a prayer list... And now we have a list, and I throw a line through them, and I move them over to the corner that says prayers answered."*

Quantitative Insights and Charts

- Before-and-after data shows engagement in consistent spiritual practice increased dramatically, with "always" responses jumping from 18.42% before to 57.89% after Living Free (see Figure 8 and 9).

- Since participating in Living Free groups, 95% of survey respondents consistently participate in spiritual practices "often" or"always", compared to only 42% before the program (see Figure 8 and 9).

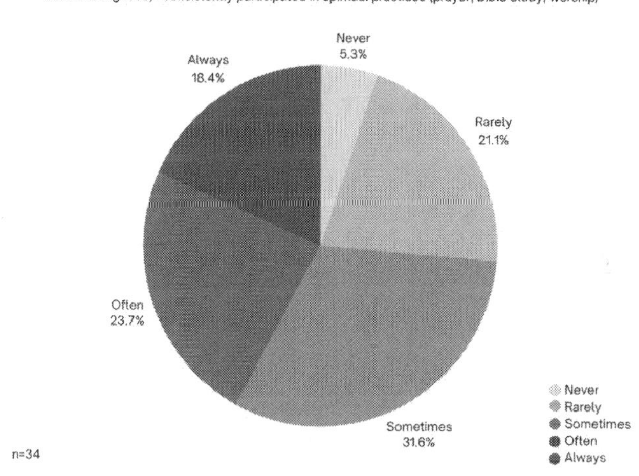

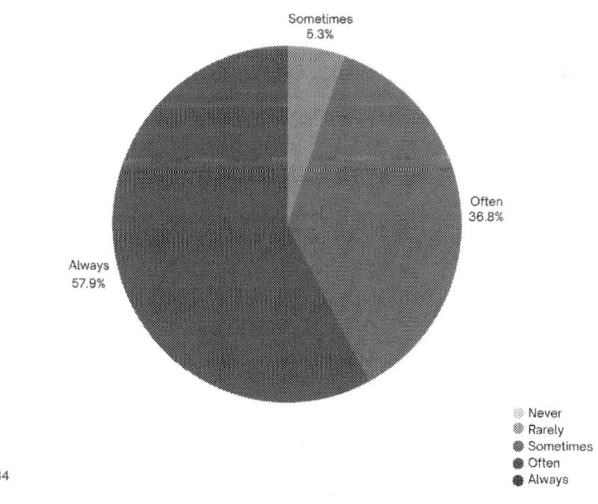

Possible Responses

- Develop resources and guides for establishing sustainable daily spiritual practices.

- Establish accountability systems within groups to maintain spiritual disciplines.
- Offer a variety of devotional resources to cater to different learning styles and preferences.
- Teach practical strategies for maintaining spiritual practices during difficult seasons.

Finding 8. Integration of Spiritual Growth with Practical Life Success.

Spiritual transformation consistently leads to practical life improvements including employment stability, business ownership, family reconciliation, health management, and financial responsibility. The data reveals that genuine faith transformation manifests in concrete life achievements. Participants not only feel better spiritually, they also experience measurable improvements in their daily lives. From Brandon's construction company, which employs recovering addicts, to Destiny achieving independent living, the integration of spiritual growth with practical success demonstrates that Living Free addresses the whole person. This holistic transformation challenges the false dichotomy between spiritual and practical life, showing how authentic faith naturally produces tangible life improvements.

Key Themes from Qualitative Interviews

- Spiritual transformation directly correlates with improved employment, finances, and relationships.
- Participants achieve practical goals previously thought impossible (business ownership, stable housing, and education).
- Faith provides the foundation and motivation for pursuing practical life improvements.
- Success in practical areas reinforces spiritual growth in a positive feedback loop.
- Participants view practical achievements as evidence of God's faithfulness, rather than as personal accomplishments.

Interview Quotes

"I own businesses. Right now, I got about 12 guys, full time employees... I want to have about three more babies and employ about 50 people and own about 300 apartment units."

"I have my own apartment. I didn't think that would ever happen... Right now I'm learning how to do a cleaning rotation, cleaning different rooms different days. I'm putting away my laundry... We've been working on a budget, saving a certain amount of money each week."

"God gave me this job. He's the one who told me to apply for it... I was offered a higher job, two grades higher than what I applied for during my interview."

Quantitative Insights and Charts

- Participants' belief in their ability to live stable, productive lives increased substantially, with those reporting "a lot" of belief rising from 26.32% before to 68.42% after Living Free (see Figure 10 and 11).
- The percentage of participants with low confidence in living productively (reporting "none" or "a little") decreased from 20.85% before to 0% after participation (see Figure 10 and 11).

Figure 10:
My belief that I can live a stable, productive life before Living Free

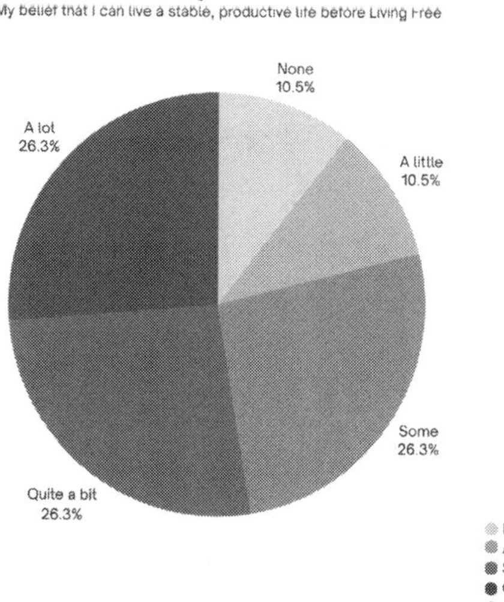

Figure 11:
My belief that I can live a stable, productive life after Living Free

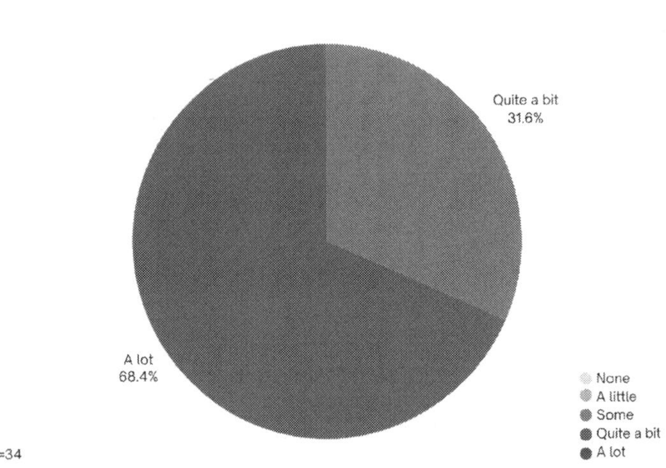

Possible Responses

- Integrate practical life skills training (budgeting, job readiness, relationship skills) with spiritual curriculum.
- Partner with vocational training programs and employers willing to hire program graduates.
- Develop metrics that track both spiritual and practical life outcomes.
- Create mentorship programs that pair participants with others who have achieved practical success.

Finding 9. Adaptability Across Diverse Contexts and Needs.

Living Free effectively serves people at vastly different life stages and circumstances - from new believers to mature faith leaders, from crisis intervention to cross-cultural ministry. The program's flexibility allows principles to be applied whether someone is in an active crisis or seeking deeper spiritual growth. The data reveals remarkable adaptability, with participants successfully implementing Living Free in Native Alaskan villages, farming communities, urban settings, and online formats. This adaptability extends to participant needs as well, serving those in early recovery alongside those with decades of sobriety, new Christians alongside ministry leaders. The program's core principles remain consistent while allowing for contextual adaptation.

Key Themes from Qualitative Interviews

- Living Free principles successfully adapt to diverse cultural contexts and communities.
- The program serves effectively across the spectrum from crisis intervention to spiritual maturity.
- Flexible delivery formats (in-person, online, hybrid) accommodate various life circumstances.
- Curriculum addresses both immediate needs and long-term spiritual development.
- Facilitators successfully contextualize materials while maintaining core Biblical principles.

Interview Quotes

"Part of the problem with that is I'm in a totally different culture. So learning the culture, what are the cultural expectations? That's kind of how I've done here. Moving here, I embrace the culture that I'm coming into . . . that's part of the adjusting here. It's using Living Free, but working it into this culture."

"We do get group work... from really pretty intense, like therapeutic weekend to just partnering with our local VA... we've done in person and Zoom studies, because of the farming in the country and North Dakota winters."

"Now we've gotten to some of the ones that are more like a Bible study. Now it's more instead of, you know, a time where she's trying to get sober. . . now it's more of a Bible study time with us."

Quantitative Insights and Charts

- This distribution demonstrates successful adaptation across varied environments while maintaining core effectiveness regardless of setting (see Figure 12,next page).

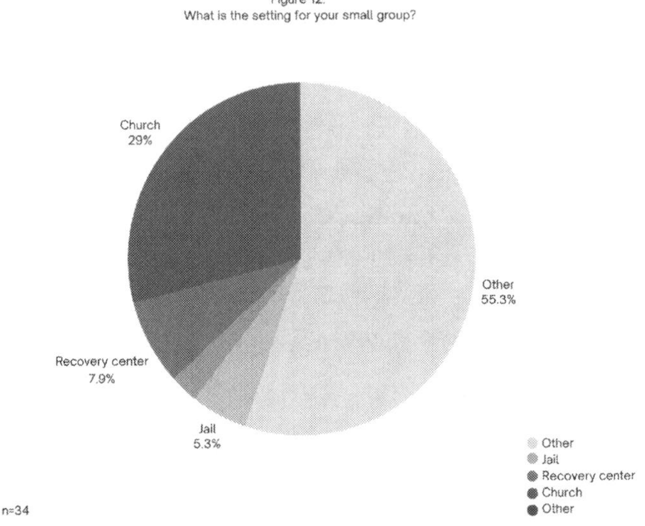

Possible Responses

- Develop cultural adaptation guides for facilitators working in diverse contexts.
- Create multiple entry points into Living Free programming based on participant readiness.
- Expand online and hybrid offerings to increase accessibility across geographic barriers.
- Train facilitators in contextualizing materials while maintaining theological integrity.

Finding 10. Family and Generational Healing Extends Beyond the Individual.

Participants consistently report transformation, extending to family relationships, with parents breaking generational patterns, adult children finding faith, marriages being restored, and family members converting from atheism. This ripple effect suggests that the program's impact extends beyond individual participants to create changes in the family system. The data reveals that as participants experience personal transformation, they become catalysts for change within their family systems. Children observe and adopt new patterns, estranged relationships are reconciled, and entire family dynamics shift from dysfunction to health. This generational impact is particularly significant as participants consciously work to break cycles of addiction, abuse, and dysfunction that may have persisted for generations.

Key Themes from Qualitative Interviews

- Individual transformation creates ripple effects throughout family systems.
- Participants actively work to break generational patterns of dysfunction and trauma.
- Children and spouses often seek their own spiritual transformation after witnessing changes in the participant.
- Family relationships previously thought to be irreparable experience healing and restoration.
- Participants develop new parenting approaches that model healthy spiritual and emotional patterns.

Interview Quotes

"There was one daughter that was serving the Lord before we started Living Free, but no one else. Since then miraculously throughout the whole family... my grandmother passed away... her greatest achievement was that the 26 of us that somehow every single one of us is serving the Lord."

"My daughter during the COVID totally flipped out, mental breakdown... every Saturday, she and I would have a sit down, and we would do a book together... My daughter has made 180 degree turn. She is on medication. Now she works couple of days a week."

"It's changed the way I pray. You know, I pray for my kids. I even pray for hard times, for them to draw them closer to Him... I got a call, Hey, I think your son's my daughter's baby's dad... Within two weeks, I took custody of her... I would have tried to run from the responsibility, but I didn't give it a second thought."

Quantitative Insights and Charts

- Understanding of healthy Godly relationships improved dramatically, with participants reporting "a lot" of understanding increasing from 15.79% before to 63.16% after Living Free (see Figure 13 and 14).

Figure 13:
My understanding of what a healthy Godly relationship looks like before Living Free

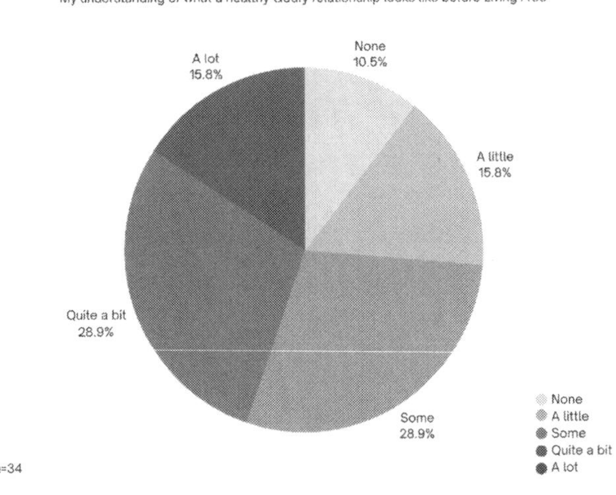

Figure 14:
My understanding of what a healthy Godly relationship looks like after Living Free

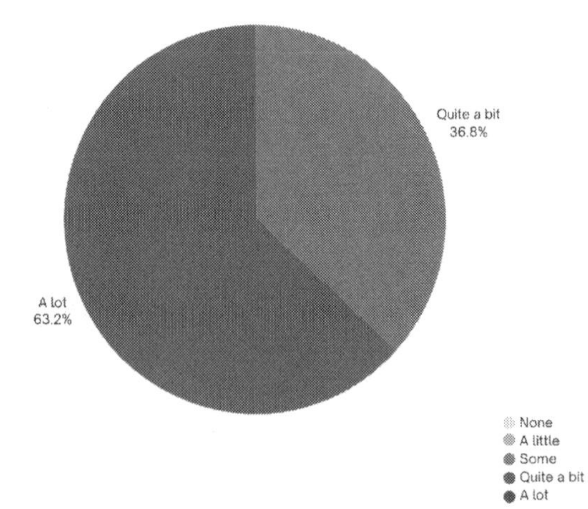

Possible Responses

- Promote existing and develop additional family-focused curriculum that addresses generational patterns and healing.

- Create opportunities for family members to participate together in appropriate groups.
- Establish support systems for participants navigating complex family dynamics during transformation.
- Document and share stories of generational healing to inspire hope for family restoration.

Conclusion

Insights Into Impact

Our evaluation findings powerfully demonstrate that Living Free is achieving its intended impacts through a comprehensive transformation process that touches every aspect of participants' lives. The journey from crisis to community leadership (Findings 1-4) directly supports participants' ability to cope with life's challenges through positive Godly choices, as they move from destructive patterns to Christ-centered solutions. The evidence of identity reconstruction, where participants shed decades-old labels and embrace their worth in Christ, combined with the establishment of daily spiritual disciplines and long-term program engagement (Findings 2, 5-7), clearly indicates substantial growth in spiritual maturity. This spiritual transformation isn't merely internal - it manifests in concrete life improvements including business ownership, stable employment, restored families, and service to others, demonstrating that participants are indeed leading productive lives rooted in their faith (Finding 8).

The ripple effects of individual transformation extending to family systems and communities (Findings 4-5, 10) reveal the program's profound impact on relationships. Participants who once lived in isolation now lead ministries, facilitate groups, and actively work to break generational patterns of dysfunction. The program's unique success where secular approaches failed (Finding 3) and its adaptability across diverse contexts (Finding 9) suggest that Living Free's integration of biblical truth with practical life application creates a sustainable framework for lasting change. Most significantly, the wounded healer dynamic reveals that participants don't simply receive help, they become conduits of transformation for others, creating a multiplier effect that extends the program's impact far beyond individual lives into families, churches, and communities.

Steps Forward

Living Free exists to facilitate hope, faith and freedom by connecting and equipping people with solutions for better living. In order to ensure that we are, and continue to meet this goal we will:

- Gather additional data on the facilitators and their experiences to evaluate their impact on the small group participants' success and offer continued support, mentoring, training and resources to the facilitators as needed based on the findings.
- Expand our efforts to survey Living Free small group participants who began a Living Free group but did not complete the course to help us understand their concerns and challenges to better minister to their needs.
- Implement a follow-up process that will allow us to gain valuable insight into the long-term impact of the Living Free program on the participants' lives and help us identify any additional support needed to ensure lasting transformation and freedom for the Living Free participants.
- In future evaluations, survey Living Free small group participants to determine additional curriculum topics desired to help the participants achieve complete freedom through Christ and examine our curriculum catalog to ensure it offers participants the level of support they seek and research and develop potential new material as needed.

Opportunities for Future Evaluation

1. Expand the sample to include Living Free small groups within the U.S. that are utilizing the Spanish versions of the Living Free curriculum.

2. Partner with our global Living Free Representatives to gather feedback from participants in Living Free small groups across 124 countries where Living Free groups are currently offered.
3. Implement a process where upon completion of each Living Free course, facilitators would administer the survey to all participants and forward the data to the Living Free headquarters so that we could continue to monitor the impact and success of the Living Free ministry.

TRANSFORMATION PROJECT

Stanley W. Bembry, *President*, George McCleskey, *Board Chairman*
Ellen Reinig, *Development Director*, Lena Leath, *Executive Assistant*

Organization and Program Overview

Introduction to Organization

The mission of the Transformation Project is to make disciples of Jesus Christ by transforming the lives of addiction-related offenders, their families, and future generations through the power of God, thereby reducing repeat offenses and crime.

Program Description

The Transformation Project exists to make disciples of Jesus Christ by transforming the lives of addiction-related offenders, their families, and future generations through the power of God. As an alternative sentencing program for addiction-related offenders and their families, we work to reduce recidivism and crime while fostering lasting personal and spiritual growth. Upon completing the program, participants should be able to be productive in relationships, employment, and society.

Our faith-based program offers pre-release services, including orientation and small group sessions, at local penal institutions. We offer transitional services for both males and females, with small group and large group meetings held twice a week for participants using the "Living Free Curriculum." Family Services are also provided using "Living Free Curriculum" such as Insight, Concerned Persons, Peacemaking: Responding to Conflict Biblically, and Growing Seasons.

Intended Impacts

Freedom in Christ. Participants are learning and applying Biblical principles that daily impact their decisions so that they are at peace with God, themselves, and others.

Positive Contributors to Society. Participants are employed, law-abiding citizens who are contributing to their communities.

Emotionally Maturing People. Participants have learned how to handle B.E.A.R.S. (behaviours, emotions, attitudes, relationships, and substance abuse) with God's help, God's way.

Evaluation Methodology

The aim of our evaluation was to assess the effectiveness of the lessons being taught by our volunteers to participants and their families. To understand this, we explored two broad evaluation questions:

1. What kind and quality of impact are we having on our participants?
2. What aspects of the Transformation Project are causing this impact?

Over the course of the project, we (a) developed and refined our ideas of intended impact and indicators, (b) designed and implemented a mixed methods outcome evaluation using both qualitative and quantitative means to collect and analyze data, (c) identified themes and findings, and (d) considered the implications to those findings for program improvement and innovation.

This project began by identifying and clarifying the intended impact of the Transformation Project. Once the ideas of impact had been developed, we utilized the Heart Triangle model to identify both qualitative and quantitative indicators of impact on the mental, behavioral, and emotional changes in our participants. We used these indicators to design a qualitative interview protocol and a quantitative questionnaire to evaluate progress toward achieving our intended impact.

Qualitative Data Collection and Analysis

For the qualitative portion of the evaluation, we designed an in-depth interview protocol to gather data on the structural and qualitative changes resulting from our program. We delimited our population to Hamilton County small group sites. Our population size for this evaluation was 20. We used a purposeful stratified sampling technique to select a representative sample from the population we serve. Our sample size was 16, drawn from the following strata of our population:

- Participants over the age of 18, past and current.
- Past and current volunteers aged 18 and above

Our interview team consisted of George McCleskey, Craig Paul, Regena Kressenberg, Beth Delaney, and Lena Leath. We conducted one-on-one interviews, each lasting between 45 minutes and one hour, and collected interview data using handwritten notes or the Otter voice-to-text transcription app.

We then analyzed the data inductively using a modified version of thematic analysis. Each interviewer analyzed the data from their interviews individually to identify initial themes. Together, we developed common themes from all of the interviews collectively. We identified the overarching and inter-interview themes that emerged from the full scope of our data analysis to illuminate the collective insights and discoveries. We mapped these themes visually and examined the dynamics among the themes, including the causes and catalysts, as well as new or surprising insights related to the themes. Additionally, we explored the relationships between the themes that were revealed in the data. We then identified the most significant and meaningful discoveries and presented them as findings.

Quantitative Data Collection and Analysis

For the quantitative portion of the evaluation, we designed a questionnaire to collect data on our quantitative indicators of impact. We administered this instrument to Transformation Project small group sites in Hamilton County, McMinn County, Warren County, Monroe

County, Rhea County, and Sequatchie County. We received 55 responses, achieving a 73% response rate. The data were analyzed primarily using measures of central tendency. We identified key insights, patterns, and gaps within the data and incorporated these discoveries into the related findings. The most significant insights from the quantitative data are described in the following narrative.

Limitations

The qualitative interviews conducted were limited to Hamilton County sites only. Additionally, our survey data encompasses responses from a diverse group that includes volunteers, program participants, and individuals who have served in both capacities, potentially creating varied perspectives within our quantitative results.

Findings

Finding 1. Small group Bible study and homework create a sense of belonging for individuals who previously felt isolated by shame.

When participants first enter the Transformation Project, they typically describe profound isolation rooted in guilt and shame. Our data reveals that many felt they only belonged among others struggling with the same addictions or life-controlling issues. Through consistent participation in small group Bible study, regular homework completion, and community support, participants experience a radical shift in their sense of belonging. They begin to see themselves not as defined by their past mistakes, but as 'God's kids' who have been adopted into a spiritual family. This transformation from isolation to belonging appears to be a foundational change that supports other areas of growth. The small group format seems particularly effective, as it provides both accountability and acceptance—two elements many participants lacked in their previous relationships. As participants describe feeling 'free, safe, supported and accepted,' they simultaneously report becoming more disciplined in spiritual practices like prayer and Bible reading. This suggests that belonging precedes behavioral change, with community connection creating the safety needed for participants to risk new patterns of living.

Key Themes from Qualitative Interviews

- Participants develop a pattern of regular church attendance after feeling disconnected from faith communities.
- Participants begin to regularly pray and apply biblical principles to daily challenges they face.
- Daily Scripture reading becomes an anchoring practice that reinforces participants' new identity.
- Participants experience feelings of freedom, security, and acceptance that replace previous shame.
- Small group Bible study provides the supportive community participants need to sustain transformation.
- Consistent homework completion helps participants internalize new beliefs about themselves and God.

Interview Quotes

"The most exciting part is knowing that I have a Lord and Savior that I can come to God with anything. He's not going to judge me. If I stay faithful to Him, He'll stay faithful to me."

"I can feel the transformation happening. My friends can see it. My family can see it"

Quantitative Insights & Charts

- 100% of respondents agree they are able to maintain consistent spiritual practices (see Figure 1, next page).
- The vast majority (98.2%) of respondents apply biblical principles to resolve conflict (see Figure 2, next page).

Figure 1:
As a result of my participation in the Transformation Project, I am better able to maintain consistent spiritual practices.

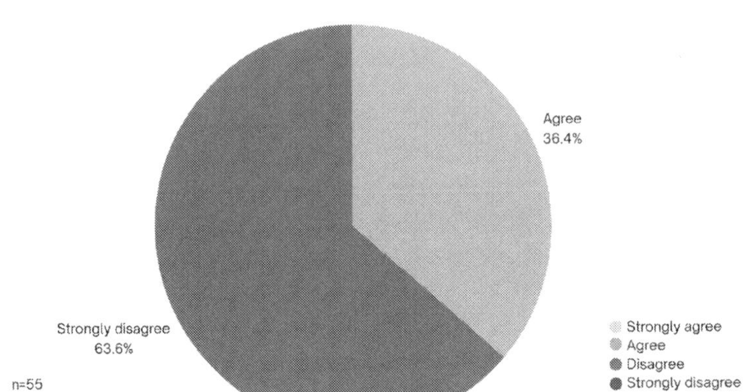

Figure 2:
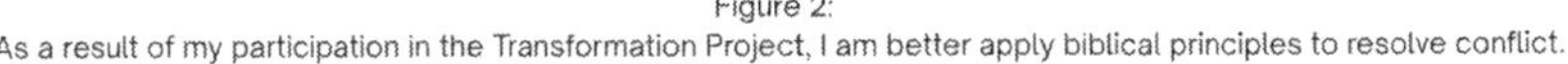
As a result of my participation in the Transformation Project, I am better apply biblical principles to resolve conflict.

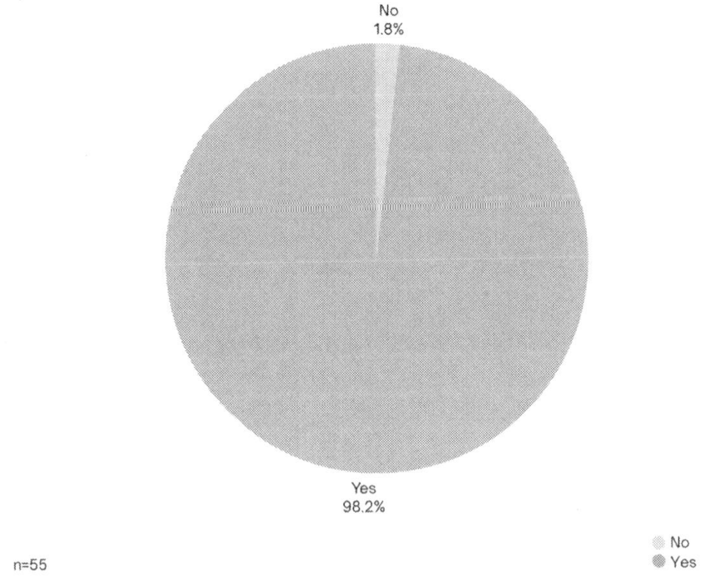

Responses

- Explore ways to better understand the belonging process. Investigate whether there might be opportunities to learn more about how participants transition from isolation to community connection, potentially informing future program enhancements.

Finding 2. Participants experience profound spiritual transformation through surrendering control to God.

Many of our participants come to us determined to try to protect themselves from pain by controlling every aspect of their lives. This approach has failed them, leaving them spiritually bankrupt and without hope when they enter our program. The data reveals a profound spiritual transformation centered on three key elements: First, participants experience a fundamental shift from self-reliance to God-reliance, surrendering control and learning to trust in God's guidance. Second, this surrender leads to emotional freedom, with participants describing feelings of being 'redeemed,' 'saved,' and experiencing peace where there was once anxiety. Third, this inner transformation manifests in tangible behavioral changes, particularly in relationships, where participants report becoming 'slow to anger' and 'slow to speak.' The program's emphasis on Bible study and community support appears to create the conditions for this surrender process, helping participants replace their failed strategies of control with a trust-based approach to life's challenges.

Key Themes from Qualitative Interviews

- Participants shift from self-reliance to God-reliance, surrendering control of their lives and trusting in divine guidance.
- Many experience emotional liberation, describing themselves as "redeemed," "saved," and finding peace where there was once anxiety and fear.
- Bible study and scripture integration become central to daily decision-making, with participants actively applying spiritual principles to their lives.
- Behavioral changes emerge, particularly in relationships, as participants become more patient, thoughtful, and "slow to anger."
- A new sense of purpose and community emerges as participants commit to maintaining their spiritual connections and helping others.

Interview Quotes

"The most exciting part is knowing that I have a Lord and Savior that I can come to with anything."

"I'm going to be more confident in my walk, spread the word and get as many people to Jesus as I can."

"He's blessing me daily in my life and working on me. I'm not who I used to be."

"I lost everything I had. I learned I never want to go back to that. I now know to line up with scripture and let the Lord lead my life."

"The world can't get to me because I won't allow it. I'm walking with Christ now. I trust he's working in me everyday"

"I am more committed now than ever in my faith"

"I know I can pray about things, I know things will be okay. I just need to keep the faith"

"I have learned that to be a child of God means that you are capable, it means you have the power to overcome anything. Can't is not a word is God's vocabulary."

"I realize that I can literally apply the scripture to my life and that's how I can overcome things, how I can fight the good fight of faith, by believing in the scripture."

Quantitative Insights & Charts

- 100% of respondents can agree that they feel more at peace with God (see Figure 3)
- 98% of survey respondents feel more committed to their faith (see Figure 4).

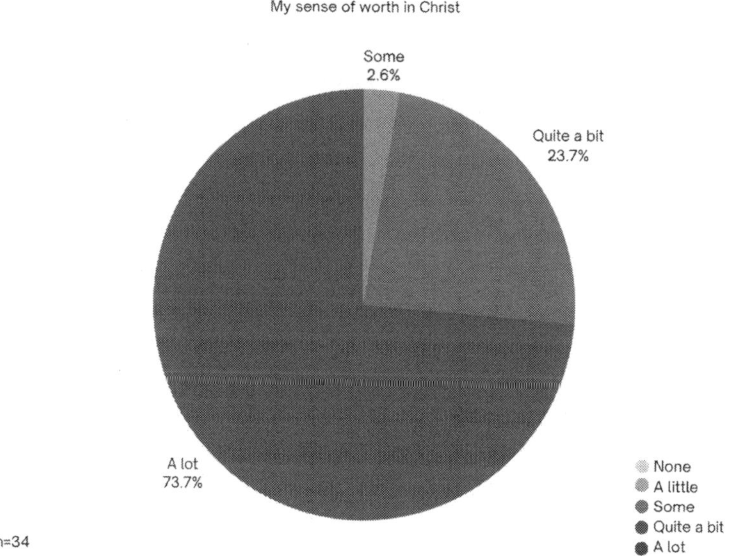

Figure 3:
My sense of worth in Christ

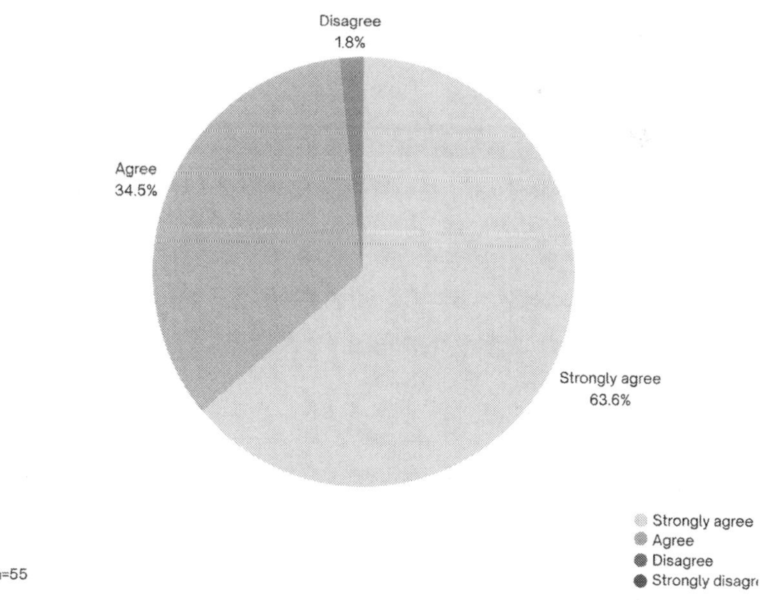

Figure 4:
As a result of my participation in the Transformation Project, I feel more committed to my faith.

Responses

- Incorporate more testimonial-sharing opportunities within the curriculum to reinforce transformation narratives.

- Develop assessment tools to better identify participants' spiritual starting points and customize approaches.
- Create follow-up resources specifically focused on maintaining spiritual practices after program completion.

Finding 3. Participants and volunteers develop renewed self-worth and improved mental health.

Many participants enter the Transformation Project struggling with depression, anxiety, and poor self-image after experiencing significant life challenges. The data reveals that through the program's combination of spiritual guidance, community support, and structured activities, participants experience substantial improvements in mental health. This transformation manifests in three key areas: first, a reduction in symptoms such as anxiety and depression; second, the development of emotional awareness and healthy coping mechanisms; and third, the emergence of a positive self-perception and sense of purpose. Interestingly, volunteers report similar benefits, suggesting the program's approach to mental wellness creates a mutually beneficial environment. Participants consistently attribute their improved outlook to both spiritual reconnection and practical tools for emotional regulation, allowing them to approach life with newfound peace and confidence.

Key Themes from Qualitative Interviews

- Participants report a significant reduction in anxiety and depression symptoms, moving from emotional distress to a state of peace and joy.
- Both participants and volunteers develop stronger self-worth and confidence, replacing negative self-perception with self-love and appreciation.
- Emotional regulation improves as participants gain understanding of their emotions and develop healthy coping mechanisms.
- A more purposeful approach to daily life emerges through engagement with healthy activities, routines, and spiritual practices.

- The combined spiritual and practical approach creates sustained mental health improvements rather than temporary emotional relief.

Interview Quotes

"I have learned depression and anxiety don't have a hold on me anymore."

"It's made me love myself more as a person because I've got the love of God in me. It's really changed my life completely."

Quantitative Insights & Charts

After the Transformation Project, 85.5% of respondents have a better understanding of their triggers and how to handle them, God's way (see Figure 5 and 6).

Figure 5:
Before Transformation Project: I have an understanding of my triggers now and how to handle them God's way

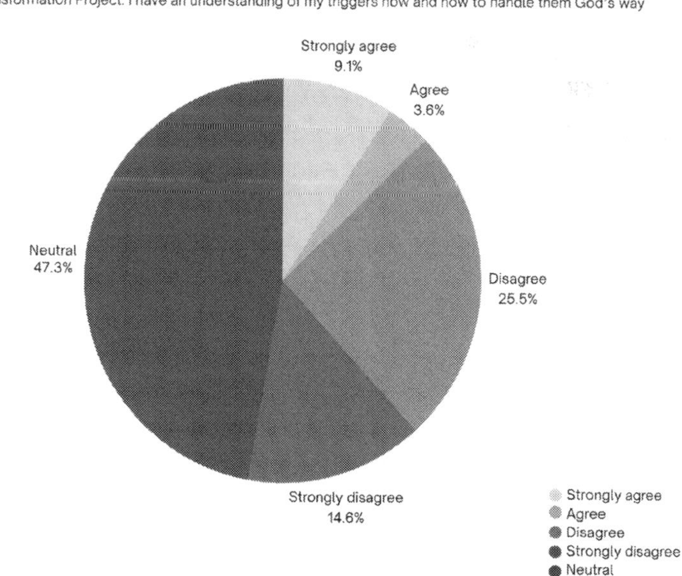

Figure 6:
After Transformation Project: I have an understanding of my triggers now and how to handle them God's way

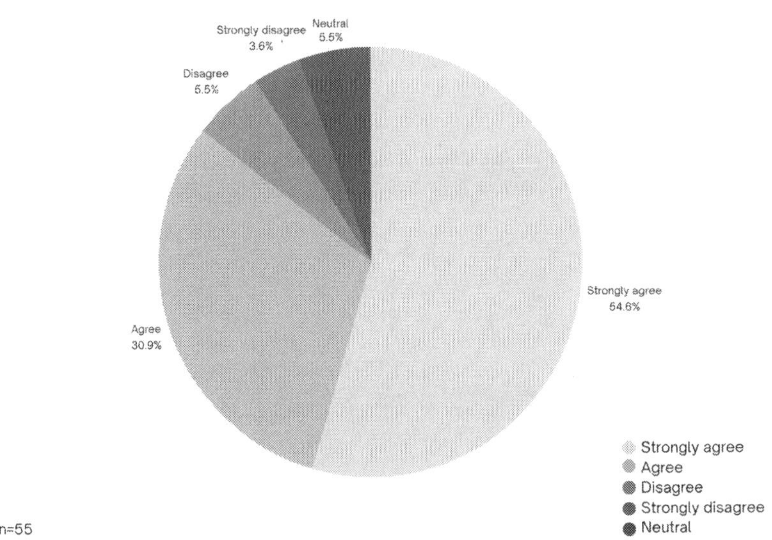

Responses

- Establish connections with mental health resources that can serve participants after program completion.
- Provide additional training for facilitators on supporting participants with complex mental health needs.
- Develop specific evaluation metrics to track mental health improvements throughout the program.

Finding 4. Participants rebuild and redefine relationships as they develop healthier boundaries and priorities.

Many participants enter the Transformation Project with severely damaged family relationships and unhealthy social connections due to addiction and lifestyle choices. The data reveals that through the program's emphasis on spiritual principles, accountability, and community support, participants experience profound transformation in their interpersonal relationships. This transformation occurs in three distinct areas: First, participants rebuild family relationships by reprioritizing their children and loved ones, reducing conflict, and becoming more active in parenting roles. Second, they develop critical boundary-setting skills, learning to distinguish between healthy and unhealthy relationships and making difficult but necessary decisions to distance themselves from negative influences. Third, they build new, supportive friendships within the recovery community, creating a sense of belonging and fellowship that many describe as 'family.' While this relationship rebuilding is described as among the most challenging aspects of recovery, participants consistently identify it as central to maintaining their transformation.

Key Themes from Qualitative Interviews

- Participants reprioritize family relationships, particularly with their children, creating more peaceful and harmonious home environments with less conflict and stress.
- Critical boundary-setting skills emerge as participants learn to distinguish between healthy and unhealthy relationships, often making difficult decisions to distance themselves from negative influences.
- The program facilitates the development of new, authentic friendships within the recovery community, providing a supportive network that many describe as a newfound family.
- Forgiveness becomes both a spiritual practice and a practical tool for healing damaged relationships and moving forward in recovery.
- Parenting skills and confidence improve significantly, with many participants reconnecting with their children and taking an active role in their lives after periods of absence or dysfunction.

Interview Quotes

"My life went from being an unstable selfish individual and not being able to see my child to now being in my child's life."

"I like being with a community of believers. There's something about being surrounded by real, loving faith believers that I know pray with me and for me. I now have no fear of fellowship."

"The most exciting thing I've learned with the Transformation Project that keeps me committed is the fellowship with other christians in recovery. It taught me the value of prayer. It's given me a sense of wholeness, togetherness and family that I didn't have before."

Quantitative Insights & Charts

- 94.6% of respondents have taken steps to improve family relationships (see Figure 7).
- Survey data indicates that respondents are becoming more aware of boundaries and actively selecting healthier ones, which contributes to improved relationships (see Figure 8, 9, and 10).

Figure 7:
As a result of my participation in the Transformation Project, I have taken steps to improve my family relationships.

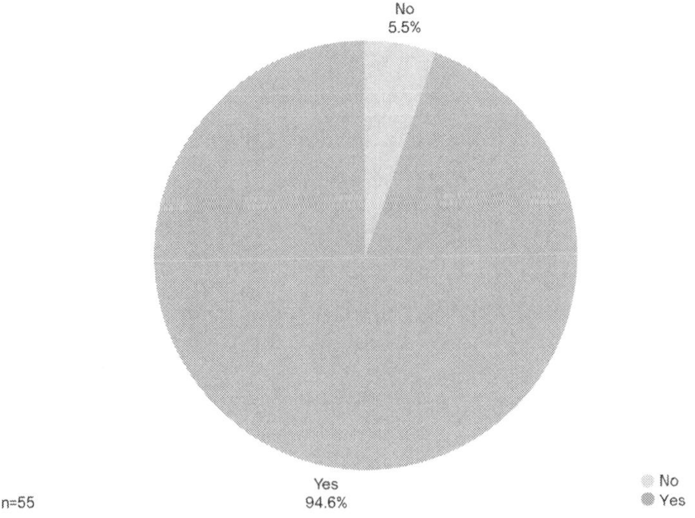

Responses

- Expand curriculum components dealing with family reconciliation and boundary-setting.
- Create resources for participants' family members to better understand and support recovery.
- Develop follow-up protocols specifically focused on relationship health after program completion.

Figure 8:
As a result of my participation in the Transformation Project, I recognize and choose healthy boundaries more now than before.

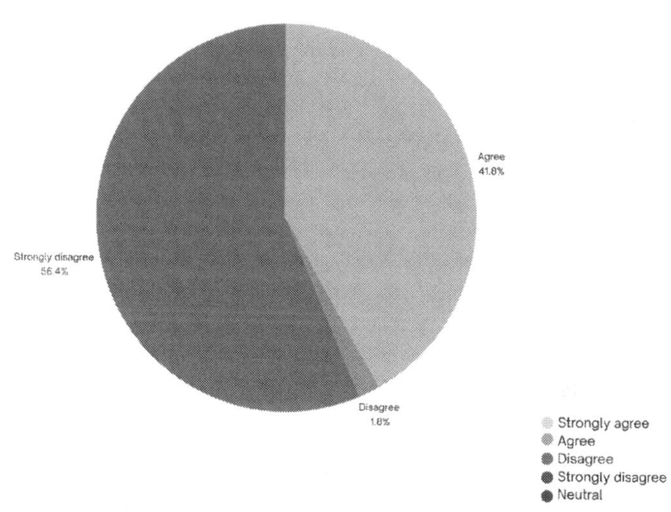

n=55

Figure 9:
Before Transformation Project: I have an understanding of my boundaries in helping others.

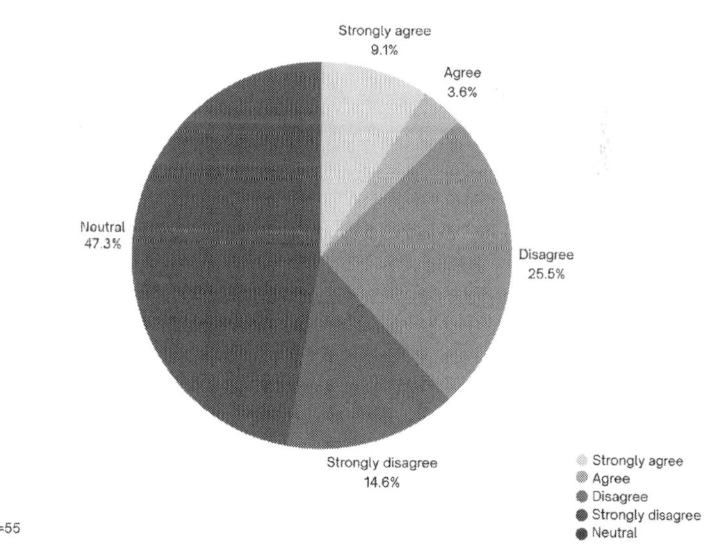

n=55

Figure 10:
After Transformation Project: I have an understanding of my boundaries in helping others.

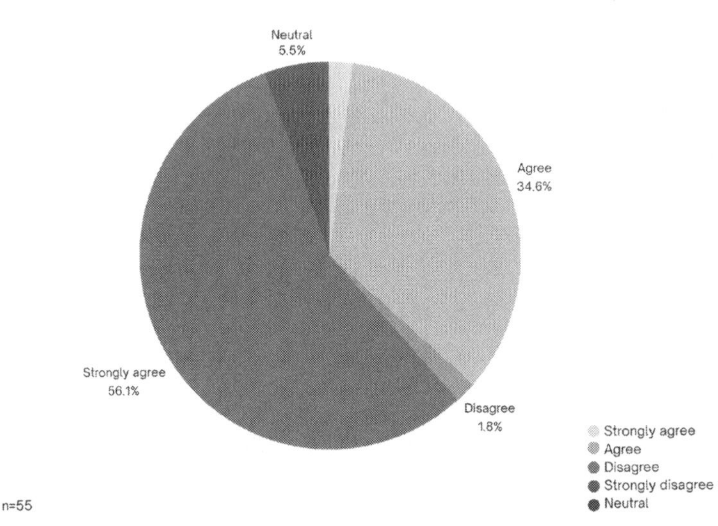

Finding 5. Participants develop concrete accountability practices through work, community engagement, and recovery commitments.

Many participants enter the Transformation Project having struggled with reliability and responsibility due to addiction and unstable lifestyles. Our data reveals that the program systematically builds accountability through interconnected spheres of practice. Initially, participants develop basic accountability through program attendance, small group participation, and sobriety commitments. This foundation then extends to employment, where participants not only secure jobs but maintain them over time, demonstrating newfound work ethics and integrity. The third sphere involves community integration, with participants consistently engaging in church activities and community service, often continuing these commitments after graduation. What makes this transformation significant is how these accountability practices reinforce each other – success in maintaining small commitments builds confidence for larger responsibilities, creating a positive cycle of growth. Participants describe this developing accountability not just as behavioral change but as a fundamental shift in identity, frequently connecting their newfound reliability to spiritual transformation and their 'new identity in Christ.'

Key Themes from Qualitative Interviews

- Participants develop consistent engagement with program requirements, including small group participation, addiction recovery meetings, and church attendance, often continuing these practices voluntarily after program completion.
- Employment accountability emerges as participants not only secure jobs but maintain them over time, demonstrating newfound work ethics, punctuality, and reliability that employers recognize and value.
- Financial responsibility improves as participants learn budgeting, begin addressing past debts, and make consistent payments for housing and other obligations.
- Interpersonal accountability develops through making and keeping commitments to others, rebuilding trust with family members, and maintaining boundaries in relationships.
- Sobriety maintenance becomes both a personal commitment and a community responsibility, with participants recognizing how their choices affect others around them.

Interview Quotes

"Integrity and work ethics is something I didn't have before, so that's one of my significant accomplishments since finding my new identity in Christ."

"I see myself continuing to grow by being a disciple of Christ, being present in church and bible study. I want to engage more in church."

"I now have a need to go to the ladies bible study class. I'm dedicated to going and have made it a priority to go every Thursday night even though I have graduated."

Quantitative Insights & Charts

- Data shows that respondents showed a significant increase from a 2.84% rating to a 4.43% rating (on a scale of 1-5, 1 being strongly disagree and 5 being strongly agree) in holding themselves more accountable & following through with commitments (see Figure 11 and 12), which lends to maintaining stability in their recovery (see Figure 13).

Figure 11:
Before Transformation Project: I hold myself accountable and follow through with my commitments.

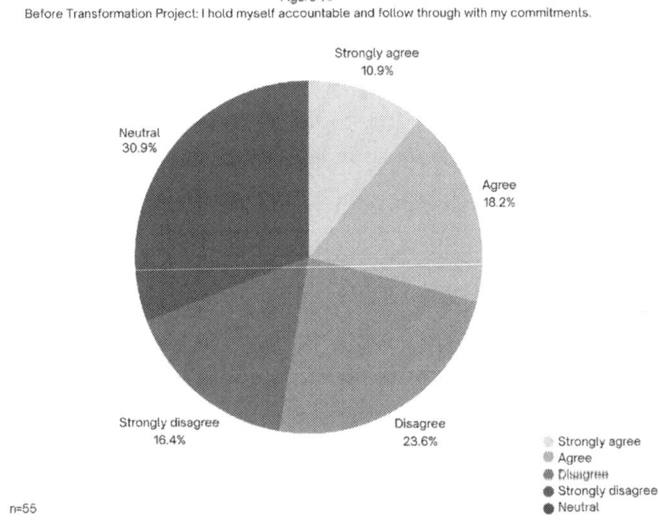

Figure 12:
Before Transformation Project: I hold myself accountable and follow through with my commitments.

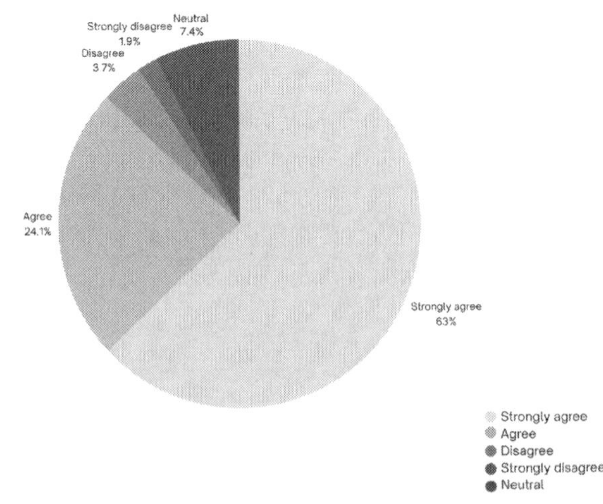

Figure 13:
As a result of my participation in the Transformation Project, I feel I can maintain stability in my recovery.

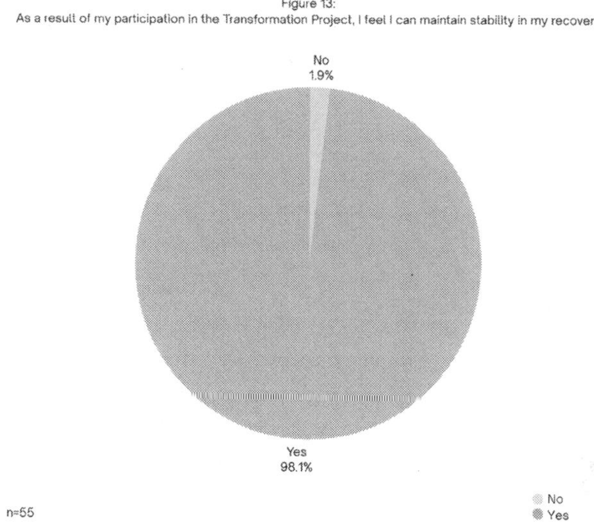

Responses

- Strengthen the assessment of participants' accountability development throughout the program.
- Expand community partnerships that provide accountability structures beyond program completion.
- Develop resources for participants transitioning from incarceration to community living.

Finding 6. Participants transform from service recipients to service providers through mentorship and community contribution.

A significant marker of transformation in the program is participants' evolution from primarily receiving services to actively providing help to others. This shift represents a fundamental change in identity and purpose for individuals who previously may have been isolated or focused primarily on their own needs. Participants demonstrate this shift in multiple ways: providing peer counseling based on their lived experiences, volunteering within the program and broader community, sharing personal testimonies to inspire others, and even taking on formal leadership roles in classes and groups. The program intentionally creates opportunities for this service through graduated responsibilities and mentorship roles. This giving orientation appears to strengthen participants' own recovery as they find meaning and purpose in supporting others.

Key Themes from Qualitative Interviews

- Participants discover purpose and meaning through helping others, transforming their self-perception into a valuable community contributor. The ability to use personal struggles as a resource for others reframes difficult past experiences as valuable wisdom that can benefit the community.
- Participants develop spiritual leadership by helping others come to Christ, which provides them with a sense of purpose and enables them to integrate their personal testimonies with their newfound faith.
- Service activities strengthen recovery by reinforcing personal transformation and fostering accountability through a sense of responsibility to others.
- Participants progress to formal leadership roles by helping facilitate classes, demonstrating both their mastery of program content and their development of leadership skills that benefit the entire community.

Interview Quotes

"Over the next year my goal is to get my certification as a care support specialist and be able to lead my daughter to Christ through my testimony."

"I'm dedicated to the Transformation Project because I get to truly see people grow and that encourages me as well."

"I'm able to share more about what I'm going through with others to help them get through it. My biggest accomplishment would be being able to counsel others who have depression & anxiety issues and be able to help them through it."

Quantitative Insights & Charts

- After participating in the Transformation Project, 94.6% of respondents have grown more confident in freely sharing their story with others (see Figure 14).
- The survey confirms that the vast majority (98%) of respondents look for opportunities to give back to others and the community (see Figure 15).

Figure 14:

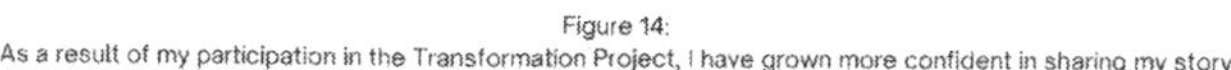
As a result of my participation in the Transformation Project, I have grown more confident in sharing my story.

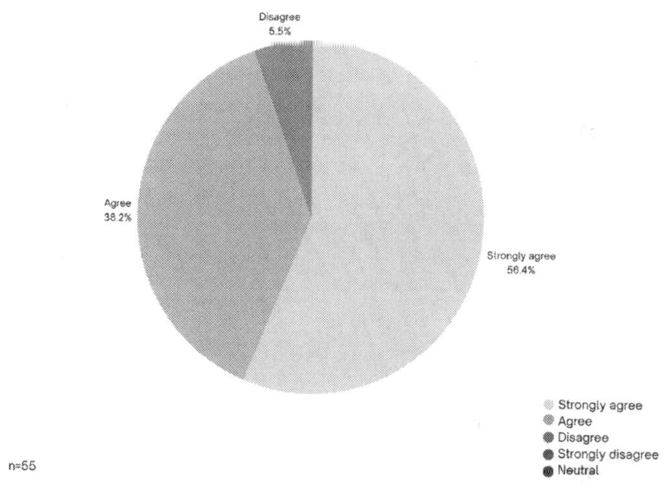

Figure 15:
As a result of my participation in the Transformation Project, I look for opportunities to give back rather than take.

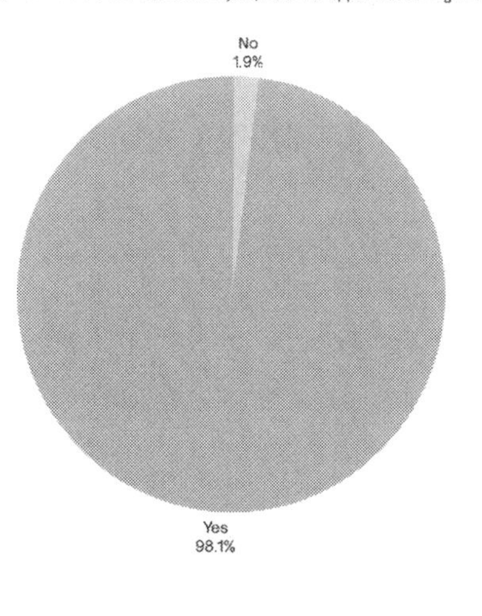

n=55

No
Yes

Responses

- Create formalized pathways for program graduates to become program volunteers or leaders.
- Develop training materials specifically for former participants transitioning into service roles.
- Establish metrics to track the impact of peer mentorship on both mentors and participants.

Finding 7. Participants develop improved decision-making skills and higher personal standards.

When participants first enter the Transformation Project, they often have a history of decision-making patterns influenced by addiction and negative peer pressure. The data reveals that through biblical teaching, accountability structures, and mentorship, participants develop significantly improved decision-making capabilities. This transformation manifests in three key areas: First, participants learn to pause and reflect before acting, often consulting scripture or trusted mentors rather than responding impulsively. Second, they begin holding themselves to higher personal standards in all areas of life, from work performance to personal hygiene to relationship choices. Third, they develop the ability to evaluate potential consequences of their actions, weighing short-term gratification against long-term goals. Participants consistently describe this improvement in decision-making as fundamental to their ability to maintain recovery and build stable lives. The program's emphasis on both spiritual principles and practical life skills appears to create a framework that helps participants rewire their approach to everyday choices.

Key Themes from Qualitative Interviews

- Participants report significant shifts from impulsive reactions to thoughtful responses when facing challenges.
- Many describe learning to "think before acting" as a crucial new skill developed through the program.
- The ability to evaluate relationships and social situations for potential risks becomes a protective factor.

- Participants develop increased consciousness about how their choices affect others, particularly family members.
- Higher personal standards emerge as participants begin to see themselves as worthy of better circumstances.

Interview Quotes

"I look at life differently. I think before I act; I just live differently. Transformation keeps me on schedule and keeps me active."

"I use the Bible daily, in all instances. I can apply spiritual principles in my life, and I know God has his arms around me. I've flooded my life with scripture."

Responses

- Enhance curriculum components focused on practical decision-making frameworks.
- Develop assessment tools to identify decision-making growth throughout the program.
- Create follow-up resources that support continued growth in this area after program completion.

Finding 8. Participants develop specific tools for processing past trauma through faith-based reconciliation.

Many participants enter the Transformation Project carrying unresolved trauma that has contributed to their addiction cycles and behaviors. Our interview data reveals that the program provides participants with specific tools and frameworks for identifying, processing, and healing from traumatic experiences through a faith-based lens. This is distinct from general emotional healing; it represents a deliberate confrontation with specific painful past events that often form the root causes of addictive behaviors. Participants describe learning to identify trauma triggers, connect these to their behavioral patterns, and apply scriptural principles to reframe these experiences. What makes this transformation notable is that participants move beyond simply managing trauma symptoms to actively engaging with their histories in ways that disarm the power these experiences hold over them. Many describe gaining the ability to "tell their story" differently—no longer as victims defined by their worst experiences, but as overcomers whose painful past now serves as testimony to spiritual restoration. This process of reconciling with their own histories appears to remove significant barriers to sustained recovery and healthy relationships.

Key Themes from Qualitative Interviews

- Participants gain specific tools for identifying connections between past trauma and current behaviors.
- Many learn to articulate and process specific painful events they previously avoided confronting.
- A spiritual framework for understanding suffering helps participants integrate traumatic experiences into a redemptive narrative.
- The concept of reconciliation extends both to self-forgiveness and to addressing relationships damaged by past trauma.
- Participants develop the ability to use their traumatic histories as resources for helping others with similar experiences.
- The program's small group format creates safe contexts for trauma disclosure and processing that many have never experienced before.

Interview Quotes

"I'm still dealing with mental health issues, but now I'm more aware of it. I've even had issues with self-worth due to life's situations, but the Transformation Project is helping me work on that."

"I've learned that even in a place of desolation and hopelessness that God has never left me."

Responses

- Provide specialized trauma-informed training for all facilitators.
- Develop better screening tools to identify trauma needs at program entry.
- Create tailored approaches for incarcerated participants dealing with institutional trauma.

Finding 9. Participants develop practical life management skills that support long-term stability.

The interviews reveal that beyond spiritual transformation, participants develop a comprehensive set of practical life management skills that are essential for maintaining long-term stability. Through structured programming and mentorship, participants develop concrete skills in time management, financial planning, and general life organization. These practical abilities appear to be critical bridges between spiritual growth and sustained recovery success. Participants consistently identify specific life management practices they've acquired—from maintaining a calendar to meal planning to budgeting—as key factors in their ability to create stability. This finding suggests that the program's holistic approach, addressing both spiritual needs and practical life skills, creates a foundation for participants to build sustainable, independent lives after completion.

Key Themes from Qualitative Interviews

- Participants learn basic time management skills, including keeping appointments and following structured daily routines.
- Financial literacy improves significantly, with participants learning budgeting, saving, and responsible spending.
- Home management skills develop, creating more stable living environments, especially for participants with children.
- Goal-setting and planning capabilities extend participants' time horizons from immediate survival to long-term aspirations.
- Participants develop organizational systems that support consistent medication management, appointments, and recovery commitments.

Interview Quotes

"I know how to maintain these changes, not because I enjoy my freedom, but because my kids are my priority now."

"The most challenging part has been letting go of people who are in active addiction. The most frustrating part for me is setting those boundaries and having to enforce them and being selfish when it comes to me getting better."

"I want to start a mental health support class in my church. I believe the Transformation Project gave me the skills and confidence to start this ministry/support group."

Responses

- Enhance life skills curriculum components based on identified participant needs
- Develop assessment tools to track life management skill development throughout the program
- Create partnerships with community resources that can support ongoing skill development

Conclusion

Insights Into Impact

Our evaluation reveals that the Transformation Project is achieving significant impact in line with our mission to make disciples of Jesus Christ. For years, we measured our success primarily through recidivism rates, noting that 75% of our graduates did not return to jail. However, this evaluation has helped us understand our impact more holistically, particularly in relation to our core mission of spiritual transformation.

The data clearly demonstrates that participants are experiencing profound spiritual growth. All survey respondents reported feeling more at peace with God and others after participating in our program. This universal response affirms that our faith-based approach is creating the conditions for meaningful transformation. Participants consistently described a fundamental shift from self-reliance to God-reliance, surrendering control and learning to trust in divine guidance.

Additionally, we've observed remarkable changes in participants' relationships, mental health, and sense of purpose. They are rebuilding family connections, setting healthier boundaries, developing accountability practices, and finding meaning through service to others. These outcomes align perfectly with our vision of holistic transformation, which impacts not just individuals but also their families and communities.

Steps Forward

Based on our evaluation findings, we are moving forward with our strategic plan focusing on External and Internal Capacity Growth. Specifically, we will:

- Review our acceptance policy to gain a better understanding of why a small percentage (less than 2%) of participants reported no spiritual growth impact. We need to determine whether some applicants are primarily seeking our program to avoid incarceration rather than for genuine transformation.
- Evaluate our curriculum to ensure it meets participants where they are spiritually. For those who may already possess spiritual maturity but have experienced legal troubles, our basic teachings may need enhancement to continue fostering their growth.
- Assess the effectiveness of all our facilitators as communicators. The quality of instruction and mentorship is critical to our participants' transformation journey.
- Expand our outreach efforts to incarcerated individuals. Our evaluation identified a need to develop methods for gathering data from those who are still incarcerated, which will help us understand their unique needs and challenges.
- Strengthen our follow-up processes with participants regardless of their graduation status. This will provide valuable insights into the long-term impact and help us identify additional support needs.

Opportunities for Future Evaluation

As we continue to grow and refine our program, we recognize several opportunities for future evaluation:

1. Expand our evaluation beyond Hamilton County to include all counties where we operate. This broader scope will help us understand how program implementation and impact might vary across different communities.
2. Develop a longitudinal study tracking participants over multiple years to assess the durability of the transformations they experience and identify factors that contribute to sustained positive outcomes.
3. Gather more comparative data between volunteers, participants, and those who serve in both capacities to better understand the mutual benefits of the program's service orientation.
4. Investigate the specific mechanisms through which spiritual transformation leads to behavioral changes and improved life outcomes, which will help us strengthen these elements in our program design.
5. Develop metrics that more directly measure discipleship outcomes, aligning our evaluation methods more closely with our mission of making disciples of Jesus Christ.

This evaluation is "not a one and done experience." We are committed to ongoing learning and program refinement based on evaluation insights, continuously improving our ability to transform lives through the power of God.

THE KNOBLE

Financial Institution Membership

Amanda Maxfield, Doug Bennett, and Evan Hokrein

Organization and Program Overview

Introduction to Organization

Established in 2019, The Knoble exists to ignite a global movement of professionals working together to disrupt Human Crime. Perpetrators of Human Crime - a broad category that includes human trafficking, online child exploitation, elder financial abuse, and scams - target vulnerable people and exploit them for profit. The Knoble believes that following the money trail is the key to stopping this flood of exploitation, abuse, and enslavement. By empowering financial services professionals and their partners to recognize and disrupt the financial activity behind these crimes, we get closer to our vision of a world in which no one is enslaved, abused, or scammed.

Program Description

The Knoble's membership program brings together a global network of professionals who are committed to protecting people from exploitation. Members represent the intersection of crime prevention and financial services, including, but not limited to financial services professionals and law enforcement agents. Currently, there are over 2000 members of The Knoble, with over 1000 members from financial institutions.

Through collaboration, shared learning, and practical initiatives, the program empowers members to turn their expertise into meaningful action against Human Crime.

Intended Impacts

Financial service professionals are awakened to the reality of Human Crime and their role in preventing it. Financial professionals understand that human trafficking, child sexual exploitation, financial scams, and elder financial exploitation occur and have a direct connection with the movement of money through financial institutions.

Financial service professionals are mobilized in their workplaces and communities to disrupt Human Crime. Financial professionals enhance the detection, investigation, reporting, intervention, and prevention of human crime within their workplace, working groups, and communities.

Financial service professionals are equipped with tools and knowledge for how to detect and report specific Human Crimes. Financial professionals learn about current methods used by scammers, abusers, and traffickers to fund their crimes. They improve their knowledge of red flags associated with the crimes that allow them to detect and report Human Crime through their normal work in fraud prevention and anti-money laundering.

Evaluation Methodology

The aim of our evaluation was to see what kind and quality of impact Knoble membership is having on the financial institution professionals. To understand this, we explored two broad evaluation questions:

1. What kind and quality of impact are we having on our members?
2. What aspects of our program are causing this impact?

Over the course of the project, we (a) developed and refined our ideas of intended impact and indicators, (b) designed and implemented a mixed methods outcome evaluation using both qualitative and quantitative means to collect and analyze data, (c) identified themes and findings, and (d) considered the implications to those findings for program improvement and innovation.

This project began by identifying and clarifying the intended impact of Knoble membership. Once the ideas of impact had been developed, we used the Heart Triangle™ model to identify qualitative and quantitative indicators of impact on the mental, behavioral, and emotional changes in our members working at financial institutions. We used these indicators to design a qualitative interview protocol and a quantitative questionnaire to evaluate progress toward achieving our intended impact.

Qualitative Data Collection and Analysis

For the qualitative portion of the evaluation, we designed an in-depth interview protocol to gain data about the structural, qualitative changes resulting from our program. While our membership spans multiple industries, we delimited our population to include only members from financial institutions who had participated in a Knoble webinar or initiative in the past year. Our population size for this evaluation was 303. We used a purposeful stratified sampling technique to select a representative sample from the population we serve. Our sample size was 12, drawn from the following strata of our population:

- Type of Institution: Bank, Credit Union
- Size of institution: Large Bank, Midsize Bank, Small Bank, Large Credit Union, Midsize Credit Union, Small Credit Union
- Employment Seniority: VP, Director, Manager, Mid-Level Professional

Our interview team consisted of Amanda Maxfield, Doug Bennett, and Evan Hokrein. We convened one-on-one interviews lasting between 30 minutes and one hour in length and collected interview data using handwritten notes and voice transcription through Microsoft Teams.

We then analyzed the data inductively using a modified version of thematic analysis. Each interviewer analyzed the data from their interviews individually to identify initial themes. Together, we developed common themes from all of the interviews collectively. We identified the overarching and inter-interview themes that emerged from the full scope of our data analysis to illuminate the collective insights and discoveries. We mapped these themes visually and examined the dynamics among the themes, causes and catalysts of the themes, new or surprising insights related to the themes, and relationships between the themes that were revealed in the data. We then determined the most significant and meaningful discoveries and brought them forward as findings.

Quantitative Data Collection and Analysis

For the quantitative portion of the evaluation, we designed a questionnaire to collect data on our quantitative indicators of impact. We administered this instrument to 930 members (all our financial institution members) and had a response of 45, a 4.8% response rate. The data were analyzed primarily using measures of central tendency. We identified key insights, patterns, and gaps within the data and incorporated these discoveries into the related findings. The most significant insights from the quantitative data are described in the following narrative.

Limitations

The primary limitation in the study is the low response rate for the quantitative survey. We expanded the population size to include all financial institution members, a population three times greater than the qualitative population. Thus, the connection between quantitative and qualitative results may not be as strong, and the response rate for the quantitative survey is very low.

Findings

Finding 1. Increased confidence in affecting change, finding purpose in work.

The data from the interviews indicated that participating in The Knoble increased members' confidence in their ability to make meaningful change. Rather than simply checking the box on compliance, they have a deeper motivation for their work. Many members reported that The Knoble helped them reconnect with their purpose, feeling like they are contributing to something bigger. The survey data appears to complement these interview findings, showing an increase from 45% to 73% in members who report feeling "Quite a bit" or "Very much" empowered in their institution to champion ideas for fighting human crime after joining The Knoble. Members described taking more initiative to share about human crime with their coworkers, families, and friends. Several members also mentioned that supplying information to law enforcement made their jobs more meaningful, even if they never found out the end result of the reported case. Others mentioned the reality of the people behind the transaction: compliance work becomes more meaningful when there is a possibility of saving a child or a vulnerable person. Even small actions were viewed as significant, as members have been able to see their place in a larger movement of impact.

Key Themes from Qualitative Interviews

- Increased Confidence in Making Meaningful Change
    - Members feel more equipped to take actions that go beyond basic compliance and contribute to broader financial crime prevention efforts.
    - Participation in The Knoble has given members a sense of personal and professional empowerment.
    - Greater sense of purpose atwork
    - Many members report that their participation has given them a renewed passion for their work.
    - Instead of viewing fraud detection as routine, members now see it as a way to make a tangible impact in protecting vulnerable populations.
    - Belief that small changes can have significant impacts
    - Respondents recognize that incremental improvements, such as refining detection methods or enhancing internal reporting, can lead to larger systemic change.
    - Even when immediate results are not visible, members remain committed to long-term progress.

Interview Quotes

"I'm a pebble in a huge ocean, but every little bit helps. If what you do keeps one person from being a victim, then that's a success."

"It really helps me reconnect with that purpose of everything that we're working together towards."

"I have confidence in knowing that I'm part of something bigger. And I want to share that with people."

"I wake up every day and go to work for a reason. Like yes, I get a paycheck, but the time that I put into my work and my effort, it can have impact, it can have meaning."

Quantitative Insights & Charts

- Significant increase in empowerment: Members reporting high empowerment ("quite a bit" or "very much") to champion anti-human crime ideas increased from 44.4% before joining The Knoble to 73.3% afterward—a 29 percentage point improvement (see Figure 1).
- More members reach highest confidence levels: The data shows meaningful movement from lower to higher empowerment categories, with the combined "Quite a bit" and "Very much" responses growing from 20 members to 33 members out of 45 total respondents (see Figure 2).

Responses

- Create more opportunities for "small changes" rather than few opportunities for big change.
    - Create and implement clear member journey, outlining potential opportunities for involvement.
- Develop a better feedback loop with law enforcement to reward FSPs with knowledge of results of their work.
    - Empower members (and HCS participants) to make connections with local law enforcement.

- Write a "Purpose-Driven" Report with interviews from Knoble members.
    - Communicate interview results with stakeholders on a consistent basis.

Figure 1:
I feel empowered in my institution to champion ideas for fighting human crime.

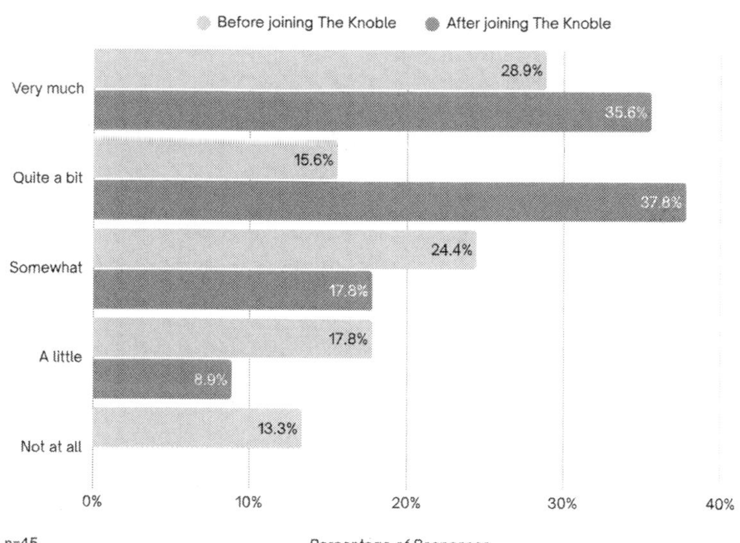

Figure 2:
Members responding "Quite a bit" or "Very much"

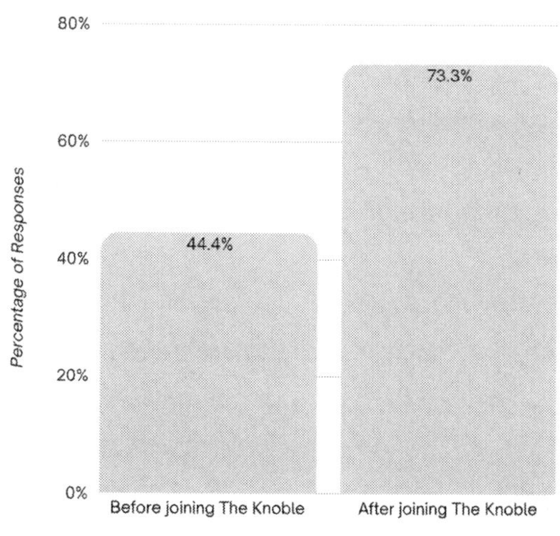

Finding 2. Increased awareness of Human Crime.

Members of The Knoble report a significant increase in awareness of the scope and magnitude of human trafficking and other forms of human crime. This awareness extends beyond their professional roles, influencing how they perceive their own communities and interactions in daily life. The survey results suggest a similar pattern, with an increase from 64% to 98% of surveyed members who report understanding "Quite a bit" or "Very much" about the connection between human crime and financial institutions after joining The Knoble. Members reported recognizing the connections between financial crime, money laundering, and human trafficking, understanding that these crimes are often interwoven. Increased awareness has led to members advocating in their institutions for more thorough detection and reporting processes. In some cases, it resulted in a suspicious transaction being reported that otherwise would have gone unnoticed.

Key Themes from Qualitative Interviews

- Increased Awareness of the Magnitude of Human Trafficking
  - Members have learned that human trafficking is far more prevalent than they previously realized.
  - The Knoble has helped to frame trafficking as a financial crime, making it more relevant to financial institutions.
  - Recognizing That Human Trafficking Can Happen Anywhere
  - Members expressed a shift in perspective, acknowledging that human trafficking is not just an international issue but one that occurs in their own communities.
  - Some reported feeling more vigilant in public spaces and at work.
- Understanding Financial Systems Used for Exploitation
  - Through The Knoble, members have gained deeper insight into how trafficking-related transactions appear in financial systems.
  - They are now more aware of how money laundering, shell companies, and fraud schemes are often connected to human trafficking.

- Awareness Translated into Action
  - Members have spread awareness in their local communities, among family members, and throughout the industry and the workplace.
  - Members reported suspicious activity that would have otherwise gone unnoticed.

Interview Quotes

"I didn't know it was so huge... Before you guys, I knew that it happened, but I didn't know that it was so widely scattered, especially in the U.S."

"I think they're using [laundered money] to fund illicit enterprise and human trafficking is likely a part of that. The Knoble helped me become more aware of that possibility."

"The Knoble awoke the fact that money laundering is tied to human trafficking. Even though it's a sex crime and a human crime, there's money involved. That's the reason they do it."

Quantitative Insights & Charts

- The detailed response distribution shows a dramatic shift toward higher understanding levels, with "Quite a bit" responses increasing substantially and "Very much" responses also growing significantly after joining The Knoble (see Figure 3).
- Members understanding the connection between human crime and financial institutions "Quite a bit" or "Very much" increased dramatically from 66.7% before joining to 97.8% after joining The Knoble (see Figure 4).

Responses

- Emphasize more human crime case studies — now that our members know that human crime exists, what are concrete examples for how to stop it?
  - Bring in more subject matter experts who can speak to specific cases.

- Continue to increase awareness for other crimes, such as sextortion and CSE.
    - Highlight different crime types in Third Thursday Talks.
- Encourage FSPs to share awareness with local community groups.
    - Create community awareness assets for members to present/share.
- Spotlight members who are involved in rehabilitation nonprofits.
    - LinkedIn features of members doing work outside of The Knoble.

Figure 3:
How would you rate your understanding of the connection between human crime and financial institutions? (e.g., identifying suspicious financial activity, such as unusual transactions or account behavior, that may indicate human trafficking or exploitation.

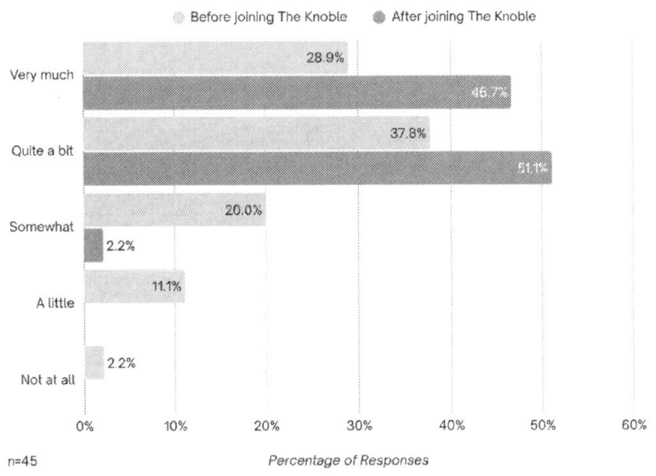

Figure 4:
Members responding "Quite a bit" or "Very much"

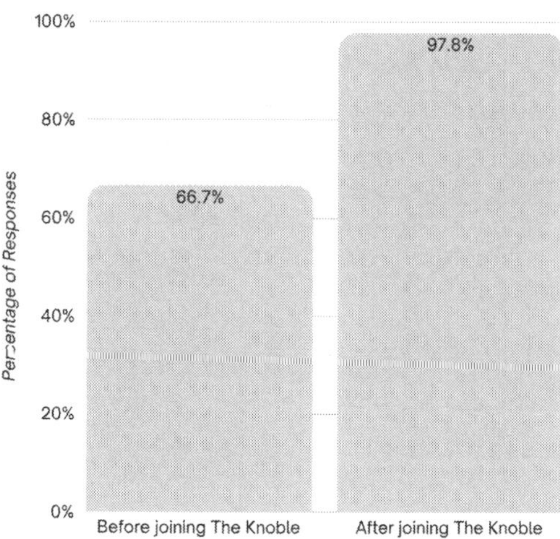

n=45

Finding 3. Knoble members are better equipped to detect and report Human Crime.

The Knoble has played a critical role in equipping financial service professionals with the skills and resources to detect and report human crime. Webinars, investigative guides, and typology reports have directly contributed to their ability to identify and respond to suspicious activity. Survey responses align with this finding, showing an increase from 43% to 70% in members responding "Quite a bit" or "Very much" when asked about their understanding of how to leverage their skills to disrupt human crime after joining The Knoble. Members in fraud, financial crimes, and AML roles reported having increased skills when it comes to detecting and reporting Human Crime. The interviews suggest that members have become more educated on how to respond to victims of scams and potential human trafficking cases. The interviews also suggest that The Knoble's resources and content are being used in the daily operations of financial professionals and as training tools within their organizations.

Key Themes from Qualitative Interviews

- Improved Knowledge and Detection Capabilities
    - Financial professionals report that The Knoble's materials provide tangible tools for identifying red flags in transactions.
    - Members have incorporated best practices from The Knoble's training into their daily fraud and compliance operations.
- Greater Application of Investigative Techniques
    - Some members have enhanced their investigative strategies based on typologies and case studies provided by The Knoble.
    - Roundtable discussions have helped members refine their approach to tracking and analyzing criminal financial behavior.

Interview Quotes

"A lot of times we see activity and not necessarily know what it means... I think that has been one of the best pieces that I have gained—knowing what to look for, what it could potentially mean, and what steps we need to take."

"I've really enjoyed your webinars... It gives me something to look at when I'm doing transactional analysis, trying to get those red flags or dig a little deeper."

"The Knoble's guidance around human trafficking has helped us to better detect this type of activity and report it."

Quantitative Insights & Charts

- The detailed breakdown reveals that "Quite a bit" became the most common response level after joining The Knoble, with notable increases in higher confidence categories and decreases in lower confidence levels (see Figure 5).
- The percentage of members responding "Quite a bit" or "Very much" about understanding how to leverage their skills to disrupt human crime rose from 44.4% before joining to 75.6% after joining The Knoble (see Figure 6).

Figure 5:
I understand how to leverage my skills to disrupt human crime.

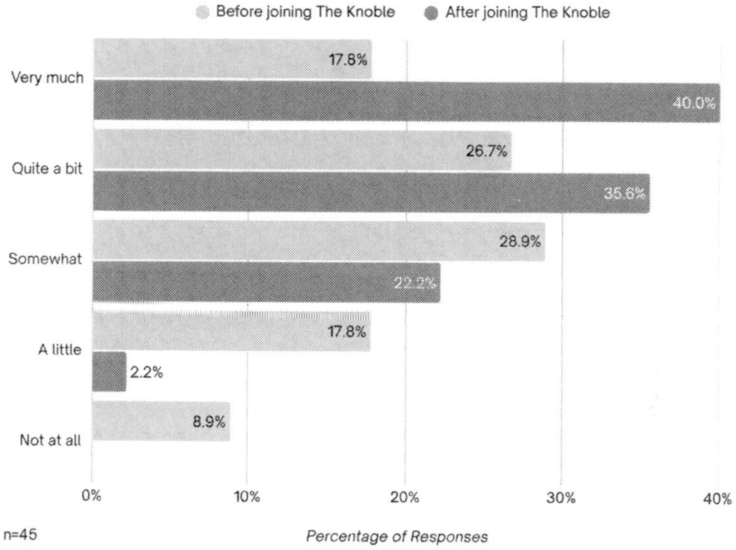

n=45

Figure 6:
Members responding "Quite a bit" or "Very much"

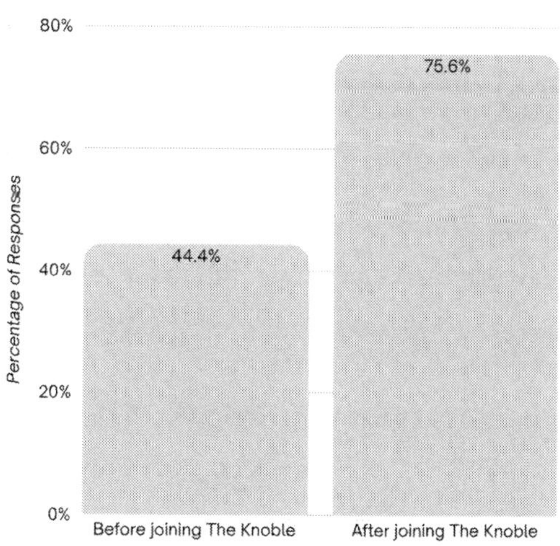

n=45

Responses

- Increase the number of investigative guides/guidances published rather than just producing webinars.
- Determine how to measure the reach of our resources (how to track how many people view the document if it is shared)
- Develop specialized educational curriculum (learning paths, certification).

Finding 4. Financial service professionals are telling their colleagues about The Knoble, but are less likely to provide trainings or implement new processes and tools in their organization.

Fighting human crime requires collective action, and many financial service professionals use The Knoble's resources to train their teams. Interviewed members reported disseminating investigative guides, webinars, and typology reports to increase awareness and equip colleagues with tools for detection. Some organizations have even incorporated The Knoble's materials into official onboarding and training programs. However, the quantitative data suggest that while our members tell their colleagues about The Knoble, they are less likely to lead trainings or implement new processes or tools in their institution. In some cases, teams reported that The Knoble's resources did not provide new information for them. Additionally, some lower-level professionals reported having difficulty convincing leaders to support training.

Key Themes from Qualitative Interviews

- Knoble Members Act as Knowledge Disseminators
    - Many members actively share The Knoble's resources with their colleagues to strengthen their institution's response to human crime.
    - Some institutions have adopted The Knoble's materials into their compliance training.

- Integration of Training into Institutional Programs
    - Organizations have started using The Knoble's content for new-hire onboarding to ensure staff members are trained in financial crime detection.
    - Some members have adapted Knoble materials for internal fraud detection training workshops.

Interview Quotes

"Even with our webinars, even with the toolkits and the different documents that are out there for us through The Knoble, it has been extremely helpful to be able to disseminate through the information that I'm getting and then push it out to those people."

"We are picking different topics that are very narrow in scope and doing deep dive training exercises for our teams... Some of the human crimes have been topics. So we've done one on elder, we've done one on CSE."

"The resources, the different artifacts that The Knoble provides… bring together like minds but give tangible things. It gives me those artifacts and those resources to share with my team."

"Some of the slides and information that have been given in the past, I've utilized to train in my most recent position."

Quantitative Insights & Charts

- While 82% of surveyed members have told one or more colleagues about The Knoble (see Figure 8), only 58.9% have trained or invited colleagues to be trained on red flags using The Knoble resources (see Figure 7).
- Among those who have trained colleagues, members reported training an average of 7 colleagues, while those who told colleagues about The Knoble reported telling an average of 8 colleagues (see Figure 7 and 8).

- Over 55% of participants reported implementing or helped develop new processes, tools, or training within their organization to better detect human crime (see Figure 9).

Figure 7:
How many colleagues have you trained or invited to be trained on red flags/indicators of potential human crime using Knoble resources?

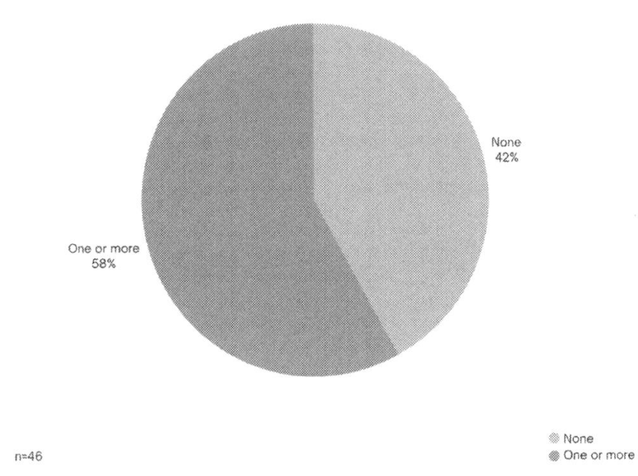

Figure 7 Note: "One or more" increases to 65% of employment roles below manager level are excluded. Of those who have trained their colleagues using Knoble resources, members reported training an average of 7 colleagues.

Figure 8:
How many of your colleagues have you told about The Knoble?

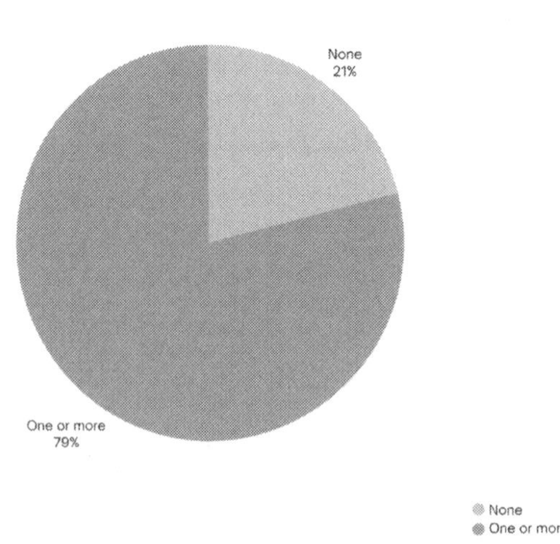

n=46

None
One or more

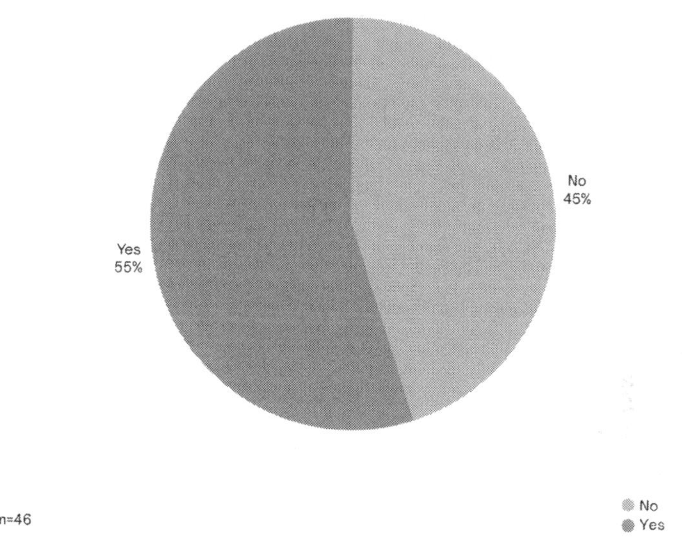

Responses

- Create easy-to-share educational content for internal training.
- Create team training hubs in the Member Center.
- Begin training entire teams around HC.

Finding 5. FSPs are becoming more aware and equipped, but it is difficult to see direct results in impacting change.

Many members of The Knoble report increased awareness of red flags and warning signs related to human crime but struggle with clear next steps. While they frequently use The Knoble's training materials, direct mobilization efforts remain limited. Institutional barriers, such as siloed decision-making in financial institutions and a lack of leadership buy-in, often prevent members from advancing human crime initiatives despite their personal commitment to the cause. Additionally, members express uncertainty about engaging law enforcement effectively, highlighting a gap in collaboration between the financial sector and investigative agencies. Time constraints further challenge engagement, as members request more actionable, concise training materials that can be quickly applied in their roles. Resource limitations within fraud and compliance teams, coupled with skepticism about the tangible impact of proactive efforts, also hinder stronger investment in human crime detection and prevention. The quantitative data reveals that the majority of surveyed members do not report human crime more frequently after joining The Knoble than before.

Key Themes from Qualitative Interviews

- **Increased Awareness Without Clear Next Steps**
    - Members acknowledge that they have a better understanding of red flags and warning signs of human crime but often do not feel they have the tools to take action beyond reporting suspicious activity.
    - They frequently use The Knoble's materials for training but do not articulate direct mobilization efforts beyond awareness-building.
- **Dependence on Institutional Support & Leadership Buy-In**
    - Many members feel limited by the structure of their financial institutions, where decision-making about risk, fraud, and compliance is siloed.
    - Despite personal passion, members express frustration that their organizations do not prioritize human crime initiatives or fail to recognize their importance.
- **Limited Engagement with Law Enforcement**
    - Members report making connections with law enforcement but do not feel confident about when or how to engage them effectively.
    - There is a noted gap between the financial services sector and law enforcement, preventing optimal information sharing and collaborative action.
- **Need for More Actionable, Concise Training**
    - Members value The Knoble's educational resources but struggle with time constraints, making it difficult to fully utilize them.

    - Requests for more "quick takeaways" or condensed red-flag summaries suggest that members want to apply their knowledge but need more practical, time-efficient resources.
- **Difficulty Justifying Resources for Human Crime Detection**
    - Fraud and compliance teams operate within tight budgets and limited staffing, making it difficult to allocate resources toward proactive human crime detection and prevention.
    - Some members express skepticism about the ability to make a meaningful impact, which may contribute to a lack of motivation for taking bolder steps.

Interview Quotes

"I think frustration sets in [when] we've provided training, we've participated in activism events, we've participated in community awareness events, right? But where are the results?"

"I would say the higher-ups not listening to, you know, the teams who see it day in and day out. You know, we see both ends. We are working for the bank and we're working for the customer... And it feels as though we don't get that support from who we need to get support from."

"Law enforcement wants the whole picture, [but] we don't have the whole picture. So, we give them this piece, and they say, 'this isn't enough.' Well, I can't give you what I don't have."

Quantitative Insights & Charts

- Despite increased awareness and capabilities, 58.8% of surveyed members report they have not reported suspected human crime more often since joining The Knoble (see Figure 10).

Responses

- Create step-by-step guides converting awareness into specific actions to address members' uncertainty about next steps despite increased knowledge.

- Organize sessions with law enforcement focused on what financial data constitutes probable cause to bridge the collaboration gap identified in interviews.

Figure 10:
Since joining The Knoble, have you reported suspected human crime more often than before?

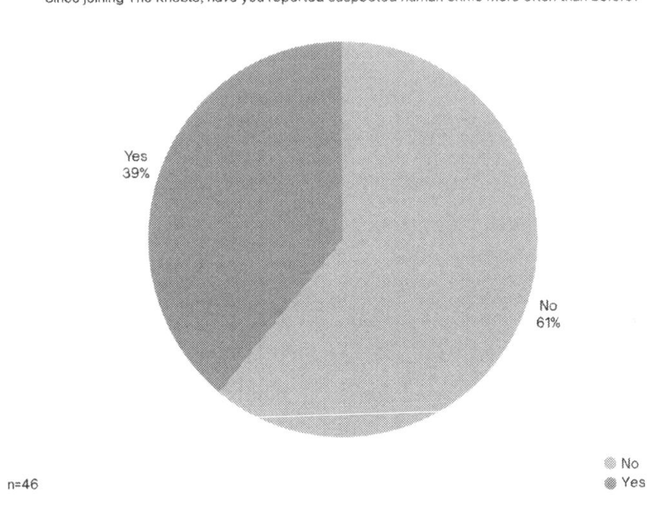

Finding 6. Connectedness and collaboration among members of our network is inhibited.

The Knoble has made great strides in facilitating collaboration in the industry, including a bank-law enforcement collaborative project around the Super Bowl and a cross-sector seminar that produced three major initiatives around preventing Human Crime. However, our interviews demonstrated that many members struggle to build meaningful connections beyond initial networking and project collaboration. Attending events and meeting industry peers often does not translate into sustained collaboration due to a lack of structured follow-up mechanisms. Additionally, members are unsure how or when to engage with others, particularly given the distinct priorities and communication barriers between financial institutions and law enforcement. This disconnect is further compounded by institutional policies and compliance restrictions, making it difficult to leverage law enforcement partnerships effectively. Within financial institutions, internal silos between fraud and financial crime compliance teams limit cross-team collaboration, preventing broader human crime prevention efforts. Some members also feel disengaged from The Knoble's ongoing initiatives, citing time constraints as a key barrier to deeper involvement and utilization of available resources.

Key Themes from Qualitative Interviews

- **Members Want to Connect but Struggle to Do So Effectively**
  - Many members recognize the value of networking through The Knoble but express difficulty in building meaningful relationships beyond surface-level interactions.
  - Several mention attending events, meeting people, and then losing touch due to lack of structured follow-up or a clear mechanism to maintain collaboration.
- **Lack of Clarity on How to Engage with Other Members**
  - Members do not always know how or when to reach out to others in the network, particularly in professional settings where financial institutions and law enforcement have distinct priorities and communication barriers.
  - Some express frustration with not knowing the best way to leverage industry contacts they make through The Knoble.
- **The Gap Between Financial Institutions and Law Enforcement Remains a Challenge**
  - While some members have met law enforcement contacts through The Knoble, they feel unsure about when to use those connections and how to facilitate better industry-law enforcement partnerships.
  - Compliance restrictions and institutional policies further prevent deeper collaboration with law enforcement agencies.
- **Fragmented Internal Structures at Financial Institutions Limit Cross-Team Collaboration**
  - Fraud and financial crime teams within institutions remain siloed, making it difficult for members to implement broader human crime prevention efforts.

  - Some members see the need for stronger connections between fraud teams and financial crime compliance teams but feel unable to drive change within their organizations.
- **Members Feel Disconnected from The Knoble's Ongoing Activities**
  - Some members appreciate the work of The Knoble but feel they are on the periphery, struggling to stay engaged.
  - A few mention time constraints preventing them from fully utilizing The Knoble's resources or participating in discussions.

Interview Quotes

"The Knoble does a great job of networking, but sometimes it feels like I'm meeting people in passing. I know these relationships could be valuable, but I don't always know how to follow up and make the most of them."

"I think a lot of the barriers are just kind of limited information sharing support within regulations... It's also a barrier just how busy everyone is... trying to find the time to commit to these various projects."

"I think networking is a big piece of it, just bringing those key players together... So, it's not just like networking where we're just talking about trends... we're actually meeting and partnering on specific objectives."

"I work very closely on a case-by-case basis with local law enforcement and FBI and Homeland Security. But that's because it's reactionary... It has really brought to me just how we can work together... to really drive meaningful change."

Responses

- Create incentives for networking within the Member Center.
- Facilitate conversation between fraud and AML teams.
- Build app so members can connect (like Slack).

- In person events, localized by city.
- Bring together executives to discuss real institutional change.

Finding 7. There's a change in how they view the customer – seeing humanity and not just a data set.

Our data shows that after financial service professionals join The Knoble they experience a change in how they view their customers. Where they once saw mainly data sets, they now see the humanity in their customers. Interviewed members expressed feelings that the customer was viewed as the "bad guy" before joining The Knoble. After joining The Knoble, there is a more holistic understanding of the crime, so the affected parties can receive appropriate responses.

Key Themes from Qualitative Interviews

- **Increased Emotional Connection to Cases**
  - Many members describe how their understanding of human crime has shifted from being purely transactional to deeply personal.
  - Instead of viewing fraud cases as just financial losses, they now recognize the real people being harmed and the devastating personal impacts of these crimes.
- **Recognizing Victims Beyond the Numbers**
  - Several members mention how they previously focused on fraud detection as a technical exercise but now see the human consequences behind the transactions.
  - There's a strong emphasis on how training and exposure to real-life stories have reshaped their perspectives on their work.
- **More Empathy and a Desire to Help Beyond the Transaction**
  - Many members describe a shift from merely identifying fraudulent transactions to actively trying to help victims recover and prevent further harm.
  - Some even mention personal outreach to customers, checking in on them, and offering resources beyond standard bank procedures.

- **Heightened Awareness of Vulnerable Populations**
  - Members acknowledge that fraud disproportionately affects certain groups, such as the elderly, immigrants, or individuals in distressing life situations.
  - Some have taken steps to engage more with their communities, especially in raising awareness about scams and exploitation.

Interview Quotes

"It brings a level of intimacy to it. Before, it was just numbers on a screen. Now, there's a face to it. You hear the stories, and it's not just black and white anymore."

"How can we be better at achieving impact rather than just kind of, you know, showing up and clearing my alert?"

"With my most recent role... I'm able to sit the customers down and actually speak to them one-on-one instead of just sending an e-mail out to them. I'm able to have that personal touch with them."

"If anything, [my increased awareness] has driven me even further. It's giving me more empathy. I embrace it more and I look at it more as, you know, helping people. I just get more passionate about it."

Responses

- Publish member testimonials/case studies by highlighting members who successfully shifted from transaction-focused to victim-focused approaches in their daily work.
- Guides for responding to victims of human crime.

Finding 8. Members believe that small, but significant influence can lead to bigger change.

Our data shows that our members believe that small, but significant influence can lead to bigger change. They described a shift in how they approach the issue of human crime. While many acknowledged feeling overwhelmed at first by the size and complexity of the problem, they also expressed a growing belief that small actions can still make a difference. Whether it's raising awareness, training their teams, or identifying a single case, members shared that these steps matter. Several also talked about the influence they have within their own organizations. They see value in spreading knowledge, improving fraud controls, and supporting colleagues. There was also a strong focus on prevention measures such as early action and training frontline associates or partnering with law enforcement before problems escalate. Across these conversations, one idea stood out: helping one person or taking one step can lead to larger change. This way of thinking has helped many move from feeling stuck to feeling like they can actually do something that counts.

Key Themes from Qualitative Interviews

- **A Shift from Feeling Overwhelmed to Recognizing the Power of Small Actions**
  - Many members acknowledge that the scale of human crime is massive and can feel insurmountable.
  - Despite this, they express that even small efforts—raising awareness, training their teams, or catching a single case—contribute to a larger impact.
- **Emphasis on Individual Influence within Their Organizations**
  - Some members mention how their role may not be directly tied to law enforcement or policymaking, but they can still drive change within their institutions.
  - They recognize that spreading knowledge, advocating for better fraud controls, and educating others are crucial steps in combating human crime.
- **A Focus on Prevention Rather than Just Reaction**
  - Members highlight the importance of proactive efforts, such as training frontline employees, implementing better fraud detection, and engaging law enforcement before issues escalate.
  - There is a sense that small improvements in fraud awareness can prevent larger-scale crimes from occurring.

- **Confidence That Every Action Matters**
  - Many members discuss how helping one person avoid fraud, educating one customer, or training one employee can create a ripple effect that leads to broader change.
  - This mindset shifts their perspective from frustration over not solving everything to empowerment in making a difference where they can.

Interview Quotes

"I don't know the outcome of that case, but I feel like I did everything I could... I slept better knowing that if it was true, I did everything I could to stop it."

"When I see my team has noticed different things when they're doing the reviews, it's like OK. We are making a difference."

"It gives me satisfaction when law enforcement tells us, 'Hey, we were able to prosecute these people because of the SAR that your team filed.'"

Responses

- Member testimonials/case studies by highlighting specific examples where members witnessed how helping individuals led to broader systemic change in fighting human crime.
- Establish feedback loop between FSPs and law enforcement.

Finding 9. Members are more confident in their ability to recognize and respond to victims of human crime.

Our data indicates that, because of The Knoble, our members are more confident in their ability to recognize and respond to victims of human crime. The survey data offers additional context for this finding, showing an increase from 52% to 86% in members responding "Quite a bit" or "Very much" about their confidence in **recognizing** potential victims of human crime after joining The Knoble. Similarly, confidence in **responding** to potential victims increased from 52% to 70%. In the interviews, members described how their approach to identifying human crime has become more focused and informed. Many said they're paying closer attention to red flags in financial transactions and are using tools and techniques to spot suspicious activity. They also shared a better understanding of how financial patterns can be linked to larger criminal behavior. When it comes to SARs, some members talked about moving beyond treating them as a checkbox exercise. Instead, they're writing reports with law enforcement in mind, trying to include clearer, more useful details. Even though there's frustration around the lack of feedback from law enforcement, there's also an awareness that these reports are an important part of the investigative process. Internally, members are sharing what they've learned with their teams. Some organizations have added training on human trafficking for fraud teams, frontline workers, and BSA officers. The Knoble's resources and events were mentioned as helpful in supporting these efforts. Members also talked about improving how they use detection tools, while others are getting more out of the tools they already have. There's a growing mindset that fraud prevention isn't just about stopping theft, it's also about identifying patterns that could be part of something bigger.

Key Themes from Qualitative Interviews

- **Increased Awareness of Red Flags**
    - Members report being more diligent in looking for specific indicators of human crime within transactions.
    - They mention leveraging new tools, software, and investigative techniques to detect suspicious activity.
    - They express a stronger understanding of how to connect financial red flags to broader criminal activity.
- **Better Use of SARs (Suspicious Activity Reports) and Law Enforcement Collaboration**
    - Some members describe a shift from simply filing SARs as a compliance measure to using them strategically to assist law enforcement.

  - There is growing frustration over lack of law enforcement feedback, but also a realization that SARs play a critical role in investigations.
  - Members discuss efforts to fine-tune SAR narratives and ensure they include useful, actionable information.
- **Expanded Internal Training and Information Sharing**
  - Members are passing down their knowledge to frontline employees and internal teams, ensuring a broader culture of awareness.
  - Some institutions have introduced specific human trafficking training for fraud teams, frontline employees, and BSA officers.
  - The Knoble's materials and events have been cited as valuable resources for this internal education.
- **Enhanced Use of Detection Tools and Risk Assessments**
  - Several members mention implementing new transaction monitoring systems or refining how they use existing fraud detection software.
  - Some have started using phone number and website checks to match suspicious transactions with known illicit activity.
  - There's a shift from traditional fraud prevention toward a more comprehensive view of how fraudulent transactions contribute to organized crime.

Interview Quotes

"I started paying closer attention to the SAR narratives—are we including the right details? Are we labeling things correctly? That matters more than I realized before."

"We utilize our monitoring system well... anytime we have those high-risk types of businesses...I try to monitor those types of individuals more closely... Having my team highly educated, watching The Knoble, watching other webinars, staying up to date really does help us."

"I've learned more in depth about pig butchering [since being at The Knoble]. In fact, some of the slides and information that has been given in the past, I've utilized to train in my most recent position."

"It's important to know the red flags out there. How do we detect this? It gets us like a guidance, like a starting point of, OK. This I may have to look at this a little bit further, right."

Quantitative Insights & Charts

- The detailed breakdown for recognition shows substantial increases in "Quite a bit" and "Very much" responses after joining, with corresponding decreases in lower confidence categories (see Figure 11).
- Confidence in recognizing potential victims of human crime "Quite a bit" or "Very much" increased from 53.3% before joining to 88.9% after joining The Knoble (see Figure 12).
- The detailed breakdown for response capability shows similar positive shifts, though with somewhat less dramatic increases than recognition confidence (see Figure 13).
- Confidence in responding to potential victims increased from 51.1% before joining to 68.9% after joining The Knoble (see Figure 14).

Responses

- Create a recognition program celebrating members who demonstrate exceptional skill in detecting and responding to human crime cases within their institutions.
- Develop video and social media content featuring success stories that showcase specific red flags members identified and the effective response techniques they employed.

Figure 11:
I am confident in my ability to recognize potential victims of human crime.

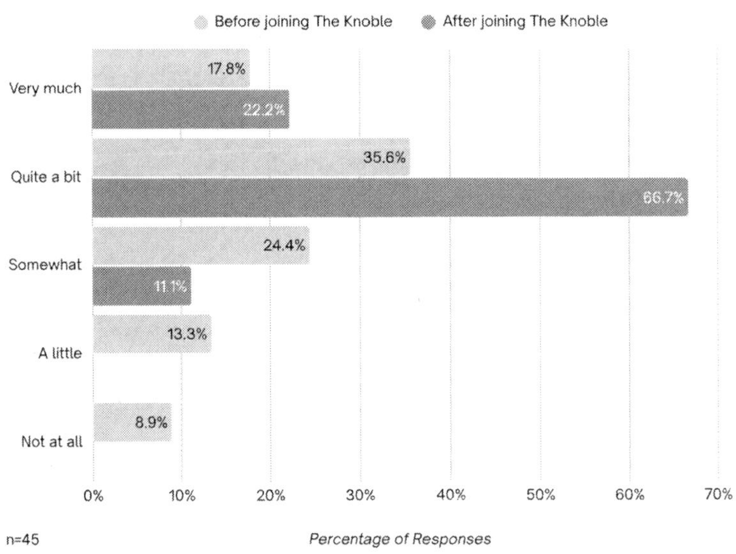

n=45

Figure 12:
Members responding "Quite a bit" or "Very much"

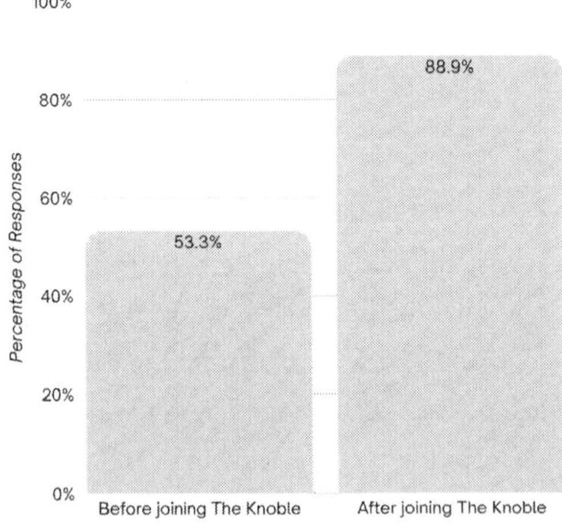

n=46

Figure 13:
I am confident in my ability to respond to potential victims of human crime.

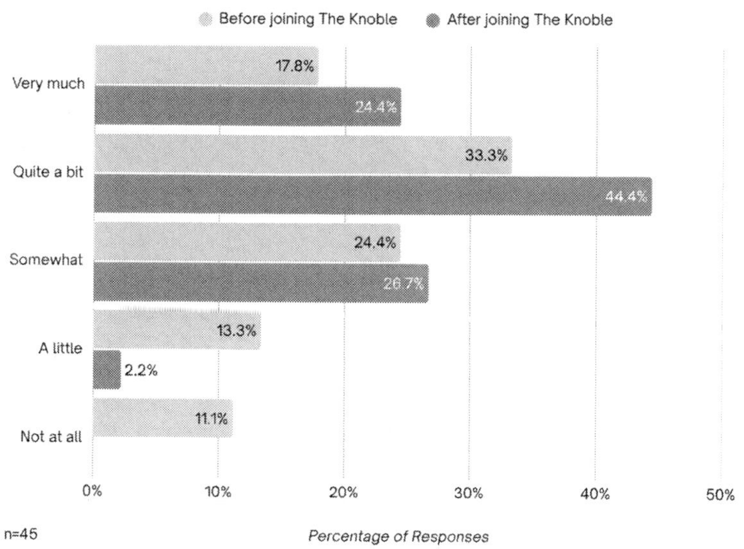

n=45

Figure 14:
Members responding "Quite a bit" or "Very much"

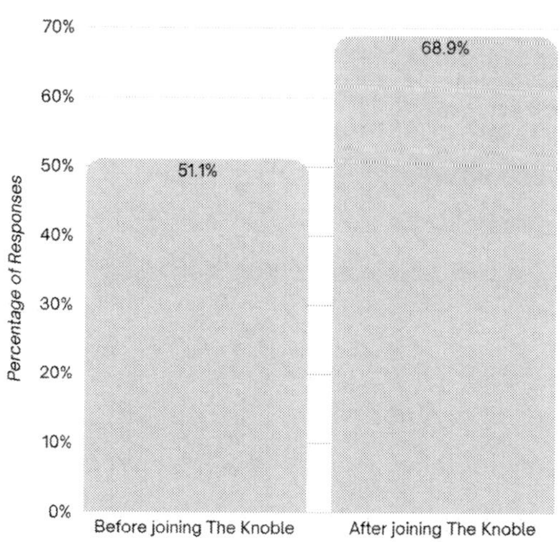

n=45

Conclusion

Insights Into Impact

The Knoble's intended impacts for the membership program are threefold: to awaken financial professionals to the reality of Human Crime, to equip them to recognize the indicators of specific Human Crimes and report them effectively, and to take action in their workplaces to disrupt Human Crime.

Awaken

Findings 2, 7, and 8 reveal that members experience an increased awareness of Human Crime, a change in the way they view their customer, and a belief that small changes can make a large difference as a result of being a Knoble member. These all contribute to the intended impact of awakening financial professionals to the reality of Human Crime and their role in preventing it. First, Knoble members become more aware of Human Crime, followed by a change in their beliefs and actions toward the customer and industry.

Equip

Findings 3 and 9 reveal that members experience an increased ability to recognize and respond to potential Human Crime as a result of being a Knoble member. These contribute to Knoble members becoming more equipped to detect indicators of Human Crime and report them effectively. Members utilize Knoble resources to increase their understanding and leverage their skills to improve their detection and reporting.

Mobilize

While the study found ample data supporting the first two intended impacts, the third intended impact is a clear area for improvement. Findings 1, 4, 5, and 6 illustrate that while Knoble members may have an increased confidence in effecting change, they may lack a clear path to take actions that drive that change. Problems reported in this study included a lack of law enforcement collaboration, low levels of change implementation, and difficulty in getting leadership involved.

Steps Forward: Strategic Pathways for The Knoble

Based on these insights, we recommend three strategic pathways that address our core challenges while building on existing strengths:

Elevate Member Journey Through Purpose-Driven Engagement

The evaluation findings reveal that The Knoble has successfully ignited a sense of purpose and confidence among members (Finding 1), fundamentally shifting how they view customers from data points to human beings (Finding 7), and cultivating belief in incremental yet meaningful change (Finding 8). To harness this transformative potential, The Knoble should develop a comprehensive member journey framework that creates clear progression opportunities aligned with members' growing sense of purpose. This framework should begin with the creation of clear entry points for new members that immediately connect their professional expertise with opportunities for meaningful impact. As Finding 1 demonstrates, members experience greater workplace satisfaction when they can see how their daily work protects vulnerable populations.

Building on members' increased confidence in recognizing and responding to human crime (Finding 9), The Knoble should establish tiered skill development pathways that create visible progression opportunities. These pathways should incorporate both recognition of developing expertise and practical application opportunities.As Finding 6 reveals, many members struggle to build meaningful connections despite valuing the network's potential. By integrating interactive learning modules, virtual collaboration spaces, and case-based discussion forums, our membership platform can facilitate the cross-institutional knowledge exchange that distinguishes The Knoble's approach.

Bridge Institutional Implementation Gaps

The evaluation findings reveal a critical disconnect between individual member transformation and institutional implementation. While members report increased awareness (Finding 2), improved detection capabilities (Finding 3), and greater confidence in recognizing human crime (Finding 9), they struggle to translate this individual growth into organizational change (Finding 4). To address this challenge, The Knoble should develop targeted resources for institutional champions that specifically address the challenges members face when attempting to implement new processes or conduct internal training. Finding 4 reveals that while 65% of members at manager level or above have trained colleagues using Knoble resources, implementation of new processes remains limited.

The evaluation also highlights the need for cross-functional integration within financial institutions. Finding 6 specifically notes the problematic silos between fraud and financial crime compliance teams that limit broader human crime prevention efforts. The Knoble should create structured frameworks for cross-team collaboration, including joint training programs, shared detection protocols, and success metrics that incentivize cooperation.The Human Crime Specialist (HCS) concept emerged in our interviews as a potential solution to these institutional implementation challenges. By formalizing this role within financial institutions, The Knoble could create dedicated champions with explicit responsibility for human crime prevention.

Strengthen Impact Visibility Through Collaborative Ecosystems

A persistent theme across evaluation findings is the difficulty members experience in seeing the tangible impact of their efforts (Finding 5). Despite increased awareness, detection capabilities, and reporting, members express frustration about limited feedback on outcomes, particularly regarding law enforcement actions resulting from their reports.To address this critical challenge, The Knoble should establish structured feedback mechanisms between financial institutions and law enforcement agencies. Finding 5 specifically notes members' uncertainty about engaging law enforcement effectively, highlighting a gap in collaboration between these sectors.

The evaluation also reveals significant untapped potential in member-to-member collaboration. Finding 6 highlights that while members value networking opportunities, they struggle to build meaningful ongoing relationships that facilitate collaborative problem-solving. The Knoble should implement structured collaborative initiatives that bring members together around specific human crime challenges.Finally, The Knoble should develop comprehensive impact measurement frameworks that capture both immediate outputs (reports filed, trainings conducted) and longer-term outcomes (cases prosecuted, victims protected). Finding 8 demonstrates members' belief that small actions can lead to significant change, but this belief requires reinforcement through concrete evidence of impact

These strategic pathways address our core challenge: while The Knoble has successfully raised awareness among financial professionals about fighting human crime and equipped them with detection tools, converting this awareness into consistent action remains our biggest hurdle. By strengthening the connections between individual transformation, institutional implementation, and collective impact, The Knoble can fulfill its vision of building a global movement that transforms how financial systems protect against exploitation.

Opportunities for Future Evaluation

Opportunities abound for future evaluation. Should the next steps outlined above be implemented as planned, there will be a need to evaluate the member journey, law enforcement feedback, and the Human Crime Specialist training. However, to build on this study, the intended impacts of awaken, equip, mobilize must remain embedded in the evaluation. Along with the member journey should come an intake survey that sets a baseline for incoming members' awareness, skills, and actions. This instrument can be administered again at certain stages in the member journey, including after the completion of initiatives or after a set period of time. This rhythm of evaluation will provide The Knoble with a robust collection of data, proving the intended impact or suggesting areas for improvement.

GREEN|SPACES

Build It Green

Laura Bass, Wayne Brown, Emma Walker, Dexter Talley, and Keyta Young-Price

Organization and Program Overview

Introduction to Organization

Green|spaces has served as a Chattanooga-based nonprofit organization dedicated to advancing sustainability throughout the region since 2007. The organization's mission focuses on progressing the way we live, work, and build in Chattanooga and the surrounding region, taking a multifaceted approach to environmental stewardship and community development. Through a diverse portfolio of initiatives—including advocacy campaigns, educational workshops, incentive programs, and workforce development programs—green|spaces has established itself as a catalyst for sustainable practices across residential, commercial, and community contexts. The organization continuously evolves its programming to meet emerging environmental challenges while simultaneously improving quality of life for area residents and visitors. Through this work, green|spaces embodies its commitment to environmental responsibility while creating practical pathways for individuals, businesses, and communities to embrace more sustainable practices.

Program Description

Build It Green (BIG) prepares young adults ages 18-24 for careers in green building and energy services through a 6-month to 1-year workforce development program. Launched in 2018 as a partnership between green|spaces and AmeriCorps' Opportunity Youth Service Initiative, BIG addresses two critical challenges: creating pathways out of poverty for youth while improving energy efficiency in low-income Chattanooga neighborhoods.

Participants receive comprehensive support, including technical training in weatherization, industry certifications, a paid living allowance, educational awards up to $6,000, and job placement assistance. The program's unique approach combines hands-on skills development with personal growth and community engagement, producing workforce-ready individuals while addressing real community needs.

BIG intentionally recruits diverse participants who represent the communities they serve, creating a supportive learning environment where individuals gain valuable skills while making meaningful contributions to neighborhood sustainability. This dual-impact model creates lasting change for both participants and the communities they serve, offering an innovative solution to both workforce development and environmental challenges.

Intended Impacts

Build It Green members develop green building skills. Build It Green members will be equipped with the skills to perform home energy audits and assessments by attending educational workshops and earning industry certifications.

Build It Green members discover their untapped potential. Build It Green members "break the cycle" by developing self-confidence, perseverance, financial freedom, and independence.

Build It Green members become role models by building and strengthening their community. Build It Green members engage in community-building and take advantage of networking opportunities and mentorship.

Evaluation Methodology

The aim of our evaluation was to see what kind and quality of impact Build It Green is having on the population we are serving. To understand this, we explored two broad evaluation questions:

1. What kind and quality of impact are we having on our participants/members?
2. What aspects of our program are causing this impact?

Over the course of the project, we (a) developed and refined our ideas of intended impact and indicators, (b) designed and implemented a mixed methods outcome evaluation using both qualitative and quantitative means to collect and analyze data, (c) identified themes and findings, and (d) considered the implications to those findings for program improvement and innovation.

This project began by identifying and clarifying the intended impact of Build It Green. Once the ideas of impact had been developed, we used the Heart Triangle™ model to identify qualitative and quantitative indicators of impact on the mental, behavioral, and emotional changes in our participants/members. We used these indicators to design a qualitative interview protocol and a quantitative questionnaire to evaluate progress toward achieving our intended impact.

Qualitative Data Collection and Analysis

For the qualitative portion of the evaluation, we designed an in-depth interview protocol to gain data about the structural, qualitative changes resulting from our program. We delimited our population to those who have graduated from the program. Our population size for this evaluation was 100. We used a purposeful stratified sampling technique to select a representative sample from the population we serve. Our sample size was 31, drawn from the following strata of our population:

- Strata - Ages - over 18 years old

Our interview team consisted of Wayne Brown and Emma Walker. We convened one-on-one interviews lasting between 45 minutes and one hour in length and collected interview data using handwritten notes and voice recordings.

We then analyzed the data inductively using a modified version of thematic analysis. Each interviewer analyzed the data from their interviews individually to identify initial themes. Together, we developed common themes from all of the interviews collectively. We identified the overarching and inter-interview themes that emerged from the full scope of our data analysis to illuminate the collective insights and discoveries. We mapped these themes visually and examined the dynamics among the themes, causes and catalysts of the themes, new or surprising insights related to the themes, and relationships between the themes that were revealed in the data. We then determined the most significant and meaningful discoveries and brought them forward as findings.

Quantitative Data Collection and Analysis

For the quantitative portion of the evaluation, we designed a questionnaire to collect data on our quantitative indicators of impact. We administered this instrument to 50 (the population of the program you administered the survey to) and had a response of 21 (number of people who responded), a 50% response rate. The data were analyzed primarily using measures of central tendency. We identified key insights, patterns, and gaps within the data and incorporated these discoveries into the related findings. The most significant insights from the quantitative data are described in the following narrative.

Limitations

- Maintaining current contact information limited the number of participants who could be contacted.

Findings

Finding 1. Participants develop technical and professional skills that create new opportunities within and beyond construction.

The data reveal that participants consistently acquire both technical construction skills and professional workplace skills that open new pathways for their futures. Participants enter the program with limited or no construction experience and leave with specific abilities they can apply across various contexts. Beyond learning basic tool use, participants develop specialized skills like energy assessment, insulation installation, and ramp building. These technical skills are accompanied by professional competencies like team leadership, project management, presentation skills, and client interaction. The interviews show that participants recognize how these skills transfer to multiple contexts—from helping family members with repairs to starting their own businesses, pursuing further education, or securing employment. Participants consistently describe how these skills extend beyond the workplace into their personal lives and future aspirations.

Key Themes from Qualitative Interviews

- Participants develop specialized technical abilities that range from basic tool use to complex assessment and building processes.
- The program teaches professional competencies that extend beyond construction into areas like leadership, client communication, and time management.
- Participants actively apply their technical skills outside the program in family settings, side businesses, and community service.
- Participants connect their new skills to specific career pathways, including further education, entrepreneurship, and employment opportunities.

Interview Quotes

"I learned how to supervise, and I learned how to cut, cut the wood, measure the wood."

"I started mounting TVs in my free time, because like I learned at BIG, another thing I learned at BIG, finding studs and stuff in the wall. Well, I use the stud finder now just because it's quick and it's easy."

"I can go to Lowe's, pick out a deck board, cut it, and put her step back on. I can even go into my mama's attic and do this and do that."

"When I first got to Build It Green, the skills I learned were using the different varieties of all the tools, such as the miter saw, the jigsaw, and the proper way of using the hammer, the blower doors... So like the roofing we were building on little houses and stuff. So things like that, I learned."

Quantitative Insights & Charts

- 76.2% of participants reported "Quite a bit" or "Very much" knowledge about making homes energy efficient after the program, compared to only 5% before (Figure 1 and 2).
- 90.5% rated themselves as "Quite a bit" or "Very much" good at using tools for energy-saving home improvements after completing the program, compared to only 4.8% before the program (Figure 3 and 4).
- Confidence in performing energy-saving home improvements increased dramatically, with 90.4% feeling "Quite a bit" or "Very much" confident after the program, compared to only 14.3% before (see Figure 4).

Figure 1:
How good were you at using tools for energy-saving home improvements BEFORE Build It Green?

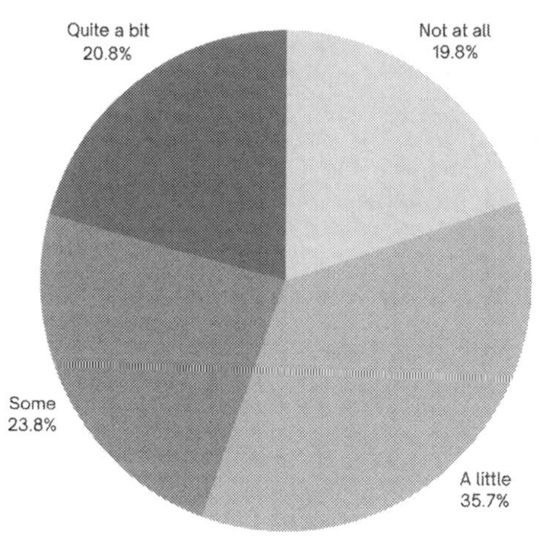

Figure 2:
How good are you at using tools for energy-saving home improvements NOW?

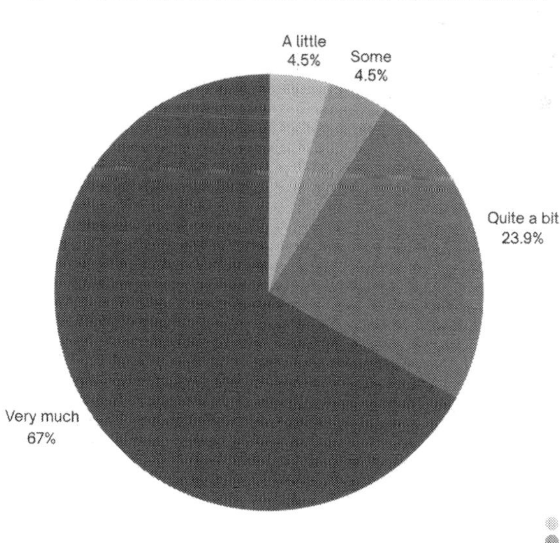

Figure 3:
How confident did you feel about doing energy-saving home improvements BEFORE Build It Green?

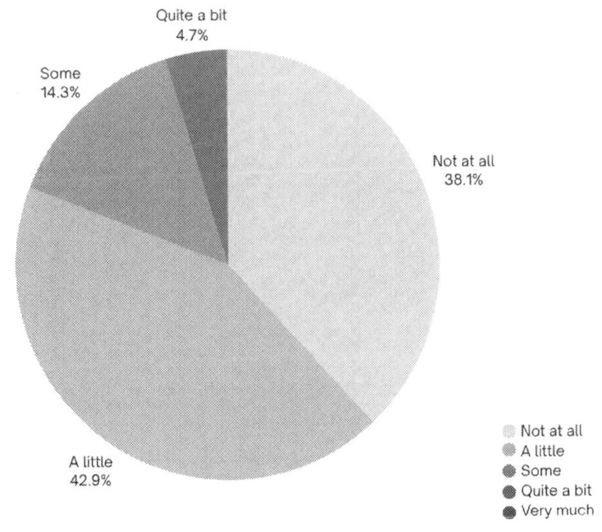

n=21

Figure 4:
How confident do you feel about doing energy-saving home improvements NOW?

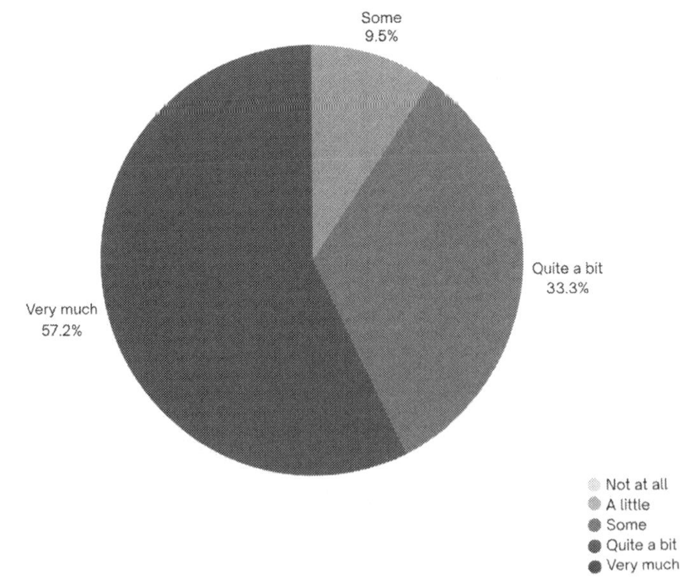

n=21

Responses

- Continue to build relationships with industry professionals and technicians to stay updated on industry trends.

- Training and industry are paramount to preparing members for the workforce.
- Continue to encourage discipline in seeing a project or goal through to completion.

Finding 2. Community service projects create purpose, satisfaction, and expanded worldview.

Throughout the interviews, participants consistently expressed deep satisfaction from helping community members through service projects like building wheelchair ramps and improving home energy efficiency. These tangible projects provide visible demonstrations of impact that foster a sense of purpose beyond personal gain. The data show that participants connect these experiences to their growing identity as community contributors rather than just program recipients. Many participants described feeling good about seeing community members' positive reactions and realizing the practical difference their work makes in others' lives. For participants with limited experience outside their immediate neighborhoods, these projects also expand their understanding of their city and community needs.

Key Themes from Qualitative Interviews

- Participants experience significant satisfaction in witnessing the direct impact of their work on community members' lives.
- Building ramps for people with mobility challenges creates a particularly powerful sense of purpose as participants see the immediate improvement in accessibility.
- Service projects take participants to different neighborhoods, expanding their understanding of the broader community beyond their immediate environment.
- Participants recognize how their work addresses specific needs that would otherwise be costly or difficult for community members to resolve.

Interview Quotes

"It made me feel good. It's like the world is so cruel. It made me feel like I'm doing good [towards] Earth, not even just that person, but like Earth... I'm doing something in life that's positive."

"It was one lady I was doing a job for and I talked to her for three weeks straight, and I finally went over there to put her equipment in because she had been sick, and she just looked at me and she was like, 'You are a beautiful soul.' She was like, you're going to be somebody one day. And just hearing those words from an older person that's been here, that means a lot."

"It made me feel good, because knowing what they would have had to go through before the ramp."

"I feel like we helped them, and now they ain't got to worry about leakage in their house, or nothing bad going over the house because we did what we had to do."

Quantitative Insights & Charts

- 100% of participants reported helping in their community more now compared to before the program, with 66.7% selecting "Quite a bit" and 33.3% selecting "Very much" (see Figure 5).
- 100% of participants reported feeling more proud about what they've accomplished in the program, with 81% selecting "Very much."
- 100% reported feeling like they're part of something important, with 85.7% selecting "Very much" (see Figure 6)

Responses

- Provide more opportunities for members to be a positive influence in their communities.
- Collaborate with other organizations making an impact in the community, which expands the meaning of "community" outside of residents who live in the area.

Figure 5:
How proud do you feel about what you've done in this program?

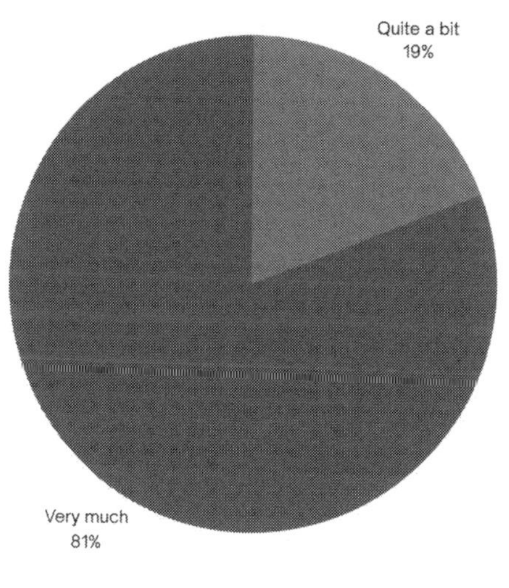

n=21

Figure 6:
How much more do you feel like you're part of something important?

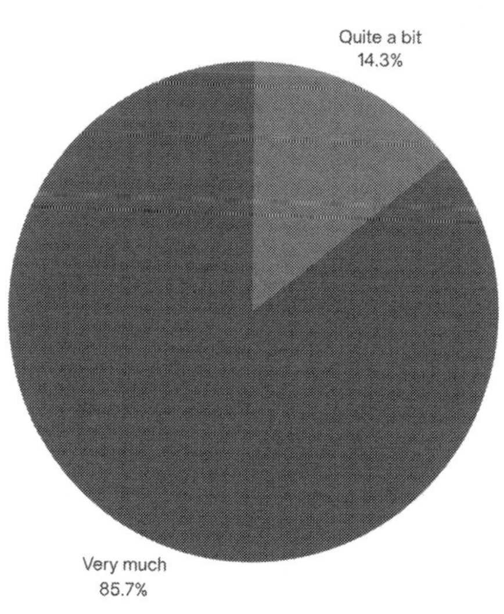

n=21

Finding 3. The program functions as an extended family, providing critical support and mentorship.

The data reveal that Build It Green creates a family-like environment that provides much more than employment or skill development for participants. Many participants explicitly described the program as "family" or a "home away from home," particularly important for those who lack strong family support systems. Program leaders function as parental figures and mentors who provide guidance, accountability, and support that extends well beyond work hours. The interviews indicate that participants find both emotional and practical support through these relationships, helping them navigate personal challenges, legal issues, housing instability, and career decisions. The data show that this family-like structure addresses deeper needs for belonging and support that many participants haven't experienced elsewhere, creating a foundation that enables their growth in other areas.

Key Themes from Qualitative Interviews

- Participants consistently describe the program as a family or home environment that provides critical emotional and practical support.
- Program leaders serve as parental figures who provide guidance, accountability, and direct assistance with significant life challenges.
- The program creates connections between participants that function as sibling-like relationships, providing peer support and accountability.
- For participants with limited family support, the program fills critical gaps in their support system that enable them to address other life challenges.

Interview Quotes

> *"When I first came into the program, I was homeless, so it kind of gave me, it was more like a family, because I don't have family, so it's a home away from home."*

"Honestly, they mean a lot to me…it's really like I got a whole group of big brothers and a daddy, so it's really like a home for me."

"Dex ain't gonna let us quit. One thing I know about Dex is, like, when it comes down to it, if you're a good worker and he sees potential in you, he's not just gonna give up on you."

Quantitative Insights & Charts

- 76.2% of participants reported feeling like they belonged to a team or group "Quite a bit" or "Very much" (see Figure 7).
- Before the program, only 42.8% knew about working well with others and being professional "Quite a bit" or "Very much" (see Figure 8). After the program, this increased to 95.2% (see Figure 9).

Responses

- Focus more on ensuring members feel less isolation and more inclusiveness.
- Enhance the sense of family through more post-graduate activities.

Figure 7:
How much did you feel like you belonged to a team or group?

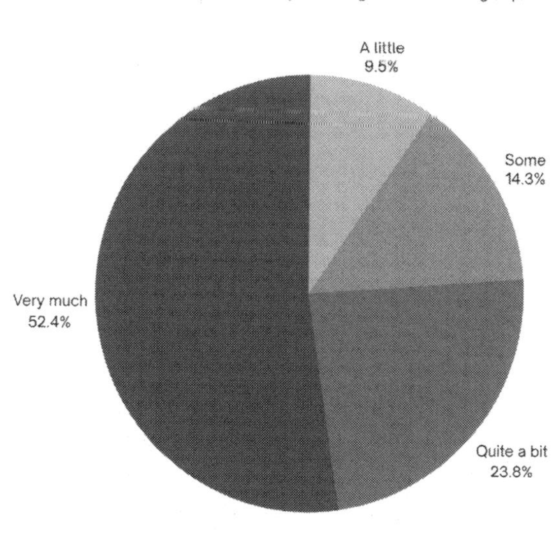

Figure 8:
How much did you know about working well with others and being professional BEFORE Build It Green?

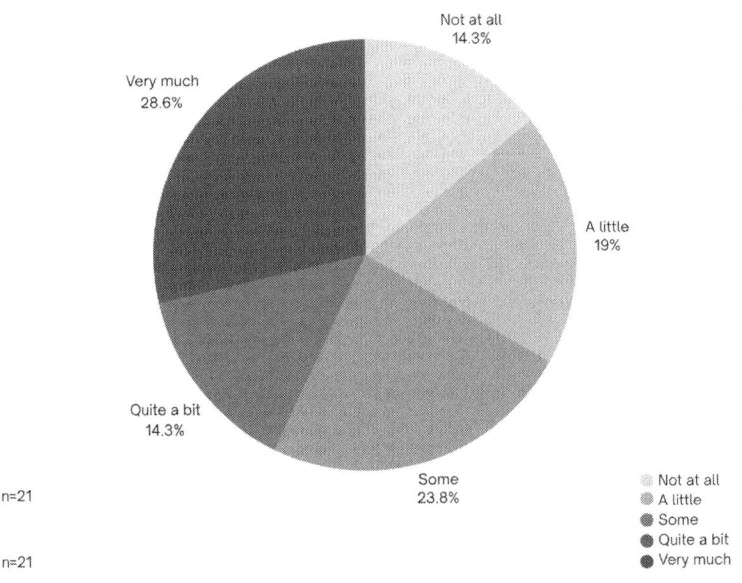

n=21

n=21

Figure 9:
How much did you know about working well with others and being professional NOW?

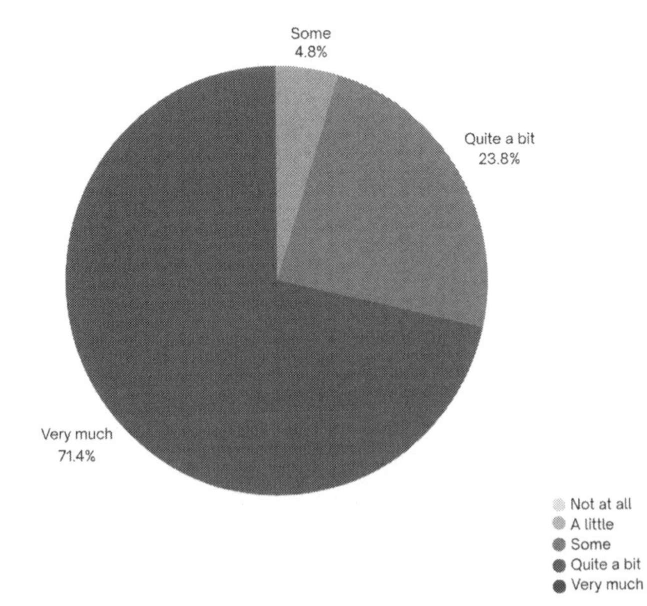

n=21

Finding 4. Participants receive comprehensive life support beyond skill training.

The interviews reveal that Build It Green provides extensive practical support that addresses multiple barriers participants face beyond employment and skill development. Participants describe receiving assistance with transportation, housing, legal issues, education, and basic needs that create a foundation for their success. The data show that program leaders actively identify participants' needs and leverage their networks to provide resources or direct assistance. This comprehensive approach addresses systemic barriers that would otherwise prevent participants from succeeding, regardless of their skills or motivation. The interviews indicate that this support is not simply about meeting immediate needs but connecting participants to lasting resources that create pathways for long-term stability and growth.

Key Themes from Qualitative Interviews

- Participants receive direct assistance with transportation barriers, including access to vehicles.
- The program provides educational support through stipends and connections to continuing education opportunities.
- Participants receive assistance with legal issues, including court advocacy and connections to legal resources.
- The program helps address immediate basic needs like housing and food security for participants facing crisis situations.

Interview Quotes

"The education stipend was a large part of me enrolling in TCAT and continuing my education. I'm thankful for the staff talking with the judge and helping to reduce my sentence and stay out of jail."

"There was a time when I was staying with my aunt, but I didn't have food or anything, so Miss Ella gave me vouchers for the food bank... she got me a room for a whole week. And if she wouldn't have done that, I would have been on the street with all my things."

Quantitative Insights & Charts

- 95.3% of participants reported becoming better at finding and using helpful resources and making connections, with 81% selecting "Very much" (see Figure 10).

Responses

- Provide members with updated information on continuing education opportunities.
- Seek to eliminate or mitigate barriers to successful completion of the program.
- Build more collaborative relationships with organizations who provide social/emotional, financial, and educational support.

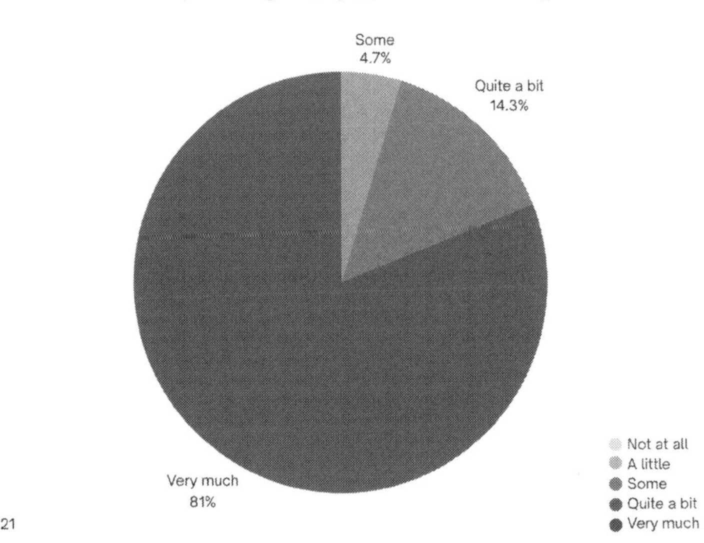

Finding 5. The program transforms participants' confidence and self-efficacy.

The data show that participants experience significant growth in confidence and self-efficacy through their program experience. When entering the program, many participants lack belief in their own capabilities or have negative self-perceptions. Through progressive skill development and accomplishment of increasingly complex tasks, participants develop a stronger sense of confidence that extends beyond specific construction skills. This transformation is evident in how participants describe their ability to tackle new challenges, speak up for themselves, and take initiative in various contexts. The interviews reveal that this confidence growth is particularly powerful for participants who have experienced previous failures or setbacks. Program leaders intentionally provide scaffolded success experiences that build upon each other, allowing participants to develop what many describe as a fundamental shift in how they view their own capabilities.

Key Themes from Qualitative Interviews

- Participants develop increased confidence through progressive skill mastery and successful project completion.
- The confidence gained extends beyond specific technical skills to general self-efficacy and willingness to tackle new challenges.
- Participants with previous negative experiences particularly benefit from structured success experiences that rebuild their sense of capability.
- Increased confidence manifests in specific behaviors like speaking up, taking initiative, and pursuing new opportunities.

Interview Quotes

"It boosted my confidence. It did."

"I was pretty cocky before, now I'm confident that if I put my mind to it, I can accomplish anything."

"My confidence level, it used to be down here. But now it's up here."

"I have grown a lot. Like I am a terrible public speaker, still am. I don't know why, it's just like talking in front of a bunch of people, my words start jumbling up and I get so flustered. But good things have grown in me where I feel confident in my ability to help these young people."

Quantitative Insights & Charts

- Before the program, only 42.9% of participants believed in themselves "Quite a bit" or "Very much." After the program, this increased dramatically to 95.3% (see Figure 11 and 12).
- 100% of participants reported being more able to do things on their own "Quite a bit" or "Very much" (see Figure 13).

Responses

- Self-confidence is paramount to members believing they can accomplish a goal.
- Our staff must continue to gain skills and knowledge to help members grow.

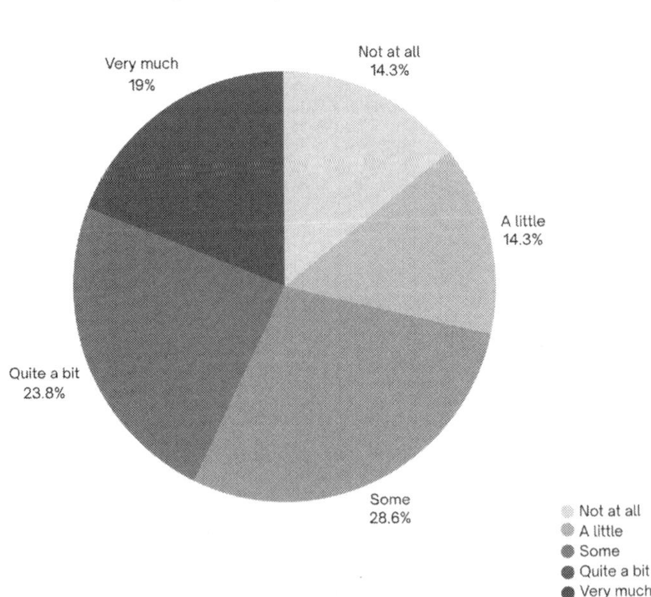

Figure 12:
How much do you believe in yourself NOW after participating in Build It Green?

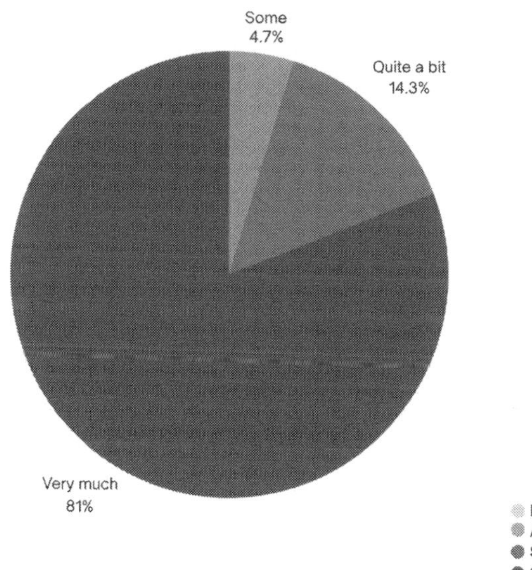

n=21

Figure 13:
How much more able are you to do things on your own after participating in Build It Green?

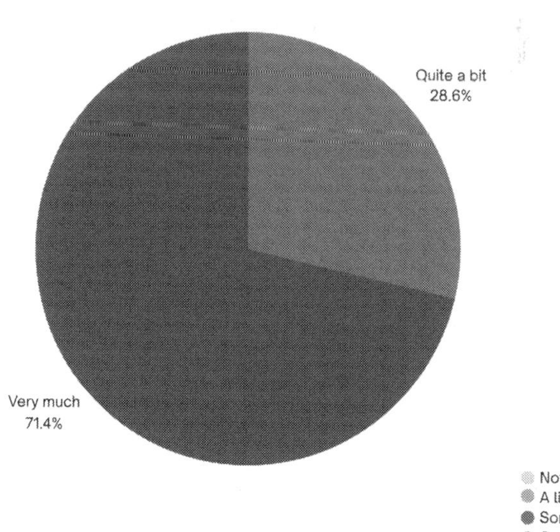

n=21

Finding 6. Participants develop accountability and responsibility that transforms relationships.

Throughout the interviews, participants consistently described developing greater accountability and responsibility that transforms how they approach relationships and commitments. The program's structure requires participants to be punctual, reliable, and accountable for their work quality, creating habits that carry over to other life areas. The data reveal that this growth in responsibility particularly impacts family relationships, with many participants describing how they've shifted from being dependent to being providers or supporters for family members. Participants also describe learning to set boundaries by holding others accountable rather than enabling unhealthy behaviors. This development of accountability appears to be catalyzed by program leaders who model and enforce appropriate boundaries while still providing support.

Key Themes from Qualitative Interviews

- Participants develop personal accountability for punctuality, attendance, and work quality that extends to other life areas.
- Many participants transition from being dependent on family to becoming providers or resources for family members.
- Participants learn to set appropriate boundaries by holding others accountable rather than enabling problematic behaviors.
- The development of accountability and responsibility directly impacts participants' self-perception and how others view them.

Interview Quotes

"If I mess up, I'm just gonna take accountability. Pull my chest out, you know, like there's always a way to fix everything. But you can't be scared to try anything."

"I learned how to take accountability for the mistakes that I made. So it's like big things that have improved since being in BIG."

"I struggle with self doubt every day, but BIG helps me to know that I'm a leader and I lead by example. So, it's basically being able to hold everybody accountable. That helps me with myself, because when it comes time for me to be accountable, I gotta do it."

Quantitative Insights & Charts

- 95.2% reported being better at keeping going when things get hard "Quite a bit" or "Very much" (see Figure 14).

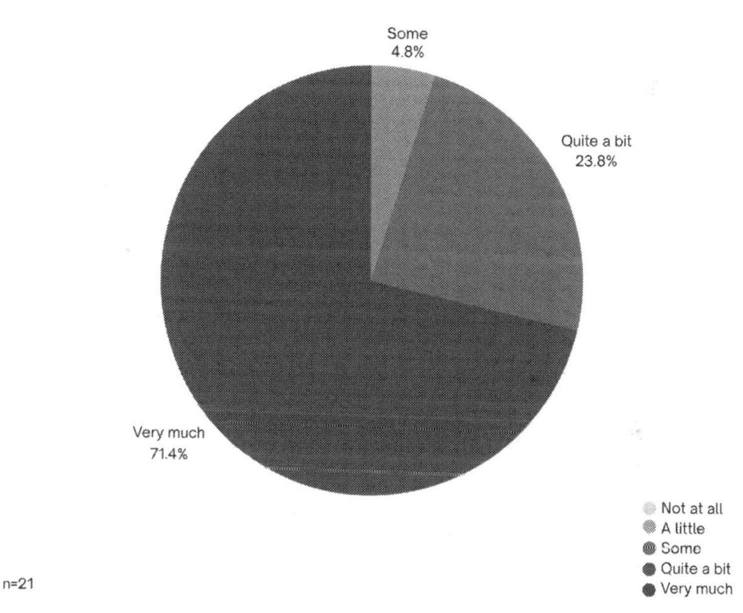

Responses

- Discipline is not exclusive to making mistakes. It must be included as a building block for success.
- Holding members, staff, clients, and partners accountable is key to the program's growth and success.

Finding 7. The program helps participants overcome adversity and life challenges.

The data reveal that the program provides crucial support for participants facing significant life challenges and adversity. Many participants enter the program at critical junctures in their lives, dealing with homelessness, legal issues, family challenges, or educational setbacks. The interviews show that the program's structure, relationships, and resources help participants develop resilience and problem-solving abilities that enable them to overcome these challenges. Rather than simply providing temporary relief, the program equips participants with mindsets and skills to navigate ongoing and future challenges more effectively. This includes developing perseverance, emotional regulation, boundary-setting, and strategic thinking about long-term goals despite immediate obstacles.

Key Themes from Qualitative Interviews

- Participants face significant life challenges including homelessness, legal issues, family problems, and educational barriers.
- The program provides both immediate assistance and long-term strategies for overcoming adversity.
- Participants develop specific resilience skills including perseverance, emotional regulation, and strategic problem-solving.
- Success in overcoming program challenges builds confidence for addressing other life difficulties.

Interview Quotes

"It was just the fact that I just felt like I didn't have anybody...I do love my mom, but at the end of the day, I know she's not a good individual for me."

"I was getting suspended, and then were telling me, 'Hey, it's time for you to get ahead, get it together with graduation coming up.'"

"Ever since [BIG], I have been in no type of trouble, like none."

"BIG was pretty tough on me about not being a morning person...I have never been a morning person. I'm known for being very late, but, you know, that kind of helped whip me into shape to the point where it's a big pet peeve of mine to be not punctual now."

Quantitative Insights & Charts

- Before the program, only 47.6% felt hopeful about their future "Quite a bit" or "Very much." After the program, 100% reported feeling hopeful, with 90.5% selecting "Very much" (see Figure 15 and 16).

Responses

- We must intentionally individualize our approach in supporting our members. Each person has a unique lived experience.
- We will continue to enhance our follow up interaction with graduate members, it is crucial to post-graduation success.

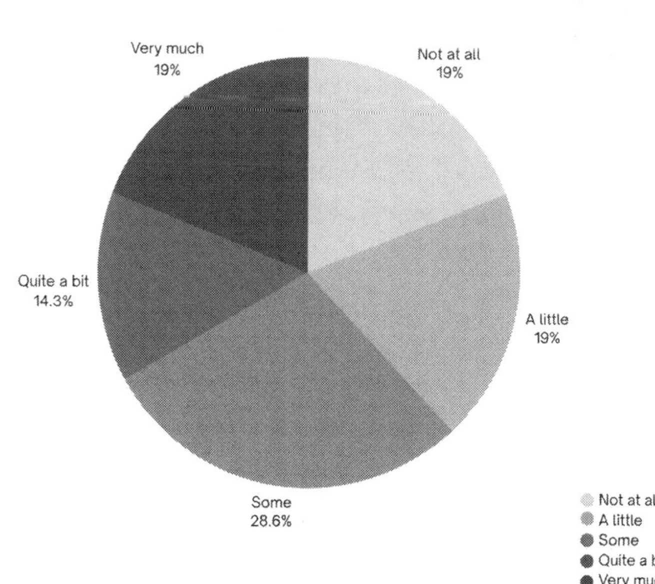

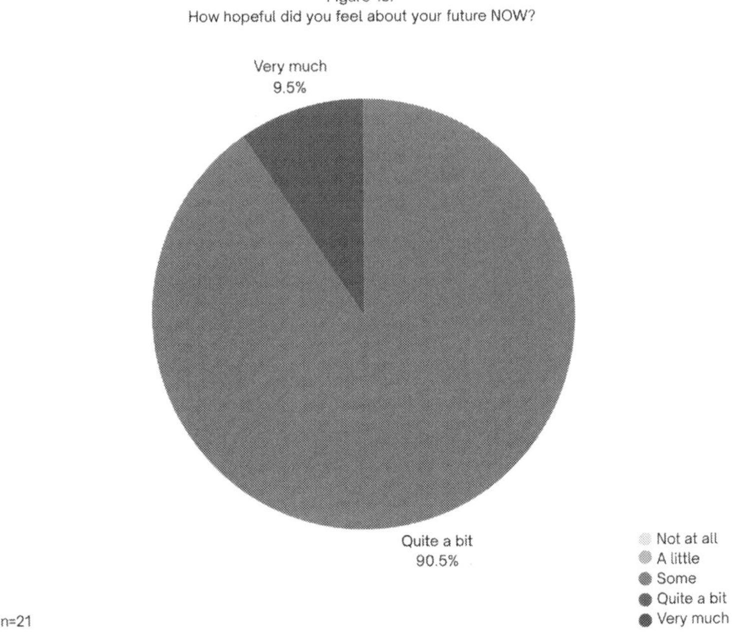

Finding 8. The program creates clear pathways for continuing education and career development.

The interviews reveal that the program consistently connects participants to education and career pathways that extend beyond their program participation. Participants describe receiving concrete assistance with educational opportunities through stipends, connections to schools, and support for certification programs. The data show that program leaders actively help participants identify career interests and connect them to relevant opportunities aligned with their strengths. Many participants indicate that the program helped them envision career possibilities they hadn't previously considered or believed were accessible to them. For participants who had negative educational experiences or dropped out of school, the program provides a bridge back to education that feels relevant and attainable.

Key Themes from Qualitative Interviews

- Participants receive education stipends and assistance with enrolling in further education or certification programs.
- The program helps participants identify career interests and strengths that align with viable employment paths.
- Participants discover career possibilities they hadn't previously considered or believed were accessible.
- For participants with negative educational histories, the program provides a bridge back to education through practical, relevant learning.

Interview Quotes

"This spring, I will complete my project management certification and plan to continue in the building industry."

"I know I want to start a demolition business so that in two years, I know for a fact I have that business, and within the next six months, I will have my GED in the name of Jesus, because I'd be procrastinating because I'm scared of failure."

"I want to look into a trade school. Learn all the trades I want to learn. Like a general contractor."

"I'm gonna use my money from BIG, my school money, I'm gonna go back to school, get an Associates. I'll probably go get my CDLs and my welding license."

Quantitative Insights & Charts

- Participants' readiness for green building jobs increased from 52.3% feeling "Quite a bit" or "Very much" ready before the program to 90.5% after (see Figure 17 and 18).
- 95.3% of participants reported knowing more about applying for jobs and doing well in interviews "Quite a bit" or "Very much" (see Figure 19).

Figure 17:
How ready did you feel to work in green building jobs BEFORE Build It Green?

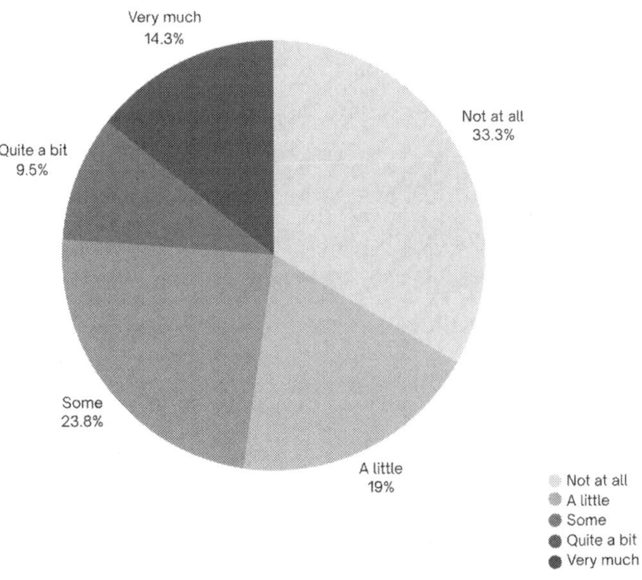

n=21

Figure 18:
How ready do you feel to work in green building jobs NOW?

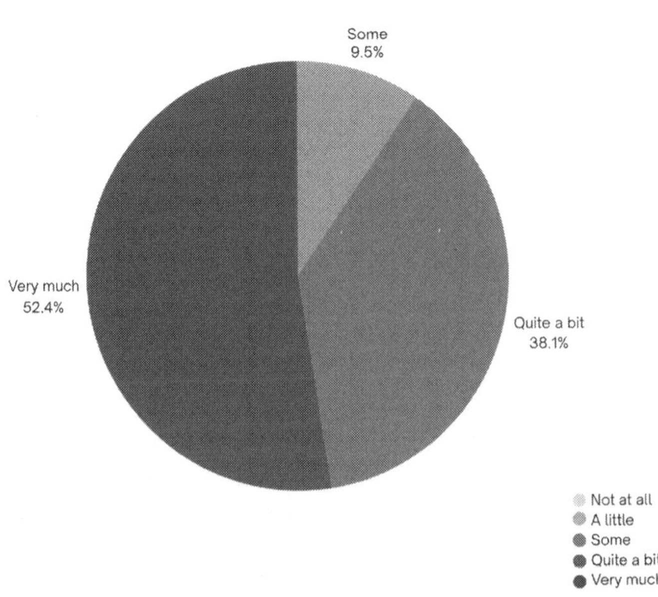

n=21

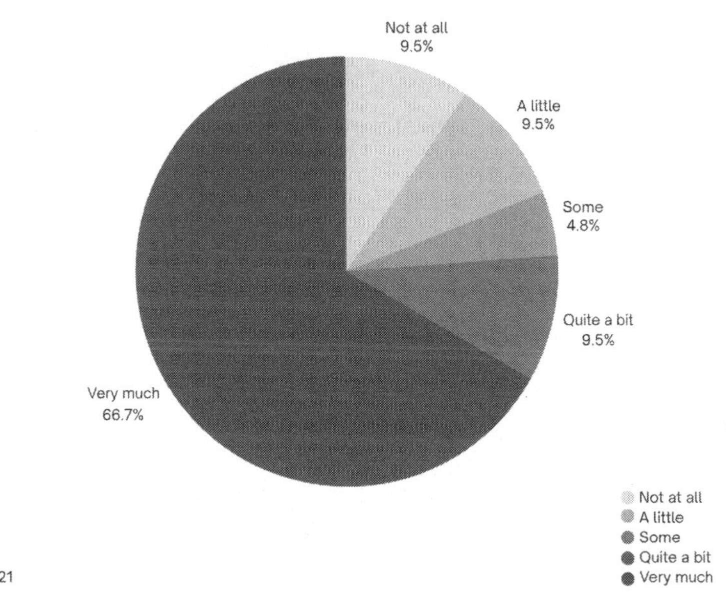

Responses

- Because the construction industry is ever advancing, we must explore and find new opportunities for certifications and training.
- Provide aptitude testing and guidance for members for choosing career paths

Finding 9. The program facilitates intergenerational relationships that benefit participants of all ages.

The data show that the program creates valuable intergenerational relationships that benefit participants across age groups. The program brings together participants from diverse age ranges, from teenagers to adults in their 40s and beyond. Rather than creating divisions, these age differences become assets within the program environment. Older participants describe finding purpose in mentoring younger members, while younger participants gain from the life experience and perspective of older participants. The interviews reveal that these cross-age relationships often develop naturally as participants work together on projects, with mutual respect developing through shared accomplishment. The data indicate that these relationships help break down age-related stereotypes and create unexpected connections that serve both groups.

Key Themes from Qualitative Interviews

- The program intentionally brings together participants from diverse age ranges.
- Older participants find purpose and meaning in mentoring and supporting younger members.
- Younger participants benefit from the life experience and perspective of older participants.
- Intergenerational relationships develop naturally through shared work and accomplishments.

Interview Quotes

> *"I'm pretty sure I'm about the oldest person that joined the program, but I don't regret it at all because it taught me some things that I didn't know before I went there."*
>
> *"It doesn't make me feel any different because we actually grow a family bond with them. I have grandkids around that age, so, you know, it doesn't make me feel any different because, you know, I'm here to learn."*
>
> *"I do one-on-ones with some of them [participants] now, like counseling and talk to them. You know, you got some that had trouble in their lifetime, some of their parents and stuff. So, you know, being there as an older person, you know, I got really respected, and was able to have a time to communicate by meeting with them."*
>
> *"You know, it's people that get construction jobs that don't have any experience. I already got at least some experience."*

Quantitative Insights

- Survey demographics show a diverse age distribution: 45% ages 18-20, 30% ages 21-24, and 25% over 24.

Responses

- Engage with participants' family members to provide them services and referrals as needed.
- Our impact is multigenerational, therefore, we must help members see how they are interconnected with family and community.

Finding 10. The program creates transformative relationships with mentors and leaders.

The interviews consistently highlight the transformative impact of relationships with program leaders and mentors. Participants describe program leaders who go beyond typical supervisor roles to provide guidance, accountability, and personal investment in their success. The data reveal that these relationships are characterized by high expectations paired with high support, creating an environment where participants are simultaneously challenged and encouraged. Many participants specifically reference program leaders who saw potential in them that they didn't see in themselves and persistently invested in their development despite setbacks. These mentoring relationships appear to be particularly significant for participants who lacked positive adult role models or had previous negative experiences with authority figures.

Key Themes from Qualitative Interviews

- Program leaders function as mentors who provide guidance, accountability, and personal investment beyond typical supervisor roles.
- Mentoring relationships combine high expectations with high support, challenging participants while providing necessary assistance.
- Participants describe mentors who recognized potential in them that they didn't see in themselves.
- These relationships are particularly meaningful for participants who lacked positive adult relationships or had negative experiences with authority figures.

Interview Quotes

"I think being paired with Keyta, she's made me more professional as far as how I deal with the young people in the program."

"I go to court with some of our justice involved kids and have met with all the Hamilton County judges and talked about the program."

"If it wouldn't have been for Dex taking me off of the streets the day he saw me in 2022, there's no telling where I would be."

"Dex ain't gonna let us quit. One thing I know about Dex is, like, when it comes down to it, if you're a good worker and he sees potential in you, he is not just gonna give up on you."

Quantitative Insights & Charts

- 100% of participants reported feeling like they're part of something important "Quite a bit" or "Very much," with 85.7% selecting "Very much," suggesting strong leadership influence (see Figure 20).
- 90.5% indicated they are better at knowing when to ask others for help "Quite a bit" or "Very much," suggesting development of trust with mentors (see Figure 20).

Responses

- Leadership is an ongoing process, not a destination. We must help members to see their future selves and the impact they can have on others.
- Give members, especially graduate members, the opportunity to become mentors to new members and younger students in the community.

Finding 11. Participants develop improved communication and conflict resolution skills.

The interviews reveal that participants develop significantly improved communication and conflict resolution skills through the program. Many participants enter with limited abilities to express themselves

Figure 20:
How much more do you feel like you're a part of something important?

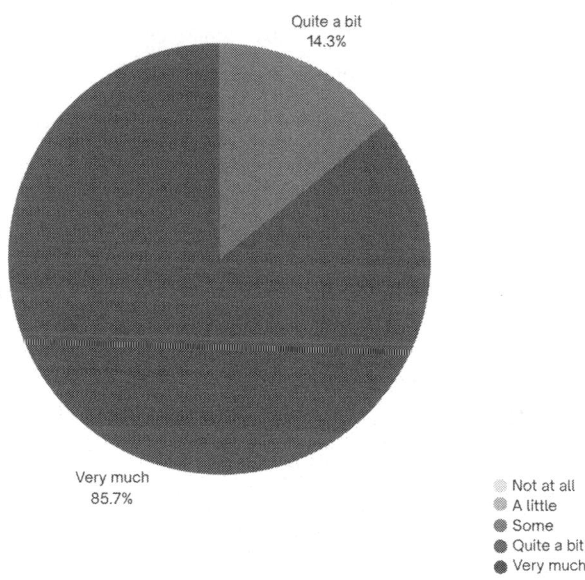

n=21

Figure 21:
How much better are you at knowing when to ask others for help?

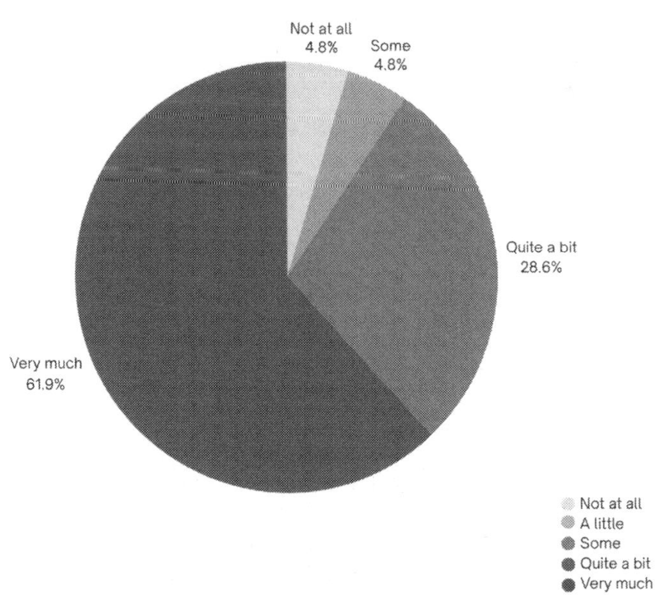

n=21

professionally, manage disagreements constructively, or communicate effectively in diverse contexts. The data show that through the program's structure, participants learn to adapt their communication for different audiences, express themselves clearly, and resolve conflicts without escalation. Participants repeatedly describe situations where they've learned to pause, listen, and respond thoughtfully rather than reacting impulsively. This growth in communication skills appears to be particularly valuable for workplace readiness and improving relationships outside the program.

Key Themes from Qualitative Interviews

- Participants learn to adapt their communication for different audiences and contexts.
- The program develops conflict resolution skills through real situations that arise in the work environment.
- Participants learn to pause, listen, and respond thoughtfully rather than reacting impulsively.
- Improved communication skills transfer to workplace, family, and community contexts outside the program.

Interview Quotes

"I didn't know how to communicate with people because I never had anyone put their time into me. It made me open up in different ways."

"When I first started, I was quiet. I did not communicate with anybody. But once I got used to it, my communication skills got better."

"I learned to sit back and listen and observe."

"I know how to tell somebody we can play around, we can have fun, but at the same time you're gonna still do what you need to do."

Quantitative Insights & Charts

- Before the program, 66.6% were good at talking with people "Quite a bit" or "Very much" (see Figure 22). After the program, this increased to 95.2% (see Figure 23).

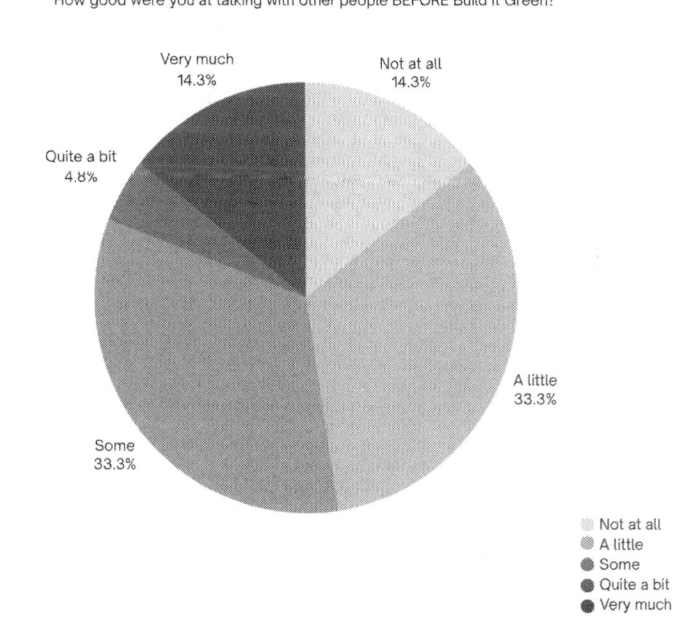

Responses

- Allow members to make mistakes in handling conflict. Not responding properly the first time can be a learning moment instead of a cause for dismissal.
- Develop more partnerships with organizations who specialize in communications and conflict resolution.

Finding 12. The program expands participants' worldview and community understanding.

The data show that the program significantly expands participants' worldview and understanding of their community. Many participants enter with limited exposure beyond their immediate neighborhoods or social circles. Through program activities, field trips, and community projects,

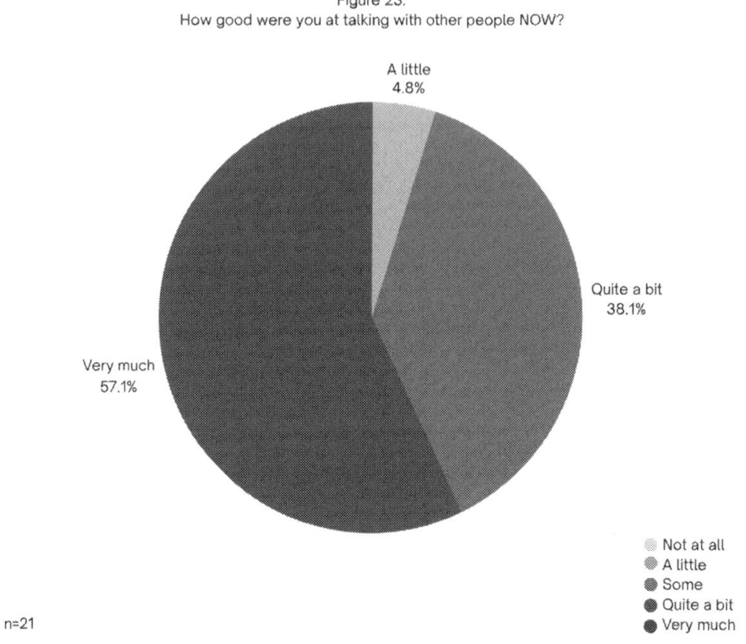

participants gain exposure to different parts of their city, diverse people, and new ideas. The interviews reveal that this expanded perspective helps participants envision different possibilities for themselves and develop a greater understanding of community needs and assets. This broadened worldview appears to reduce perceived barriers between different neighborhoods and help participants see themselves as part of a larger community where they can make meaningful contributions.

Key Themes from Qualitative Interviews

- Program activities expose participants to different neighborhoods, people, and ideas beyond their usual experience.
- Participants develop greater understanding of community needs and assets through direct engagement.
- Expanded perspective helps participants envision new possibilities for themselves and their future.
- Participants develop a sense of belonging to the broader community rather than just their immediate neighborhood.

Interview Quotes

"Me, I don't plan on staying in Chattanooga forever. So like, knowing that I know people and got connections out of state, and knowing that I can go somewhere else and eventually, like, build a new life somewhere else, it made me feel good about myself."

"When we went to Washington, I had never been there. Like, it's just certain stuff. I never did this kind of stuff before."

"Made me feel good. I felt like I was actually doing something for the community, not just for myself, but like helping out with the community, knowing that there's more out there that we can do."

"I look at it like this as long as you mind your business and do what you have to do, you ain't gotta worry about nothing. That's how it's always been. Do what I gotta do. Get the job done. Don't worry about anything else."

Quantitative Insights & Charts

- 81% of participants reported feeling connected to their community "Quite a bit" or "Very much" (see Figure 24).

Responses

- Continue to place members in situations where they have a direct positive impact for people outside of their normal surroundings.
- Challenge members to look beyond the Chattanooga area to see how their community fits into a broader community and their position within the broader community.

Figure 24:
How connected did you feel to your community?

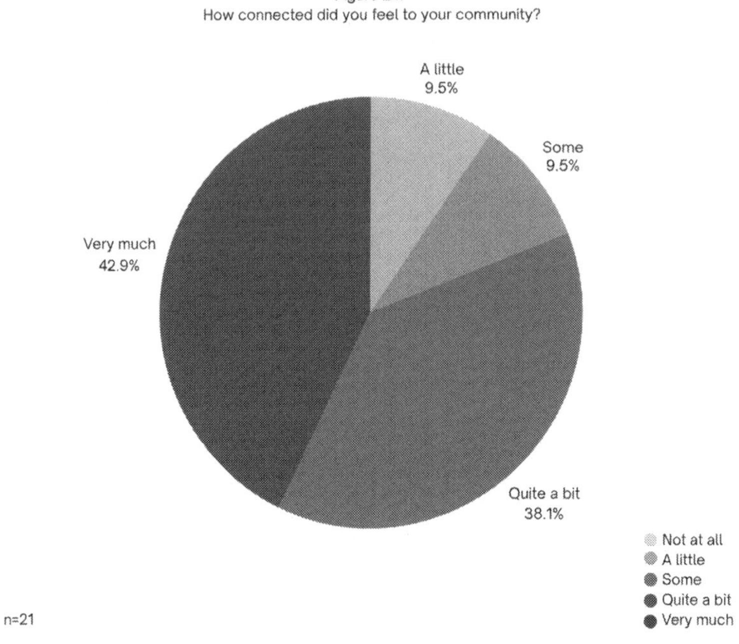

Conclusion

Insights Into Impact

Our evaluation demonstrates that Build It Green is effectively achieving its intended impacts across all three areas. Regarding developing green building skills, the findings reveal remarkable progress, with participants' knowledge about making homes energy efficient increasing from 5% before the program to 76.2% afterward, and readiness for green building jobs rising from 52.3% to 90.5%. The program is successfully helping members discover their untapped potential, as evidenced by the dramatic increase in self-belief (from 42.9% to 95.3%) and hopefulness about the future (from 47.6% to 100%). Participants consistently develop perseverance, overcome significant challenges, and connect to educational and career pathways they hadn't previously considered possible. In terms of becoming role models and strengthening community, the evaluation shows that 100% of participants help more in their community after the program, and intergenerational mentoring relationships flourish. The program's holistic approach creates its strongest impact by simultaneously developing technical skills, personal confidence, and community connection while providing practical support to overcome life barriers. While we can continue strengthening certain elements, particularly in formalizing mentorship systems and career pathways, the evaluation clearly demonstrates that Build It Green is substantially achieving its intended impacts and transforming lives in meaningful ways.

Steps Forward and Opportunities for Future Evaluation

As Build It Green continues to grow and evolve, several areas could be explored in future evaluations to deepen understanding of program impact. We might look at how participants are doing several months or years after they complete the program – are they using their skills in jobs or their personal lives? How lasting are the changes in confidence and outlook?

Another valuable area to explore would be understanding which program activities participants find most helpful and why. We could also examine how the program affects different groups of participants – does age, background, or time in the program change what people gain from their experience? Additionally, we might investigate how Build It Green's community service projects affect the neighborhoods and residents who receive them. Gathering stories from family members about changes they've noticed in participants could provide fresh perspectives on program impact. These future evaluation directions would help Build It Green continue improving while demonstrating its value to the broader community and potential funders.

CHATTANOOGA ROOM IN THE INN

Shelter to Stability

A six month residential program for women
and children experiencing homelessness

Taylor Hixson, Sara Collier, Sydni Owens

Organization and Program Overview

Chattanooga Room in the Inn (CRITI) offers a six-month residential program for women and children experiencing homelessness. Women and children coming into our program may stay at our facility, free of charge, for up to six months while they rebuild their lives in five major focus areas: Health, Housing, Finances, Family, and Career.

At CRITI, we are committed to empowering women and their children through essential support services aimed at fostering stability and independence. Our offerings include transitional housing, daily meals prepared by dedicated volunteers, life skills training, parenting classes, and mentoring. Additionally, we assist clients in locating affordable, permanent housing and provide tailored case management services. Through these initiatives, we aim to create sustainable opportunities for a successful future.

Introduction to Organization

Chattanooga Room in the Inn began in 1988 as a result of a community-wide analysis of needs in the Chattanooga area spearheaded by Christine Morrison. It revealed there were few beds available to single women and women with children who found themselves homeless. Volunteers from seven area churches organized the first program of emergency shelter. Women and children were fed a hot meal and given a safe place to stay for the night, then given breakfast in the morning. Church vans then transported the residents to the next host church for the evening. Each church was a host one night a week. The goal of shelter was met but the women and children had to move to a new location every day. This went on for four years until Congresswoman Marilyn Lloyd stepped in and a HUD grant was received and we were able to move into a permanent location in 1991, which is where we still operate today.

Founding Churches:

First Christian Church Chattanooga
Our Lady of Perpetual Help Catholic Church
Clear Creek Church
Hixson United Methodist Church
Central Presbyterian Church (now closed)
First Centenary United Methodist Church
Brainerd United Methodist Church

Program Description

This program evaluation examines the impact of the Shelter to Stability program on the lives of its participants. Through a combination of qualitative interviews and quantitative insights, this report illuminates key areas of growth and transformation experienced by individuals transitioning from homelessness to stable living. Our findings reveal significant progress across several domains, including the development of future-oriented thinking, the adoption of healthy financial habits, the prioritization of mental wellness, the cultivation of supportive networks, and the enhanced capacity for active parenting. Furthermore, the evaluation highlights the program's role in fostering self-reliance, appreciating structure, and ultimately empowering participants on their pathways to independence. This report details nine key findings that underscore the program's effectiveness in equipping individuals with the skills, resources, and mindset necessary to achieve lasting stability and envision a brighter future.

Intended Impacts

Residents prioritize well-being by focusing on physical and mental health. Families have on-site access to mental health services, are educated on additional resources in the Chattanooga area to access healthcare, and regularly receive mental health and physical health services.

Family members build stronger relationships. Family members develop healthy communication patterns, spend quality time together, and create supportive bonds that contribute to their collective wellbeing.

Residents gain stable income through full-time employment. Residents have the tools they need to achieve career advancement, to maintain employment, and financially support their families.

Residents are capable and confident in their ability to make responsible financial decisions. Residents have strong financial literacy skills, they budget, save, and have smart spending habits.

Residents support their children's educational success. Parents develop the confidence and skills to advocate for their children's educational needs, actively engage in their school experience, and create home environments that support learning.

Residents maintain stable housing. Families secure and maintain permanent housing through developing the skills, resources, and stability needed for long-term housing success.

Evaluation Methodology

The aim of our evaluation was to see what kind and quality of impact the Shelter to Stability program is having on the women and children experiencing homelessness we serve. To understand this, we explored two broad evaluation questions:

1. What kind and quality of impact are we having on the women and children experiencing homelessness we serve?
2. What aspects of our program are causing this impact?

Over the course of the project, we (a) developed and refined our ideas of intended impact and indicators, (b) designed and implemented a mixed methods outcome evaluation using both qualitative and quantitative means to collect and analyze data, (c) identified themes and findings, and (d) considered the implications to those findings for program improvement and innovation.

This project began by identifying and clarifying the intended impact of the Shelter to Stability program. Once the ideas of impact had been developed, we used the Heart Triangle™ model to identify qualitative and quantitative indicators of impact on the mental, behavioral, and emotional changes in our program participants. We used these indicators to design a qualitative interview protocol and a quantitative questionnaire to evaluate progress toward achieving our intended impact.

Qualitative Data Collection and Analysis

For the qualitative portion of the evaluation, we designed an in-depth interview protocol to gain data about the structural, qualitative changes resulting from our program. We delimited our population to encompass current program participants, program graduates, and program participants who did not complete the program. In addition, we also delimited the population to ensure both single women and women with children were represented. In June of 2023, our programming model shifted slightly and our five focus areas (Health, Housing, Finances, Family, and Career) were adopted. Our population size for this evaluation was 46 and reflects program participants who received services under this updated programming model. We used a purposeful stratified sampling technique to select a representative sample from the population we serve. Our sample size was 15, drawn from the following strata of our population:

- Single Women
- Women with Children
- Current participant, program graduate, or program participant who did not graduate

Our interviews were conducted by Sydni Owens, Intern and Occupational Therapy Doctorate Student. We convened one-on-one interviews lasting from between 45 minutes and one hour in length and collected interview data using the voice-to-text transcription service, Otter.ai.

We then analyzed the data inductively using a modified version of thematic analysis. The evaluation team analyzed the data from the interviews individually to identify initial themes. Together, we developed common themes from all of the interviews collectively. We identified the overarching and inter-interview themes that emerged from the full scope of our data analysis to illuminate the collective insights and discoveries. We mapped these themes visually and examined the dynamics among the themes, causes and catalysts of the themes, new or surprising insights related to the themes, and relationships between the themes that were revealed in the data. We then determined the most significant and meaningful discoveries and brought them forward as findings.

Quantitative Data Collection and Analysis

For the quantitative portion of the evaluation, we designed a questionnaire to collect data on our quantitative indicators of impact. Anticipating the likelihood that some of our past participant contact information may no longer be valid, we administered this instrument to all program participants possible. This resulted in the sending the quantitative survey to 67 individuals consisting of all current and past program participants and had a response of 8, a 11.94% response rate. The data were analyzed primarily using measures of central tendency. We identified key insights, patterns, and gaps within the data and incorporated these discoveries into the related findings. The most significant insights from the quantitative data are described in the following narrative.

Limitations

In conducting this study, the response rate to our quantitative survey resulted in fewer responses than we initially expected. After sending surveys to current and past program participants and encouraging participation through multiple attempts, the response was still not what we'd hoped. We partially attribute this to the possibility that our records may not contain the most current contact information, as details such as phone numbers often change within the population we serve. This challenge in maintaining current contact information is common when working with individuals experiencing housing instability and affected our ability to reach all intended survey recipients.

Findings

Finding 1. Dreams Taking Shape: The Power of Future Vision.

Our findings indicate that participants in the Shelter to Stability program gained knowledge that continues to serve them well after its completion. Many clients expressed an ability to dream of future growth and opportunities in a way they hadn't been able to do so previously. In many responses, clients described actively setting goals and committing to ensuring success. This encompasses both thinking of and planning for future career potential as well as personal goals. Clients repeatedly confirmed their commitment to saving and budgeting, ensuring they are well-prepared for the future. Moreover, they value planning ahead and have contingency plans in place to handle emergencies, ensuring they are always prepared for the unexpected. This shift from crisis-focused thinking to future orientation represents a profound psychological transformation. When clients can envision a future worth planning for, they develop internal motivation that sustains them through challenges.

Key Themes from Qualitative Interviews

- Clients are dreaming of future growth and have committed to saving and budgeting.
- Sets and actively works towards goals.
- Prioritizes career and takes initiative to advance or grow in their career.
- Plans ahead/has a back-up plan for emergencies.

Interview Quotes

"I want to be able to own my own property, so I'm looking for property and building my credit to where I can buy my own property."

"I want to own my own company."

"I found out that I could do anything I set my mind to, and to stay focused and get out there and just do it."

"I am excited about my future and being financially stable. You guys give us the opportunity to regroup so that we can become stable financially. You give us the time we need to find stability."

"Because of my new stability, I have a better insight of our future on what next year might look like and how I can make that happen. Like a bigger house or nicer car. I can actually plan for the future now."

"I'm working on getting more education on things so I can be more qualified for better employment with better pay."

"The program really opened my eyes to the resources that are available and my own potential."

Quantitative Insights & Charts

- Before the program, 37.5% reported they were "not at all" able to prioritize setting aside money for emergencies, while after the program, 85.7% reported they could do so "quite a bit" or "very much" (see Figure 1 and 2).
- Career goal development showed significant improvement, with 75% of respondents indicating they developed or strengthened career goals "quite a bit" or "very much" since participating in the program (see Figure 3).

Figure 1:
Before the program, how well were you able to prioritize setting aside money as an emergency fund?

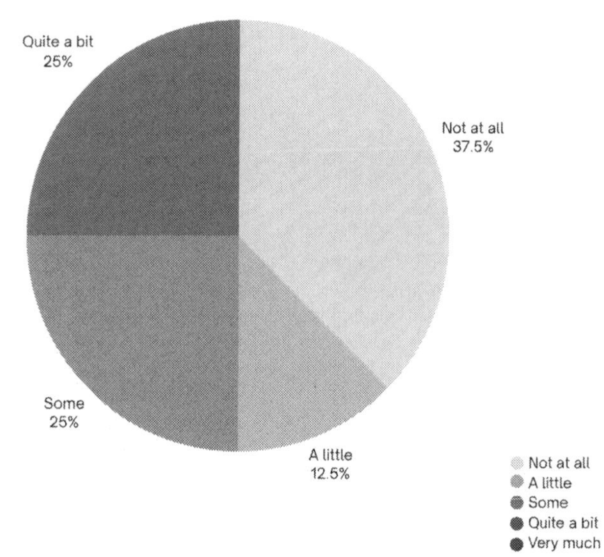

n=8

Figure 2:
After the program, how well have you been able to prioritize setting aside money as an emergency fund?

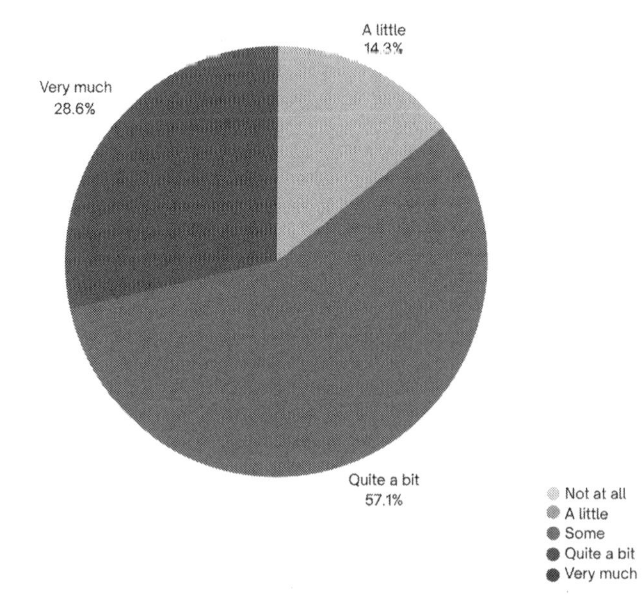

n=7

Figure 3:
Since participating in the program, I developed or strengthened career goals to work toward career advancement.

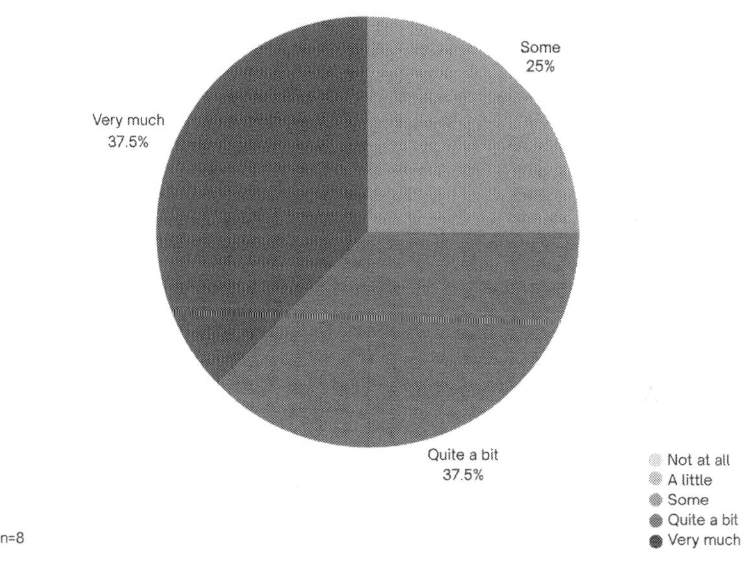

Responses

- Explore more workforce development opportunities
- Continue to empower and support women in focusing on their future and goals through expanded life skills classes and personalized case management that includes structured goal-setting and progress tracking.
- Provide a safe and supportive space for women to dream about and envision a brighter future for themselves and their children.

Finding 2. The Financial Transformation Journey.

Throughout the study, clients in the Shelter to Stability program continually identified a change in how they prioritize healthy financial habits. Before the program, many clients did not regularly budget or save. Now, they actively maintain budgets and contribute to savings accounts, representing a distinct shift in financial management. While participating in our program, clients attend financial literacy classes that teach these core skills. We were surprised to learn that many clients continued to seek out additional opportunities to build these skills and knowledge beyond what was required. Many clients now report being more aware of what products and services cost and actively look for cost-effective alternatives, such as cooking at home instead of eating out. These habit changes indicate a fundamental shift in how clients understand and value their earned income.

Key Themes from Qualitative Interviews

- Actively saving and budgeting/making it a habit and priority.
- Aware of costs and intentional with spending.
- Continues to learn and grow in financial education/literacy.
- Takes responsibility for finances.

Interview Quotes

> *"I don't do a lot of traveling. I used to put gas in my truck and just hit the road. Now I'm more aware of things, like car maintenance. I am just planning ahead more."*

> *"They had a program about saving, and that pretty much helped me with the savings I had. I've always known how to save, but I was never applying to it. So they taught me to put back your savings, so it's there when you need it. They have taught me to really value my savings."*

> *"I learned that you do not have to spend your money like just recklessly. Before I had bad habits and ate out a lot. I was definitely a spender. Now, I cook a lot more and I am actually more aware of what I am spending.*

Quantitative Insights & Charts

- Survey respondents showed marked improvement in financial confidence, with 87.5% reporting they have "quite a bit" or "very much" more confidence in managing personal finances since participating in the program (see Figure 4).
- Participants demonstrated increased preparedness for financial challenges, with 87.5% indicating they now know what to do when facing financial struggles (see Figure 5).

Figure 4:
Since participating in the program, I have more confidence in how to manage my personal finances.

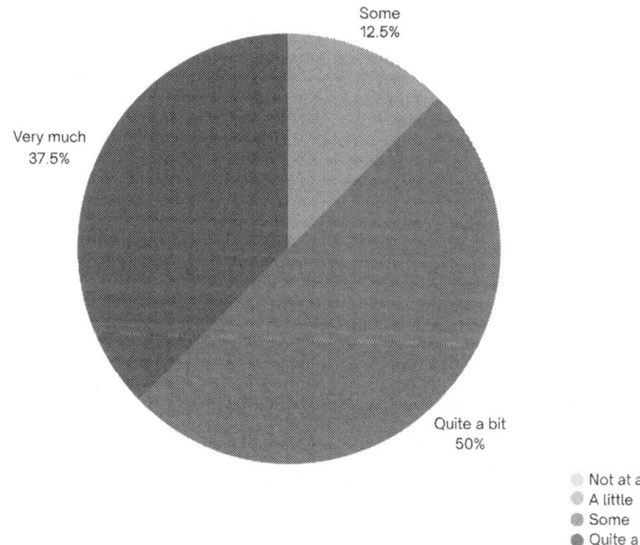

n=8

Figure 5:
I know what to do if I am facing financial struggles.

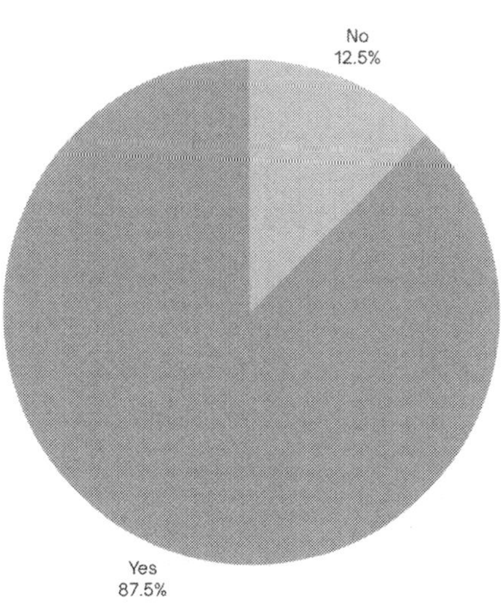

n=8

Responses

- Provide connection to additional financial literacy and growth opportunities after clients have graduated the program so that they can continue to build on the financial skills they've already developed.
- Explore implementing a "next steps" financial literacy program in aftercare that builds on foundational skills and introduces more advanced concepts like investing and building credit.

Finding 3. Mental Wellness as Foundation.

Throughout our interviews, clients consistently shared that they had learned they mattered and needed to include themselves in the equation. They realized that prioritizing their own health care, mental health care, and self-care was essential to being able to care for their children and families. Many also gained a better understanding of what healthy relationships look like and the importance of having a strong support system.

The therapy and counseling provided have been instrumental in helping them build confidence, develop a positive self-image, and cultivate a strong mindset—enabling them to navigate challenges without giving up. Many clients reported that they now recognize when they need help and are more willing to reach out for support. Additionally, they continue to meet with their therapist, with some seeing multiple therapists. Overall, these elements: therapy, self-care, healthy relationships, and a strong support system seem to be foundational to their success in all other aspects of the program. The data reveals that mental health work isn't just a nice addition to our program—it's the essential foundation that makes all other progress possible. Without addressing trauma and mental health needs first, clients struggle to benefit from other program elements.

Key Themes from Qualitative Interviews

- Prioritizes health care, mental health care, and self care.
- Recognizes healthy relationships.
- Reaches out to find help when needed.

- Has a healthy support system.
- Self confidence and positive self image.

Interview Quotes

"Being at the Room in the Inn and talking to the counselors really gave me the opportunity to dig deep and find out what some of my triggers and things like that are. I'm a very upbeat, smiling person, so if I was frowning, then you knew I was upset. I thought I was okay, or that I was just not having a good day. But what it really was is that I had so much stuff that I was always smiling about. But deep down, I was dealing with it all mentally, just trying to close it off. You know how you trying to pack everything into a drawer, and you're like, I'll deal with it later, type of thing, and you don't realize it. So that drawer is so full that it starts overfilling and these things start spewing out. Having those counselors there definitely made me realize how I was feeling and made me realize that I wasn't feeling it in a right way, and I needed someone to talk to. I needed someone to say, "Hey, I understand. I got you." I was so used to being strong, that I forgot that it's okay to feel weak. Sometimes you need that help and need that support, so I definitely appreciate it. I'm by far not at my 1,000% or where I want to be, but I would definitely say that I'm way better than where I was at."

"I've learned that mental health is very important. When I was here, it felt like the roof came in on me, because I've never been in a situation like this. I do and did have mental problems before coming here, and then when I was here I felt like I was always on edge, because I'm not used to this.....I'm still seeing my therapist. I see all of them still.....I found out that I could do anything I set my mind to, and to stay focused and get out there and just do it."

"I'm more aware than I used to be. I used to be in lala land, but now I am more aware of what I need to do. My head is in a better place.... I have learned that I matter too. I know that I have to take care of myself so that I can take care of my daughters."

"That is important to notice when I'm struggling and finding different ways to cope with it. Again, reaching out for help when I need it instead of fighting something alone."

"They did teach me a lot about that. That it is very important, and I can't really maintain a stable family if I'm not stable….It has helped me prioritize, and I do appreciate that. I didn't quite take care of my own health. When I did come to them, my children were taken care of so, you know, so I had a chance to take care of myself and prioritize myself. So, they did teach me to put myself in that loop if I was going to continue to be here for my children."

"Without your mental health, there's no way you'll be able to take care of anything else. And I understand, as far as myself, that I need to take some time for myself so that I can take care of other people. I've learned to talk to someone. I still talk with counseling through the program. It's hard. I'm not gonna say I have it figured out, but I'm still working on it. Because I have an autistic child and I need mental counseling every once in a while, so I really look forward to that."

Quantitative Insights & Charts

- Before the program, 25% of participants knew "not at all" or "a little" about accessing physical and mental healthcare resources (see Figure 6), while after the program, 50% reported knowing "quite a bit" or "very much" about these resources (see Figure 7).

Responses

- Continue to connect clients to multiple mental and physical health resources through expanded partnerships with healthcare providers and community programs.
- Provide more trauma informed care and trauma informed training to staff to better support clients' mental health needs and recovery journeys.
- Explore adding group therapy to programming opportunities to create peer support systems and shared healing experiences.

Figure 6:
Before the program, how much did you know about accessing physical and mental healthcare resources?

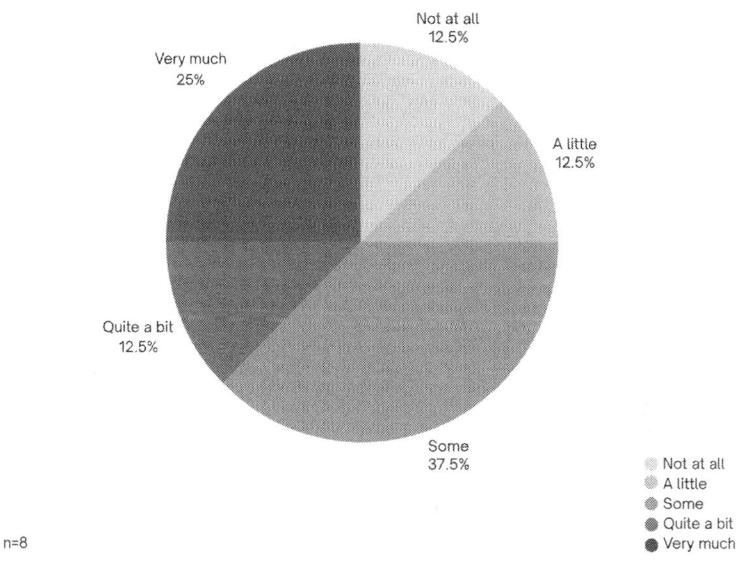

Figure 7:
After the program, how much do you know about accessing physical and mental healthcare resources?

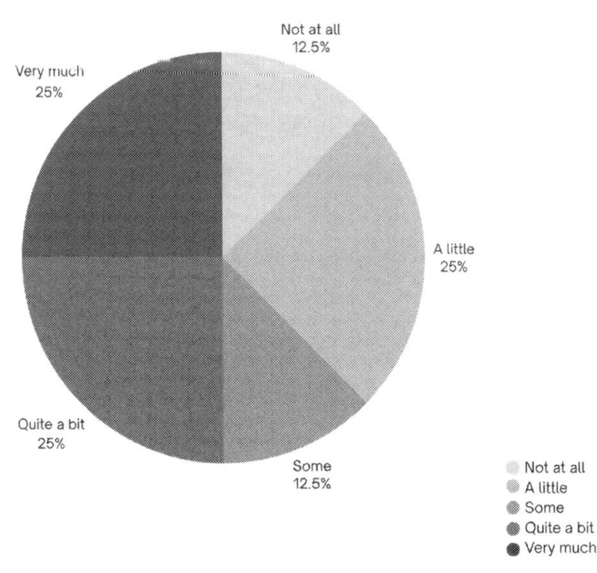

n=8

Finding 4. Lifelines of Connection.

Our findings indicate that long-term success for our clients is closely linked to their ability to access resources and build strong relationships. Developing a support network and social capital creates a "village" that empowers them in their goals. Providing access to resources enables clients to continue growing beyond their time in the program. Partnerships connect them with experts in key areas—family, health, career, financial literacy, and housing—ensuring they have long-term support tailored to their specific needs. Even after graduating from the program, these partnerships serve as an ongoing source of guidance and stability, helping clients navigate any challenges they may face.

Key Themes from Qualitative Interviews

- Building a village and social capital.
- A broader support system allows for engagement in children' s school and academic success .
- Providing access to resource to enable continued growth.

Interview Quotes

> *"Some of us have things that we need to deal with, mentally or whatnot. And I honestly feel like the ladies that were involved with helping me, from the lady from the bank to the counselors that would come there and talk to me, like Street Grace and Ms. Lafreeda. I honestly think they are amazing, absolutely amazing. I think those programs in itself are definitely helpful. And even while there, I was able to get my first aid certification. I took advantage of that, because I felt like, hey, this is an opportunity for me to get something that I had years ago. Those are great programs."*

> *"I feel like I'm not alone anymore. I feel like I have a support system and access to resources that I may need. The program allowed us to just get back on track. We got into our own home, which that was very exciting for me. My girls were overly excited about having their own place. We are just excited about it all. All of the resources that*

we now have, the counselors, family support, and family therapists have really helped us."

"I would say the resources and the different skills that I've gained without even knowing, like time management, budgeting. The program really opened my eyes to the resources that are available and my own potential."

"I will also say that the sisterhood is something great that came out of it."

"So [my daughter] being there has been great. She has a wonderful guidance counselor, social workers, it's amazing. So I got [her] into that school because of being at the shelter, and I'm forever grateful. She would tell you that she doesn't like the school part, but she loves her teachers. She has a very good support system. They all love her. They care about her. And she said last night, she said, "I know that the people there actually care about me."

Quantitative Insights

- Even though we did not have a survey question that directly correlated to the effects of partnerships, we found that clients brought this up consistently in their interviews and the impact connection to services and partners had made in their success and well being.

Responses

- Explore additional partnerships, especially those who stay with the client past program graduation to provide ongoing support during transition.
- Provide a comprehensive resource guide for community partners that clearly outlines services, eligibility requirements, and contact information.
- Continue to develop partnerships with organizations and companies that align with our program goals.

Finding 5. Stability makes active parenting possible.

During the program, residents who have children staying with them at the shelter are provided with tools and resources to gain and develop parenting skills. While working with a child advocate, residents are given the opportunity to develop a personalized parenting plan. While working through this plan, the mothers gain skills in playing an active role in their children's academic success, including how to communicate with their children's teachers or counselors and providing consistency with school attendance. In the study, the interviewed mothers expressed their desire to be emotionally available for their children and a positive role model. The mothers are learning the importance of spending quality time with their children and playing an active role in their children's lives.

Key Themes from Qualitative Interviews

- Mothers of school aged children are building relationships with their children's teachers and counselors, which is positively impacting their children's academic success.
- Mothers are striving to be emotionally available for children.
- Mothers are playing an active role in multiple aspects of their children's lives.
- Mothers are prioritizing quality time with their children.

Interview Quotes

> *"I can see him actually trying. He has a tutor, and I've been getting him enlisted in his special ed classes and stuff like that. I've been going to the school to have meetings. It's like, as we've been here, the school has been more open to what's going on to him."*

> *"I learned that sometimes we overlook our kids and their emotions. And then nowadays, kids are shut down. So, I try to make sure every day I ask them, "how was your day with school, did you meet some new friends?" It's just basically taught me how to be more open minded to my kid's feelings. I want them to always know that they can talk to mom."*

"Due to what we've gone through, I don't want them feeling like they don't have anyone to talk to. So I make sure that I am available."

"I felt like I was making a difference in their lives and actually being the positive role model that they needed."

Quantitative Insights & Charts

- Family relationship strength showed notable improvement, with 85.8% of respondents reporting their family feels stronger "quite a bit" or "very much" since participating in the program (see Figure 8).
- School engagement data revealed that 57.2% of participants feel "quite a bit" or "very much" more confident in communicating with their child's school, while 85.7% reported increased engagement in their child's academic success "quite a bit" or "very much" (see Figure 9 and 10).

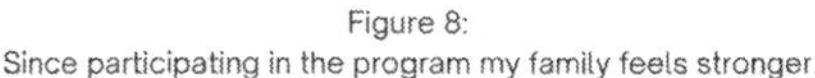

Figure 8:
Since participating in the program my family feels stronger.

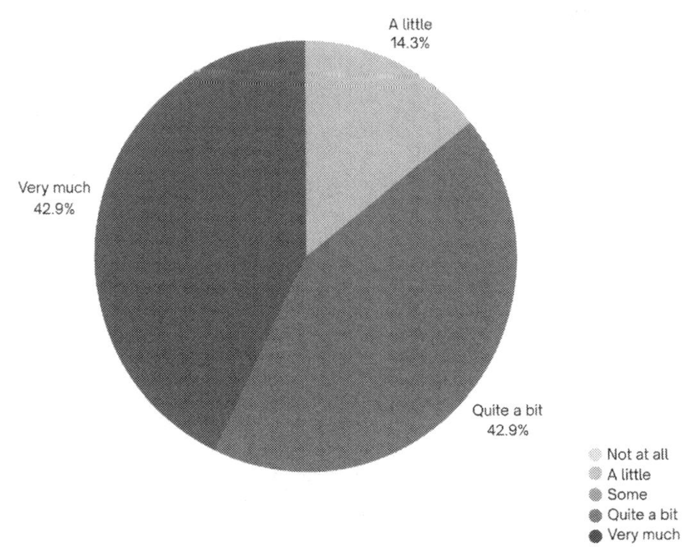

Figure 9:
ce participating in the program, I feel more confident in being able to communicate and connect with my child's sch

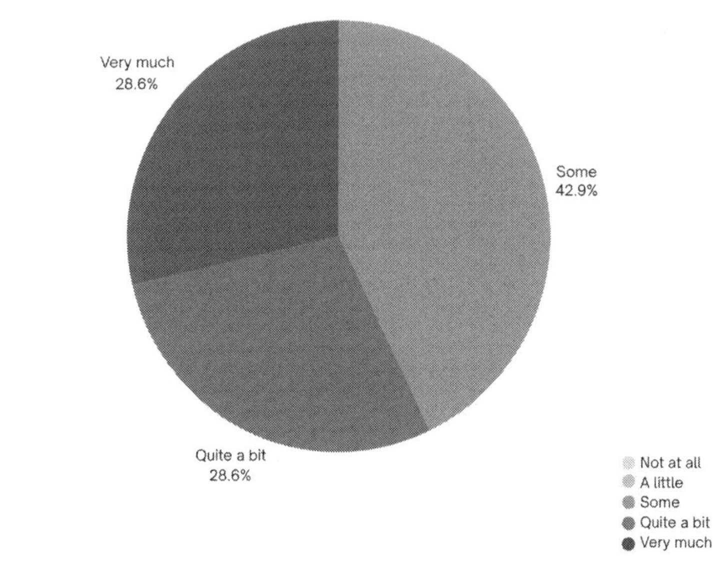

Figure 10:
Since participating in the program, I am more engaged in my child's academic success.

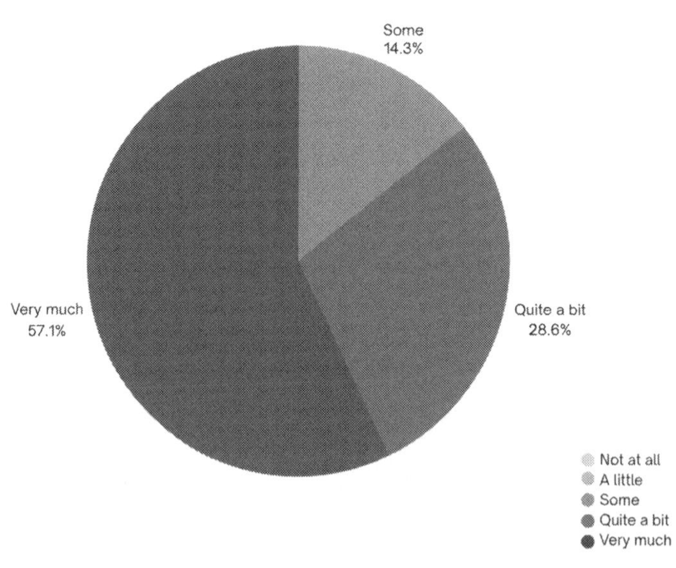

Responses

- Explore community building such as parenting support groups where parents can share experiences and strategies.
- Provide more targeted education and support for single parents addressing their unique challenges and needs.
- Continue to challenge parents to be involved in academic success and play an active role in their children's lives.

Finding 6. Room for growth in advocacy and policy addressing systemic issues.

Throughout the study, it is evident that there are many systemic barriers that inhibit stability and success, even for the families who have graduated from the program. Many of the interview participants expressed the challenge of finding consistent and reliable transportation. Other participants revealed that a lack of childcare was still an ongoing issue and impacting their ability to maintain employment. With the rising cost of living in our community, finding affordable housing that can be supported by entry-level wages remains difficult.

While our program successfully addresses immediate housing needs and builds individual capacity, time constraints and limited resources prevent us from fully addressing these systemic issues during program participation. These findings highlight important opportunities for our organization to expand into advocacy work and policy change efforts that could address these persistent barriers to stability for all families in our community.

Key Themes from Qualitative Interviews

- Transportation and childcare continues to be a barrier to success/stability.
- Low wage jobs/finding affordable housing.
- Acknowledging the systemic problem, and taking responsibility to advocate for change.

Interview Quotes

"I don't mind going to work, it's the getting there that is the hard part. If I had a car or something like that, then, I would have no problem."

"My situation is always the same. It's just that I don't have childcare on the weekends, and the jobs that I have require you to rotate the weekend."

"I'm learning that the process is very long. I'm not used to that. I'm used to getting something like just like that, whenever I need or want it. But this time around, I've been having to do all the steps. So it's a very good wake up call."

"Balancing my work and the kids at the school is sometimes hard too with their bus schedule."

Quantitative Insights

- While our survey focused on individual-level outcomes, the qualitative interviews revealed valuable insights about systemic barriers such as transportation challenges, childcare access, and wage adequacy, highlighting opportunities for future quantitative measurement that could strengthen program evaluation and advocacy efforts.

Responses

- Explore what advocacy looks like for our organizations and innovative approaches to addressing and resolving systemic barriers for our clients.
- Continue to systematically gather and document client feedback on barriers that negatively affect them and their ability to be successful.
- Provide life skills classes on self-advocacy techniques and systems navigation to help clients effectively advocate for themselves and their children.

Finding 7. Pathways to Independence.

Our study results indicate that program participants develop a new perspective on employment, recognizing it as a key tool for self-sufficiency and preventing a return to homelessness. Through their participation, they gain confidence in themselves and their abilities, equipping them to sustain long-term employment. Additionally, as they learn new skills and realize their capacity to overcome challenges, some participants seek further education and opportunities for career growth.

Key Themes from Qualitative Interviews

- Participants recognize employment as essential for maintaining housing and providing for themselves and their children.
- Participants build confidence in their skills and self-worth, enabling them to secure and sustain employment.
- With increased confidence, participants are proactively planning career advancement and setting goals for their future.

Interview Quotes

"In order to get out of displacement or homelessness, I had to have a safer job in order to save and build and grow to another level."

"I learned how to maintain employment. I guess I learned how to be more independent in stuff, like I wasn't independent before having a job or being in the program."

"They taught me go to work, the importance of it. Like to go to work and save. I'd say my confidence kind of grew a little bit, because normally I would work but not for a long time. But I maintained a job the whole time I was here."

"Because of my new stability, I have a better insight of our future on what next year might look like and how I can make that happen. Like a bigger house or nicer car. I can actually plan for the future now."

"I'm working on getting more education on things so I can be more qualified for better employment with better pay, things like that."

"It just made me look at how much more important it is to be employed, if anything."

Quantitative Insights & Charts

- Survey data shows 100% of respondents indicating they "quite a bit" or "very much" better understand the importance of gaining and maintaining full-time employment since participating in the program (see Figure 11).

Figure 11:

nce participating in the program, I better understand the importance of gaining and maintaining full-time employmer

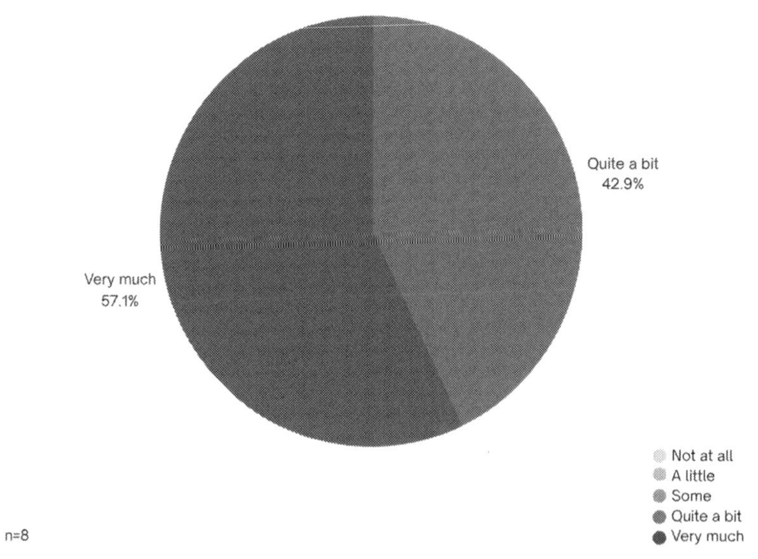

Responses

- Explore having on staff career counselors and coaches who can provide specialized employment guidance and job readiness training.
- Continue empowering and encouraging clients to dream big and invest in themselves.
- Provide more opportunities for program participants to upskill.

Finding 8. Structure Builds Capability.

Our study revealed that program participants learned to appreciate the consistency and structure that is provided by the program. During the interviews, clients shared their stories of the rules and program expectations, such as completing nightly chores and nightly curfew. Although these policies initially required an adjustment, many clients revealed that the structure of the program allowed them to feel prepared for their future responsibilities. Some clients even stated that the program's structure and consistency positively impacted their children, as they completed their chores as a family.

Key Themes from Qualitative Interviews

- Participants recognize that structure, although difficult to abide by initially, positively impacted their ability to manage responsibilities once on their own.
- Consistency and structure impacts the wellbeing of all individuals in the household, even the children.
- Participants who adhered to the program's expectations and plan were likely to find stability and independence after graduation.

Interview Quotes

"You might not like all the rules. Might not like that you have a curfew, but honestly, I didn't mind the curfew out because my kids were on a curfew before, and I wanted to be asleep in bed. I didn't want to have to do nothing. And I was used to cleaning and having, you know, like a chore or something, that I had to do because I had to clean all day anyway. Honestly, I appreciate it for what it was and what I was able to take away from it."

"I hear a lot of people complain and everything about chores and rules and stuff like that, but it's really to keep us on track, because when you go home you already have to do that, right? Versus, when you go home and you clean up once a week, or twice a week. But

being here, you going to do it every day, because you have to do it right. So your body is going to get used to you doing it every day. It's just, just a way of life."

"Then the kids, they help clean the room and stuff like that, which is fine, and I'm cool with that, because when we get our own place they will do their part, so that's cool with me. It's teaching them about other people's space and being mindful of other people."

"They really have helped me, and they have helped a lot of people. They put structure in at the end of my time there and I have kept that structure."

"If you really want it, and you follow how they are going about things, you will have structure when you leave that place. I promise you that."

Quantitative Insights

- The consistent emergence of structure appreciation themes in qualitative interviews revealed an important impact area that represents a valuable opportunity for future quantitative measurement, potentially strengthening our understanding of how program structure contributes to long-term participant success.

Responses

- Explore strategies to ease the transition into structure during the initial weeks after admission.
- Continue to provide structure and consistency to families to empower them to maintain their responsibilities after graduation.
- Provide opportunities for clients to take on greater responsibility in the house as they progress through the program, creating a pathway to independence.

Finding 9. Rising Confidence: The Self-Reliance Journey. The study revealed the program played a crucial role in helping clients develop self-reliance, confidence, and a strong sense of personal capability. By providing the right tools, resources, and support, the program encouraged individuals to take initiative and tackle challenges in order to accomplish their goals. Clients indicated that completing the program boosted their self-confidence but also empowered them to trust their own abilities and make informed decisions. As clients faced and overcame challenges, they gained a stronger belief in their abilities, which helped to build their confidence. This sense of accomplishment not only enhanced their self-esteem but also reinforced their understanding that they are capable of achieving their goals independently.

Key Themes from Qualitative Interviews

- By overcoming obstacles, clients experienced increased self-assurance, which strengthened their belief in their ability to succeed.
- Clients are committed to continual improvement and ensuring they are successful.
- Increase confidence and self-worth in program participants.

Interview Quotes

"I found out that I could do anything I set my mind to, and to stay focused and get out there and just do it."

"Because of my new stability, I have a better insight of our future on what next year might look like and how I can make that happen. Like a bigger house or nicer car. I can actually plan for the future now."

"The program really opened my eyes to the resources that are available and my own potential."

"So, it's a big deal, but it has really boost my pride up, because it let me know that I can do it. Instead of somebody handing it to me, I

can actually do it myself. Now I know what steps to go through, how to do it, and how long it would take."

"Maybe believing in myself, because I used to doubt myself a lot. But being here, you know, I learned that I can do it. You know, just take it step by step. Breathe. Just make it through the learning process, because everything is definitely a learning process. So, I've learned how to manage a lot."

Quantitative Insights & Charts

- Survey data reveals 75% of participants reporting "quite a bit" or "very much" more confidence in planning for their future since participating in the program (see Figure 12).

Figure 11:
ince participating in the program, I better understand the importance of gaining and maintaining full-time employmer

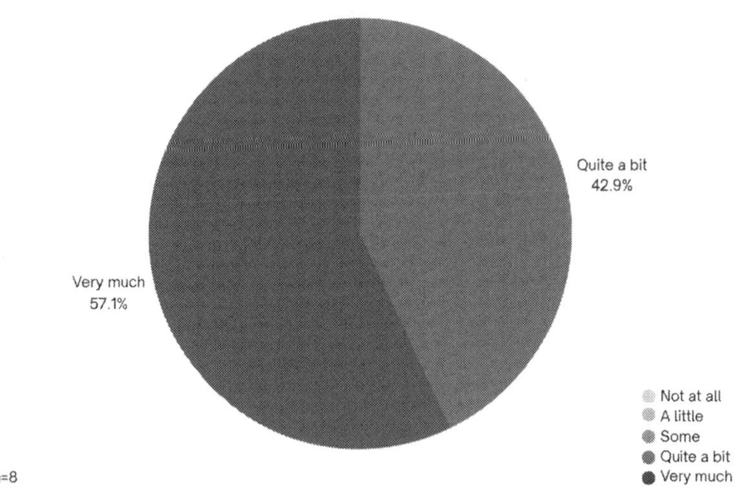

Responses

- Consider incorporating goals and growth opportunities into our aftercare program to ensure clients can continue developing even after they leave the main program.
- Maintain a culture of support and continue empowering clients through our programming and organizational values.

- Create more opportunities for clients to build skills by providing step-by-step instructions that allow them to complete tasks independently and learn through experience.

Conclusion

In conclusion, the findings of this program evaluation provide compelling evidence of the Shelter to Stability program's positive and transformative impact on its participants. The data consistently demonstrates significant growth in areas critical for long-term stability, moving individuals from crisis management to proactive planning and empowered action. The ability to envision a positive future, coupled with newfound financial responsibility, a focus on mental well-being, and the development of crucial support systems, creates a strong foundation for sustained independence. Moreover, the program fosters self-reliance and an appreciation for structure, further equipping participants to navigate the complexities of independent living and active parenting. While acknowledging the persistent systemic barriers that require broader advocacy efforts, this evaluation underscores the vital role the Shelter to Stability program plays in empowering individuals to take control of their lives, build a more secure future, and ultimately thrive in their communities. The insights gleaned from this evaluation offer valuable direction for continued program enhancement and strategic growth, ensuring its ongoing success in supporting individuals on their journey towards lasting stability.

Insights Into Impact

The evaluation of the Shelter to Stability program has shown promising evidence that women who complete the program have stronger financial literacy skills and are more confident in their ability to budget, save, and practice smart spending habits. Moreso, these financial skills were also present in the data of participants who did not complete the full program suggesting that financial education was paramount in moving women and children experiencing homelessness into self sufficiency. Additionally, the data revealed significant impact to the family's well-being attributed to mental health support and counseling available at no cost to program participants. Parents described increased confidence and skills to advocate for their children's educational needs, actively engaging in their school experience, and creating home environments that support learning. It was also noted in the data that clients still experience difficulties in many aspects of financial stability due to systemic challenges including transportation, childcare barriers, and obtaining parent friendly employment.

Steps Forward

As a result of this study, Chattanooga Room in the Inn plans to expand the workforce development opportunities offered to program participants to build job skills and confidence in seeking higher wage employment. Additionally, we learned that there was a need for continued financial literacy and financial planning support after program completion. To support this need, we plan to increase access to community resources and partnerships utilizing our aftercare services and offer new workforce development opportunities to program graduates in addition to current participants. Other opportunities for program enhancement include offering group counseling sessions for participants as well as additional internal and external support focused on parenting for single mothers.

Opportunities for Future Evaluation

Through this program evaluation process, we've gained insight into the long-term impact of the Shelter to Stability program and heard directly from those we serve. It has proven to be an invaluable resource as we continue to grow. Going forward, Chattanooga Room in the Inn is exploring ways to continue this evaluation process to listen to those we serve and improve our work. These opportunities could involve members of our board and committee leadership spearheading an annual or bi-annual program evaluation utilizing the Project Impact model. We also anticipate deploying this evaluation study across other programs, specifically our aftercare program, which supports Shelter to Stability program graduates for one year after moving into permanent housing.

CHATT FOUNDATION

Homeless Services

Rebecca Matthews, Holden Young, Holly Reeve

Organization and Program Overview

CHATT Foundation works to meet the most basic needs of hungry, homeless, and vulnerable people in our community while offering a clear path to self-sufficiency. CHATT Foundation accomplishes this by providing over 30 programs, including shelter, housing, case management, and basic daily necessities to homeless individuals and families.

CHATT Foundation provides a myriad of services to help support individuals and families experiencing homelessness. These range from housing, employment, and case management to basic daily necessities such as food, showers, laundry, and mail services.

Intended Impacts

People experiencing homelessness stabilize their daily lives through meeting basic needs. Homeless individuals will have access to basic human needs, such as shelter, food, mail services, educational services, social services, laundry services, and much more.

People experiencing homelessness establish and maintain networks of support. Individuals build connections with social services, community resources, and support systems that help them move forward. They demonstrate the ability to access and maintain these connections, from healthcare to employment support to community services.

People experiencing homelessness achieve stable and sustainable living situations. Individuals move beyond crisis living to establish longer-term stability. They create and follow through on plans that help them maintain housing, income, and overall life stability over time.

Evaluation Methodology

The aim of our evaluation was to determine the type and quality of impact our homeless services programs were having on newly homeless individuals and families in our area. To understand this, we explored two broad evaluation questions:

1. What kind and quality of impact are we having on newly homeless participants?
2. What aspects of our program are causing this impact?

Over the course of the project, we (a) developed and refined our ideas of intended impact and indicators, (b) designed and implemented a mixed methods outcome evaluation using both qualitative and quantitative means to collect and analyze data, (c) identified themes and findings, and (d) considered the implications to those findings for program improvement and innovation.

This project began by identifying and clarifying the intended impact of our homeless service programs. Once the ideas of impact had been developed, we used the Heart Triangle™ model to identify qualitative and quantitative indicators of impact on the mental, behavioral, and emotional changes in our newly homeless participants. We used these indicators to design a qualitative interview protocol and a quantitative questionnaire to evaluate progress toward achieving our intended impact.

Qualitative Data Collection and Analysis

For the qualitative portion of the evaluation, we designed an in-depth interview protocol to gain data about the structural, qualitative changes resulting from our program. We delimited our population to new homeless individuals and families from zero to ninety days and from ninety days to a year, in order to better understand the impact of our programs on newly homeless participants. Our population size for this evaluation was 25. We used a purposeful stratified sampling technique to select a representative sample from the population we serve. Our sample size was 12, drawn from the following strata of our population:

- Individuals ages 18-25,25-55, 55+
- Gender (male/female)
- Race/ethnicity

Our interview team consisted of individuals from our Hospitality Department, Development, and from the Maclellan Shelter for Families. We convened one-on-one interviews lasting between 45 minutes and one hour in length and collected interview data using handwritten notes and voice recorder for Otter. We then analyzed the data inductively using a modified version of thematic analysis. Each interviewer analyzed the data from their interviews individually to identify initial themes. Together, we developed common themes from all of the interviews collectively. We identified the overarching and interview themes that emerged from the full scope of our data analysis to illuminate the collective insights and discoveries. We mapped these themes visually and examined the dynamics among the themes, causes and catalysts of the themes, new or surprising insights related to the themes, and relationships between the themes that were revealed in the data. We then determined the most significant and meaningful discoveries and brought them forward as findings.

Quantitative Data Collection and Analysis

For the quantitative portion of the evaluation, we designed a questionnaire to collect data on our quantitative indicators of impact. We administered this instrument to 23 individuals and had a response of 23, a 100% response rate. The data were analyzed primarily using measures of central tendency. We identified key insights, patterns, and gaps within the data and incorporated these discoveries into the related findings. The most significant insights from the quantitative data are described in the following narrative.

Limitations

Limitations for data collection include the transient nature of the populations that we serve. Talking to participants and asking them to participate in this process was easy, but trying to conduct the actual interview and take roughly an hour of their time was challenging, which may have resulted in smaller qualitative sample sizes than originally intended.

Findings

Finding 1. Participants require intensive navigation support to overcome practical barriers to stability.

The data reveal that participants face significant challenges moving beyond day-to-day survival mode. Participants consistently described living "minute by minute" and "second by second," struggling to focus beyond immediate needs to work on long-term stability. Throughout our interviews, a clear pattern emerged showing participants overwhelmed by resource navigation, housing processes, and employment pathways. The data show a profound need for intensive guidance or "hand-holding" through these complex systems, as participants frequently expressed difficulty understanding available resources and completing necessary paperwork. This finding suggests that increased capacity in personalized support services would significantly impact participants' ability to progress toward stability.

Key Themes from Qualitative Interviews

- Participants need hand-holding or intense guidance on navigating resources available to them at CHATT Foundation and in the community abroad.
- Participants often become complacent in their situation because they have lived in "lawlessness" for most of their lives.

- The complexity of resource systems creates practical barriers that prevent participants from accessing available help.
- Participants need someone to help inspire hope in themselves and what they are capable of accomplishing.

Interview Quotes

"Not knowing what the next step is, feels like we will be forever stuck on what to do now."

"Before coming to the CHATT Foundation, we often faced challenges of meeting certain criteria."

"I don't want to stress or worry about anything. I really just take it one day at a time. I just try to get through the day. I hope for tomorrow, but no one is promised tomorrow."

"I've a folder full of papers, but I don't know what to do with them. I guess it's my lack of following through, to see what all is out there."

"CHATT Foundation makes it easier when you don't have to worry about when your next shower will be, or where to get soap or deodorant."

Quantitative Insights & Charts

- When asked how much CHATT Foundation has helped connect them with other helpful community services, 95.6% indicated help, emphasizing the importance of relationship-building approaches to service connection (see Figure 1).
- 91.3% of respondents reported that CHATT Foundation has helped them identify other helpful community services (see Figure 2).

Figure 1:
How much has CHATT Foundation helped you connect with other helpful community services?

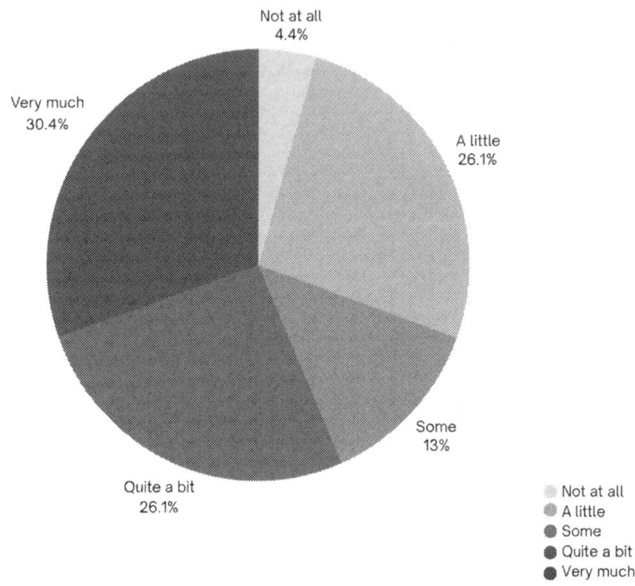

n=23

Figure 2:
As a result of CHATT Foundation's program, how many more local support organizations can you now identify that could help meet your needs?

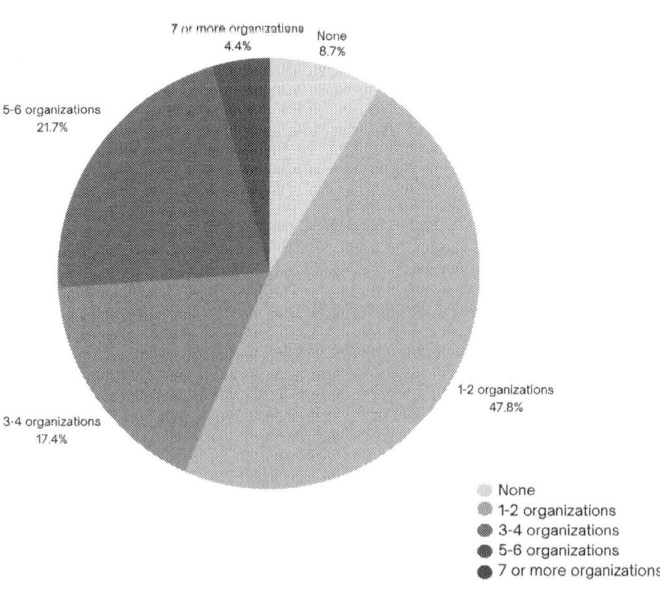

n=23

Responses

- Create a comprehensive resource binder to help staff direct and navigate participants toward available community resources.
- Develop Community Center activities that would increase participant engagement levels.
- Create a dedicated Donation Department to manage donations and distribute them to the appropriate departments, thereby reducing the burden on Hospitality staff and allowing them more time to engage with participants on workforce development.
- Increase the number of peer navigators and outreach workers to provide more direct support for participants and help them navigate complex systems.
- Establish a volunteer/peer navigator committee to advise on classes, events, and community happenings, which would in turn ensure programming remains relevant to participant needs.

Finding 2. Participants experience significant emotional and psychological barriers requiring specialized approaches.

Findings from our qualitative analysis show multiple areas of concern as they relate to participants emotional and psychological well-being. Throughout our interviews, participants consistently expressed struggling with anxiety, timidity, fear, and constantly operating in survival mode. These emotional barriers create a complex psychological landscape that participants must navigate alongside their practical challenges. The data show that these emotional experiences are not peripheral but central to participants' journeys toward stability. Many participants described experiencing a lack of privacy and challenges with basic self-care. The data suggest that addressing these psychological barriers through appropriate intervention approaches is essential for meaningful participant progress.

Key Themes from Qualitative Interviews

- Participants express overwhelming emotions, which include feelings of being anxious, timid, scared, out of control, fear, and constantly being in survival mode.
- Participants mentioned often living "day-to-day," and wondering how they were going to make it to tomorrow.
- Participants report experiencing challenges with basic self-care and sanitation.
- Lack of privacy and a general lack of trust amongst their peers and supportive services create additional barriers.

Interview Quotes

"It gets discouraging when others are being housed. Brandy is here in the field every day. I had my name in before the others. I've found stability through my own resources."

"I was in a relationship with a man, and had to get away from him. So I tried to stay with my dad in Coleman, AL, and decided to come to [Chattanooga] to stay with my grandparents. Me and my Dad got in a disagreement and he told me I couldn't stay there anymore..........I was kind of stuck in the situation with the [bad] relationship and no other family would help me. Every time I tried to get away, they just told me to keep going back [to that person]."

"I don't want to stress or worry about anything. I try not to because it's bad for the body. I really just take it one day at a time. I just try to get through the day. I hope for tomorrow, but we're not promised tomorrow."

Quantitative Insights

- While stress levels have decreased, they remain relatively high, indicating that emotional and psychological barriers persist even with support services (see Figure 3 and 4).
- Comparing pre- and post-intervention stress levels reveals that while CHATT Foundation services reduce overall stress, participants still report significant residual stress (average 2.9

on a 5-point scale), suggesting that specialized mental health services are needed in addition to basic needs services (see Figure 3 and 4).

Figure 3:
Rate your level of stress about meeting your basic daily needs before CHATT Foundation: (1 being the lowest)

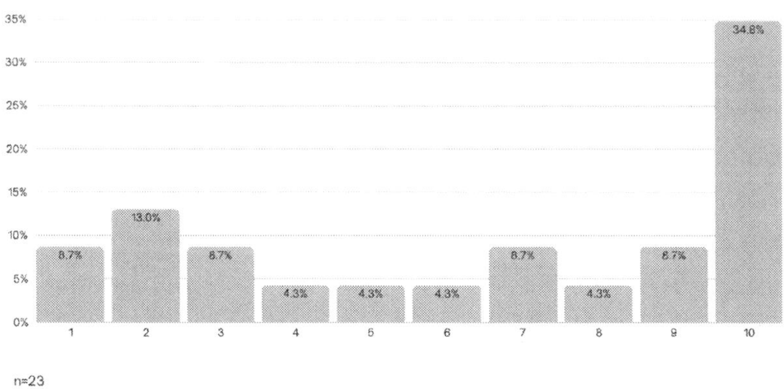

Figure 4:
Rate your level of stress about meeting your basic daily needs after CHATT Foundation: (1 being the lowest)

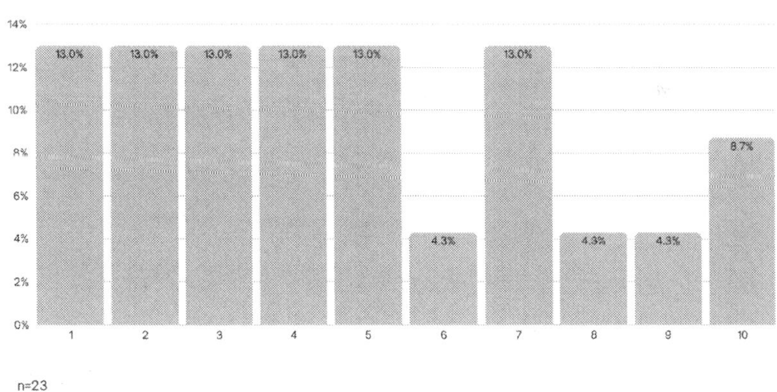

Responses

- Identify internal or external accredited trainers for core modalities, including Trauma-Informed Care, Motivational Interviewing, Critical Time Intervention, and De-Escalation skills.
- Create standards for regular staff training with each of these modalities, establishing a schedule that might include monthly,

quarterly, or bi-annual refreshers depending on the complexity of each approach.
- Develop ongoing education and training programs that would ensure all staff maintain these critical skills over time, leading to more consistent trauma-informed interactions with participants across all service points.

Finding 3. Participants often face a "perfect storm" of interconnected causes that have led to their current homeless episode.

The data reveal that participants' homelessness typically results from a "perfect storm" of interconnected challenges rather than a single cause. Throughout our interviews, participants described complex situations involving broken family relationships, housing instability, economic hardship, and limited support networks that combined to create their current circumstances. This finding demonstrates that addressing homelessness requires comprehensive approaches that recognize and respond to these multiple factors simultaneously. The data show that when these factors compound, participants become increasingly overwhelmed by both their situation and the complexity of navigating available resources, thus developing intense feelings of mistrust and uncertainty about their future.

Key Themes from Qualitative Interviews

- Broken relationships with past family members or people they were living with often directly lead to homeless episodes.
- Participants feel overwhelmed by the amount of resources available to them, unsure of where to start or how to start the process.
- Multiple factors including relationship breakdowns, economic hardship, and housing instability typically combine to create homelessness.

Interview Quotes

"My mom...she didn't want to see my face because of my prior drug addictions. Now that I've moved to Chattanooga, she has opened up dialogue again with me. She never would talk with me [before]."

"When I talk to people, they get very confused with all the paperwork. People can't read."

Quantitative Insights & Charts

- Survey data on participants' current housing situations reveals the diversity and complexity of the circumstances participants face. 43.5% report living unsheltered, 34.8% in emergency shelters, 8.7% in transitional housing, 8.7% in other temporary arrangements, and 4.3% stable housing (see Figure 5).

Figure 5:
What is your current housing situation?

Unsheltered 8.7%
Permanent supportive housing 21.7%
Emergency shelter 47.8%
Transitional housing 17.4%

- Unsheltered
- Emegency shelter
- Transitional housing
- Permanent supportive housing
- Stable housing

n=23

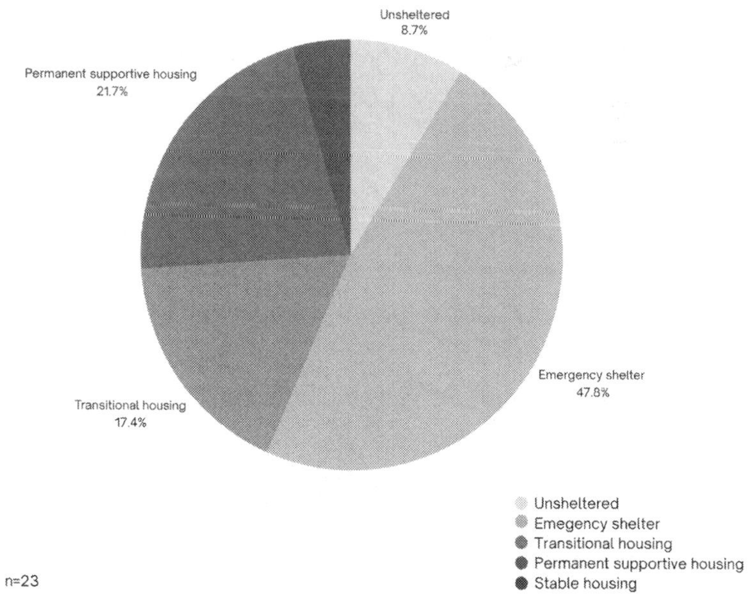

Responses

- We recommend CHATT Foundation further invest in growing and building our Development Department, hopefully leading to increased revenue for the CHATT Foundation and thereby increasing the ability for us to hire and retain qualified and knowledgeable social services staff (i.e. case managers, social workers, peer navigators) to better serve our participants' daily needs.
- Restructuring to include oversight from key committees:
    - Grants Committee (Internal)
    - Properties Committee (External)
    - Investment Committee (External)
    - Audit Committee (External)
    - Development Committee (External)
- These committees will work to better inform Development and the agency as a whole on new approaches to fundraising and grant & private funder opportunities.

Finding 4. CHATT Foundation excels at meeting the practical basic needs of the hungry, homeless, and vulnerable in our community.

The data consistently reveal that CHATT Foundation demonstrates significant strength in meeting participants' basic immediate needs. Throughout our interviews, participants expressed appreciation for accessible services including laundry, showers, mail, food services, computer lab access, and employment resources. The data show that these services provide essential stability touchpoints that help participants meet immediate needs while working toward longer-term goals. Participants specifically highlighted the ease of accessing these services and the valuable role they play in meeting daily hygiene and nutritional requirements. This finding demonstrates that meeting basic needs effectively creates a foundation from which participants can begin addressing more complex challenges.

Key Themes from Qualitative Interviews

- Participants report easy access to basic hygiene and social services at CHATT Foundation.
- Welcome desk staff effectively direct participants to appropriate services within the facilities.
- The streamlined process allows participants to efficiently meet multiple needs in a single day.

Interview Quotes

"[Services] are readily available…there's never any obstacles. If I have to get laundry, mail, and showers in one day, I can get them done in one day."

"I believe that what you have given me here specifically, is an opportunity for responsibility."

Quantitative Insights

CHATT Foundation, in partnership with the National Institute for Medical Respite Care, CommonSpirit, and Hamilton County Tennessee's Homeless Health Care Center, a division of the county's health department, operated a pilot respite care program from September 25, 2023, to June 30, 2024. The overarching intent of the pilot program was to establish a funding model, ensure effective processes, identify need, and assist with housing. During the pilot program, 73 individuals sought respite care through referrals.

- Patient Demographics and Days in Respite Percentages:
  - Gender: 82% Male, 18% Female
  - Race: 81% White, 18% Black, 01% Asian
  - Age Group: 1% 20-29, 3% 30-39, 8% 40-49, 38% 50-59, 36% 60-69, 14% 70+
  - Days in Respite: 38% (5 days, 34% 6 to 14 days, 17% 15 to 21 days, 11%) 22 days

- Percentage of Patients with Specific Diagnoses:
  - Pneumonia: 11%
  - Wound Care: 10%
  - Post Amputation: 10%
  - Other: 69%

Cost breakdown for a permanent medical respite care program: Staffing for the program would require a certified nursing assistant (CNA), a case manager, and after-hours security. To meet the needs of future programming, a respite care program would need approximately $360,000 per year.

Responses

- CHATT Foundation should continue to actively pursue funding for re-opening Respite Care. Respite care provides essential services to homeless participants who are being discharged from hospitals and area providers, without any place to rest and recuperate from major surgeries or procedures.
- Now that CHATT Foundation has determined the best model for operating an ongoing, onsite Medical Respite Care Program, discussion with prospective funders is currently being pursued.

Finding 5. Participants facing physical limitations and hardships need to be stabilized through medical intervention to better help meet their basic needs.

Our study reveals that health crises represent critical intervention opportunities where targeted medical support shows significant impact. Throughout our interviews, participants who experienced serious health issues emphasized the life-changing and often life-saving role of respite care services. The data show that CHATT Foundation can effectively meet the immediate basic needs of participants who have faced catastrophic health crises when agency partners are engaged and when participants can access appropriate levels of care. This finding demonstrates that addressing medical needs creates a foundation for addressing other stability challenges and that the timing of these interventions is often crucial.

Key Themes from Qualitative Interviews

- Health crises often precipitate or exacerbate homelessness for participants.
- Medical respite care provides essential support for participants with acute health needs.
- Transitions from hospital to street without intermediate support create dangerous gaps in care.
- Health stabilization creates a foundation for addressing other needs.

Interview Quotes

"I had a heart attack and Respite Care saved my life."

"I ended up there [Respite] because I was in the hospital for two days and they let me out. I was still so sick........I think I would have been dead if I hadn't gone over there. I could hardly walk."

"I was working two jobs until I started to lose weight. I [ended up] needing open heart surgery and lung surgery."

"I might make it a week [living outside], and that would be it for me."

"If I don't have that machine or those tanks, I won't make it a day."

Quantitative Insights

CHATT Foundation, in partnership with the National Institute for Medical Respite Care, CommonSpirit, and Hamilton County Tennessee's Homeless Health Care Center, a division of the county's health department, operated a pilot respite care program from September 25, 2023, to June 30, 2024. The overarching intent of the pilot program was to establish a funding model, ensure effective processes, identify need, and assist with housing. During the pilot program, 73 individuals sought respite care through referrals.

Patient Demographics and Days in Respite Percentages:

- Gender: 82% Male, 18% Female
- Race: 81% White, 18% Black, 01% Asian
- Age Group: 1% 20-29, 3% 30-39, 8% 40-49, 38% 50-59, 36% 60-69, 14% 70+
- Days in Respite: 38% (5 days, 34% 6 to 14 days, 17% 15 to 21 days, 11 %) 22 days

Cost breakdown for a permanent medical respite care program: Staffing for the program would require a certified nursing assistant (CNA), a case manager, and after-hours security. To meet the needs of future programming, a respite care program would need approximately $360,000 per year.

Responses

- CHATT Foundation should continue to actively pursue funding for re-opening Respite Care. Respite care provides essential services to homeless participants who are being discharged from hospitals and area providers, without any place to rest and recuperate from major surgeries or procedures.
- Now that CHATT Foundation has determined the best model for operating an ongoing, onsite Medical Respite Care Program, discussion with prospective funders is currently being pursued.

Finding 6. Participants experience significant stigma and shame that impedes their progress toward stability.

The data reveal that participants face overwhelming stigma and internalized shame related to their homeless status. Throughout our interviews, participants consistently expressed feeling judged by society, service providers, and even family members about "how they got there" and their perceived inability to improve their circumstances. The data show that these experiences of judgment and shame create significant psychological barriers that compound the practical challenges participants face. Many participants have internalized these negative perceptions, viewing themselves as failures due to their homeless episode, which further diminishes their confidence in seeking assistance and navigating complex systems. This finding demonstrates that addressing the psychological impact of stigma is essential for creating effective pathways to stability, as shame and judgment directly impact participants' willingness to engage with available services and their belief in their own capacity for change.

Key Themes from Qualitative Interviews

- Participants voiced a fear of failure and how they already see themselves as failures due to their current homeless episode.
- Respondents mentioned an immense feeling of judgment towards them, with multiple people asking them "how they got there," and what they plan on doing to get themselves out.
- Participants report experiencing loss of dignity, shame, and challenges with basic self-care and sanitation.
- Lack of privacy and a general lack of trust amongst their peers and supportive services creates additional barriers.

Interview Quotes

> *"Not knowing what the next step is, feels like we will be forever stuck on what to do now."*
>
> *"It gets discouraging when others are being housed. Brandy is here in the field every day. I had my name in before the others. I've found stability through my own resources."*
>
> *"I've a folder full of papers, but I don't know what to do with them. I guess it's my lack of following through, to see what all is out there."*
>
> *"Before coming to the CHATT Foundation, we often faced challenges of meeting certain criteria."*

Responses

- CHATT Foundation should prioritize and actively pursue funding for Peer Navigators to hire on staff. Recruitment and training of Peer Supports are a leading best practice in the area of homeless services and social services. Peer Navigators provide the ability for someone with lived experience, to come alongside homeless participants and help advocate for their sobriety, while also helping them navigate the network of housing and social service resources available to them, all of which ultimately contribute to the stability of the participant. Additionally, Peer Navigators work with participants on building community relationships with faith based organizations, other social services, and like-minded individuals in the area.

Finding 7. Relationship-building and dignity-centered approaches significantly enhance participant engagement and outcomes.

The data consistently show that the relationship quality between staff and participants fundamentally impacts service effectiveness and participant progress. Throughout our interviews, participants emphasized the value of interactions that preserved their dignity and treated them with respect. The data reveal that consistent, trusting relationships with staff members significantly increase participant engagement with services and willingness to work toward longer-term goals. Participants specifically highlighted how being treated with dignity restored their sense of self-worth and provided "an opportunity for responsibility." This finding demonstrates that beyond the practical value of services offered, the manner in which those services are delivered—with respect, consistency, and attention to human dignity—creates the psychological safety necessary for participants to engage meaningfully in their journey toward stability.

Key Themes from Qualitative Interviews

- Participants value staff interactions that preserve their dignity and treat them with respect.
- CHATT Foundation staff training on trauma-informed care and motivational interviewing are key to help participants feel dignified and inspired to put in the work to achieve their goals.
- CHATT Foundation property improvements and program improvements are key towards helping participants feel more dignified, and help them establish healthy boundaries in their lives.
- The atmosphere and environment of service provision significantly impacts participants' sense of self-worth.

Interview Quotes

"I believe that what you have given me here specifically, is an opportunity for responsibility."

"CHATT Foundation makes it easier when you don't have to worry about when your next shower will be, or where to get soap or deodorant."

"[Services] are readily available...there's never any obstacles. If I have to get laundry, mail, and showers in one day, I can get them done in one day."

Quantitative Insights & Charts

- Survey data shows that 78.2% of participants agree or strongly agree that having their basic needs met through CHATT Foundation has helped them feel more dignified, indicating the importance of dignity-centered approaches (see Figure 6).

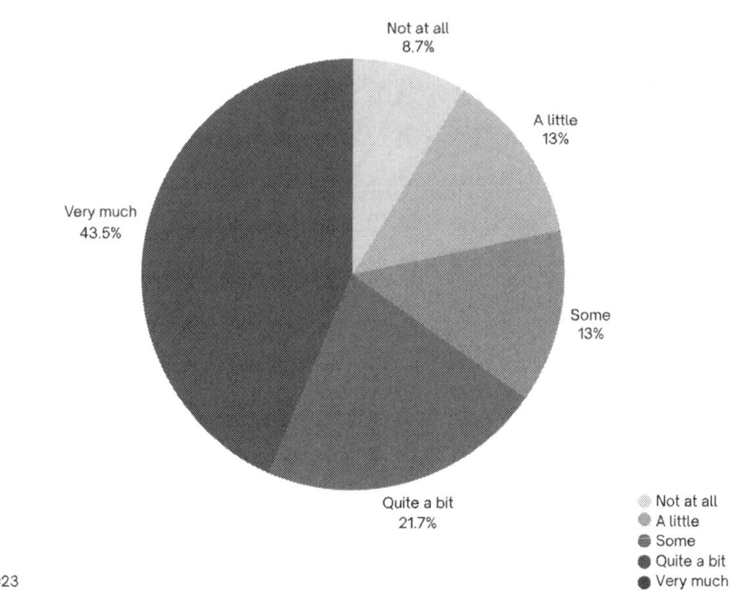

Responses

- Maintaining relationships with community partners that have common goals and shared visions will allow us to expand our resource availability, improve our coordination of services, and encourage a comprehensive approach to addressing homelessness in our community.
- Partnerships and Memorandums of Understanding (MOU) with collaborating organizations can help us use a more comprehensive approach to addressing the needs of our participants, and allow for a clear delineation of responsibilities for each organization.

Finding 8. Mental health and substance use issues present significant barriers requiring specialized interventions.

The data reveal that mental health challenges and substance use issues are prevalent and often unaddressed factors contributing to homelessness among participants. Throughout our interviews, participants described how mental health difficulties and substance use have damaged family relationships, depleted support networks, and complicated their pathway to stability. The data show a significant gap in specialized mental health and substance use services that participants can access consistently. Participants specifically identified the need for dedicated mental health counseling as a critical missing component in their journey toward stability. This finding demonstrates that comprehensive approaches to homelessness must include specialized mental health and substance use interventions that are accessible, consistent, and integrated with other support services to effectively address these complex and often co-occurring challenges.

Key Themes from Qualitative Interviews

- Mental health issues frequently co-occur with homelessness and complicate recovery.
- Substance use problems have damaged family relationships and support networks.
- Participants express overwhelming emotions, which include feelings of being anxious, timid, scared, out of control, fear, and constantly being in survival mode.
- Current service models may not adequately address the depth of mental health needs.

Interview Quotes

> *"The only thing that I have to say is that mental health is a big issue. I would suggest one day to have the budget to hire a mental health counselor.........a good part of these participants need mental health and substance abuse counseling."*

> *"My mom.....she didn't want to see my face because of my prior drug addictions. Now that I've moved to Chattanooga, she has opened up dialogue again with me. She never would talk with me [before]."*

> *"I don't want to stress or worry about anything. I try not to because it's bad for the body. I really just take it one day at a time. I just try to get through the day. I hope for tomorrow, but we're not promised tomorrow."*

Responses

- Expand mental health services at CHATT Foundation by maintaining a partnership with Volunteer Behavioral Health (VBH) Care System.
- Provide crisis counselling services at CHATT Foundation through the Volunteer Behavioral Health Liaison staff.
- Maintain a Memorandum of Understanding (MOU) with agency partners to provide Certified Peer Support Recovery Specialists in Mental Health.
- Consider investing in talk-therapy options through a Licensed Professional Counsellor to support participants with non-serious mental illness.
- Continue to refer participants to partnering agencies, such as VIP: an outpatient substance abuse treatment program through the Homeless Health Care Center, as well as other agency partners.

Conclusion

Insights Into Impact

After the conclusion of gathering our data and compiling our report, we discovered several things as they related to our intended impacts. First, our findings showed that we were meeting and exceeding the expectations laid out in our first finding. Both qualitative and quantitative data showed that participants regularly and frequently used our basic services and felt that these services provided a degree of stability in their lives. As they relate to impacts two and three, our findings showed that while CHATT Foundation has made good progress in helping our participants establish and maintain networks of support and helping them work towards stability, we still have work to do towards providing better comprehensive care to participants. Quantitative data showed that 48% of respondents stated that because of CHATT Foundation's programs, they are now connected to only one or two more support systems in the area, than before our intervention. The steps we plan to take to address these issues are outlined in the responses to our findings and highlight the areas of focus we believe will be essential to providing a quality level of care to our participants which will ultimately help put them on the path to stability and out of their current homeless episode.

Steps Forward

Moving forward, CHATT Foundation will implement two key initiatives to deepen our understanding of impact and enhance our services:

1. **Enhanced Annual Reporting Through Mixed Methods Evaluation** We will integrate the qualitative interview and quantitative survey approach developed through Project Impact into our annual reporting cycle. This systematic approach to data collection will allow us to consistently measure and demonstrate the transformative changes occurring in the lives of those we serve. By making this evaluation methodology a standard part of our operations, we can track progress over time, identify emerging needs, and communicate our impact more effectively to stakeholders and funders.
2. **Year-Round Interview Initiative with Newly Homeless Individuals** We will establish an ongoing interview program, utilizing interns to conduct regular conversations with individuals and families experiencing homelessness for the first time. These interviews will serve a dual purpose: providing real-time insights into the immediate challenges and barriers faced by those entering homelessness, while simultaneously informing our staff's approach to case management and support services. By maintaining this continuous feedback loop, we aim to develop more responsive interventions that can meaningfully shorten the duration of homelessness episodes for those we serve.

Both initiatives reflect our commitment to listening deeply to those we serve and using their experiences to continuously improve our programs and practices.

Opportunities for Future Evaluation.

CHATT Foundation has an ongoing commitment to serve people experiencing homelessness and their complex needs. We intend to continue to evaluate our individual programs based on the needs of our participants. Two opportunities of future evaluation that presented in our findings included (1) investing in reopening our medical respite program, and (2) leveraging our ability to serve participants not under our direct case management by interviewing them using this Project Impact approach. We discovered enhanced synergy of coordination of services with partnering agencies through insights gained from interviews. From these interviews we were able to advise participants as to practical next steps to take on their individual path to housing without having them assigned to our case management workload.

SCENIC CITY WOMEN'S NETWORK

Faith-Based Leadership Symposium

Renee Nail, Phyllis James, Roxanne Fulkerson, Linda Waterman

Scenic City Women's Network's recent impact project focused on analyzing the outcomes of our leadership symposiums. This work is in preparation for developing a Christian leadership curriculum to be offered by Scenic City Women's Network. The goal of the leadership program is to provide practical guidance and insights on integrating faith into the workplace. It will begin by identifying foundational Biblical principles and exploring their application in various professional settings. The goal is to impact business leaders' decision-making, resulting in spiritual and professional growth.

Introduction to Organization

Founded in 1994, Scenic City Women's Network is a non-profit ministry designed to Encourage, Equip, and Energize Christian business and professional women to reflect Jesus Christ in their world! Our Vision is to fulfill Christ's mission by encouraging women with a sense of belonging to God and each other; equipping women to develop spiritual maturity and to become all they are to be in Christ; and energizing women to bless others with the love, grace, and truth of Jesus Christ.

Program Description

The Scenic City Women's Network Leadership Symposium is a professional development initiative designed to equip women leaders and emerging leaders with insights on integrating Christian principles into workplace leadership. Held annually, the symposium brings together local business professionals and aspiring leaders for focused learning and networking opportunities.

The success and positive response from the 2023 and 2024 symposiums inspired the Scenic City Women's Network to explore developing a more comprehensive curriculum that would provide deeper, ongoing engagement opportunities for women seeking to integrate their faith with their professional leadership development. This potential expansion would build upon the foundational conversations and connections established through the annual symposium format.

Intended Impacts

Leaders embody God-centered practices in their business practices and organizational culture. Leaders will impact work and the Kingdom by implementing God-centered practices through a Christian World & Life View. Through quality, character, and ethics of work, leaders learn to bring their faith to the office, understanding that God owns it all and leadership is stewardship of His business. The pursuit of that calling and purpose, working with excellence, transforms the life of the leader, their staff, and work environment, ultimately impacting the bottom line. Leaders grow in faith and learn to see themselves from God's perspective and the world from His viewpoint, becoming driven by Biblical mandates, using Biblical methods, and living by Biblical character.

Leaders achieve meaningful alignment between their faith, family, and professional lives through People Centered Practices. Leaders embrace God's structured approach to work/life balance by putting God first, family second, and career third. By creating and living out their mission, vision, and values across all three areas of life, they make meaningful impact in the workplace, the home, and the greater

Kingdom. Leaders actively invest in relationships across all these areas, influencing people in their faith while showing genuine care for others. They demonstrate servant leadership principles and seek wisdom to see situations and circumstances through a Biblical lens.

Leaders steward their organizations as a reflection of their faith calling. Leaders embrace their role as stewards of God's business, implementing leadership practices aligned with Biblical principles. Drawing from wisdom like that found in David Green's "Leadership NOT by the Book," they learn to lead in God's way, creating organizational cultures that honor both Kingdom principles and business excellence. Leaders demonstrate transformed understanding of stewardship by managing resources, leading people, and making decisions in ways that reflect their faith commitment and God's ownership of all things.

Evaluation Methodology

The aim of our evaluation was to see what kind and quality of impact the two pilot events were having on women in the workplace. To understand this, we explored two broad evaluation questions:

1. What kind and quality of impact are we having on working women at all ages and positions?
2. What aspects of our program are causing this impact?

Over the course of the project, we (a) developed and refined our ideas of intended impact and indicators, (b) designed and implemented a mixed methods outcome evaluation using both qualitative and quantitative means to collect and analyze data, (c) identified themes and findings, and (d) considered the implications to those findings for program improvement and innovation.

This project began by identifying and clarifying the intended impact of Leadership-God's Way. Once the ideas of impact had been developed, we used the Heart Triangle™ model to identify qualitative and quantitative indicators of impact on the mental, behavioral, and emotional changes in our attendees. We used these indicators to design a qualitative interview protocol and a quantitative questionnaire to evaluate progress toward achieving our intended impact.

Qualitative Data Collection and Analysis

For the qualitative portion of the evaluation, we designed an in-depth interview protocol to gain data about the structural, qualitative changes resulting from our program. We defined our population by including only participants who had attended both the 2023 and 2024 leadership symposia. Our population size for this evaluation was 65. We used a purposeful stratified sampling technique to select a representative sample from the population we serve. Our sample size was 14, drawn from the following strata of our population:

- Participants of both the 2023 and 2024 symposiums.
- Participants who were in middle or upper management work positions.

Our interview team consisted of Roxanne Fulkerson, Phyllis James, Renee Nail and Linda Waterman. We convened one-on-one interviews lasting from between 45 minutes and one hour in length and collected interview data using handwritten notes and voice recordings that were transcribed in full.

We then analyzed the data inductively using a modified version of thematic analysis. Each interviewer analyzed the data from their interviews individually to identify initial themes. Together, we developed common themes from all of the interviews collectively. We identified the overarching and inter-interview themes that emerged from the full scope of our data analysis to illuminate the collective insights and discoveries. We mapped these themes visually and examined the dynamics among the themes, causes and catalysts of the themes, new or surprising insights related to the themes, and relationships between the themes that were revealed in the data. We then determined the most significant and meaningful discoveries and brought them forward as findings.

Quantitative Data Collection and Analysis

For the quantitative portion of the evaluation, we designed a questionnaire to collect data on our quantitative indicators of impact. We administered this instrument to 134 participants and received a response rate of 20%, with 27 responses. The data were analyzed primarily using measures of central tendency. We identified key insights, patterns, and gaps within the data and incorporated these discoveries into the related findings. The most significant insights from the quantitative data are described in the following narrative.

Limitations

Several limitations may have affected the accuracy and depth of our findings. The quantitative survey was distributed to all symposiums, which limited our ability to analyze potential differences in impact across various participant demographics such as career stage, industry, or leadership experience level. This approach may have missed important nuances in how different groups of women experienced and applied the symposium content.

Additionally, the symposium was a single-day event, which may have limited our ability to assess longer-term impact or sustained application of the principles discussed. The timing of our evaluation may not reflect the deeper, more durable changes that could develop over time as participants have opportunities to implement what they learned in their workplace contexts.

Findings

Finding 1. There is a need for faith-based leadership training for wmen in the workplace.

The data consistently reveal that all interviewees recognized a significant need for leadership training that helps integrate faith into everyday work life. Throughout our interviews, participants expressed a strong desire for practical application of Biblical principles as demonstrated by successful business leaders. This desire stems from both a personal need to better apply faith in professional settings and a perceived gap in the Chattanooga leadership development landscape. All participants stated that opportunities for faith-based leadership training in Chattanooga were scarce, and none knew of any leadership training specifically designed for women. This finding directly relates to our intended impact of equipping women to lead with Biblical principles in their workplaces, highlighting both a community need and an opportunity for our organization.

Key Themes from Qualitative Interviews

- Leadership training that integrates Biblical principles in daily work life is needed and desired by Christian women in business.
- Participants specifically value practical examples where leaders describe actual Biblical application scenarios in workplace situations.
- Leadership programs to train young Christian women in the workforce are virtually non-existent in the Chattanooga area, creating a significant gap in professional development resources.

Interview Quotes

> *"It is a faith-builder when we see like-minded leaders facing the same challenges in the workplace and learn from their experiences."*

> *"I would want to go to a leadership conference because I'm not very good at applying Biblical passages or Biblical teachings to everyday life. Until you guys even offered this, I never really thought about how to apply faith-based leadership. That's why I'm interested. I want to know how faith-based and work go together."*

> *"I don't think there's a lot of leadership training in Chattanooga. I mean, I just, I don't think there's a lot. So that would be my biggest miss. There's just not, or if it is, it's not so in your face that I would think about it. And I do think, because there is so limited opportunity, this could be a real signature event in Chattanooga."*

"No leadership ministry in Chattanooga is women focused. So, the women specific angle, I think makes sense. I don't know of another organization that has anything specific to women."

Quantitative Insights & Charts

- 45.2% of survey respondents reported that the symposium increased their likelihood of seeking additional faith-based leadership training "quite a bit" or "very much" (see Figure 1).

Figure 1:
How much has the symposium increased your likelihood of seeking additional faith-based leadership training?

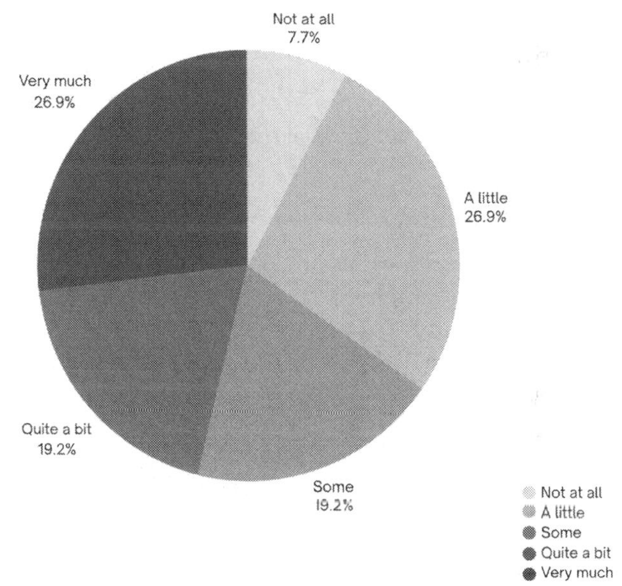

Responses

- Develop a comprehensive faith-based leadership curriculum specifically designed for businesswomen with multiple skill levels.
- Create workshops featuring different aspects of Biblical leadership principles applied to workplace scenarios.
- Partner with local churches and business organizations to promote and expand access to faith-based leadership training opportunities.

Finding 2. The need to define Biblical principles is the first step in faith-based leadership development.

The data reveal that most interviewees struggled to identify and articulate specific Biblical principles they would seek to integrate into their professional lives. This finding presents a fundamental challenge that must be addressed before deeper leadership training can take place. Throughout our interviews, many participants could only identify two to four principles, often naming broad concepts such as integrity and servant leadership rather than specific Biblical teachings or applications. This gap in knowledge suggests that before training women to apply Biblical principles in leadership, we must first help them identify and understand these principles. This finding highlights the importance of beginning with a clear foundation of Biblical principles that are relevant to workplace settings as a prerequisite for effective leadership development.

Key Themes from Qualitative Interviews

- Many leaders have limited training in identifying specific Biblical principles, making it difficult for them to intentionally integrate these principles into their leadership practices.
- When asked directly, most participants could only identify a few general principles (like integrity, honesty, or servant leadership) rather than specific Biblical teachings applicable to workplace leadership.
- There appears to be no clear, agreed-upon framework of Biblical principles specifically applicable to leadership in professional settings that participants can readily access.
- Establishing a clear definition and understanding of relevant Biblical principles must be prioritized before training in the practical application of these principles can be effective.

Interview Quotes

"I would say I'm drawing a blank because that would be why I would want to go to a leadership conference. Because I'm not very good at applying whatever Biblical passages or Biblical teachings to everyday life. So, here's where I really am...I'm not the best Christian, because I'm sure you could list the Biblical principles, but I couldn't."

"One is the idea of servant leadership. The second one that comes to my mind is abundance mentality. Yeah, it's so easy to get caught up in a scarcity. You know, there's never enough...there's not enough money, there's not enough time, there's not enough about that."

"Coming at it from a Biblical perspective we are called to maybe lead differently than what the world perceives as leadership. I think that we would exhibit the fruit of the Spirit. So, we would be more gracious, we would be more self-controlled in our role as a leader... that we would reflect Him, as opposed to being in it for our ego or the money, or, whatever else might be a distraction from that."

"'He has shown you, O man, what is good; And what does the Lord require of you. But to do justly, to love mercy, and to walk humbly with your God' (Micah 6:8). We need more of His love, justice, and mercy. This is missing, as well as diversity."

Quantitative Insights & Charts

- 65.4% of survey respondents reported their understanding of Biblical business leadership principles increased "quite a bit" or "very much" as a result of the symposium (see Figure 2).

Responses

- Create a foundational workshop or module that clearly defines and explains core Biblical principles relevant to workplace leadership.
- Develop a reference guide or workbook that participants can use to identify and understand specific Biblical principles.

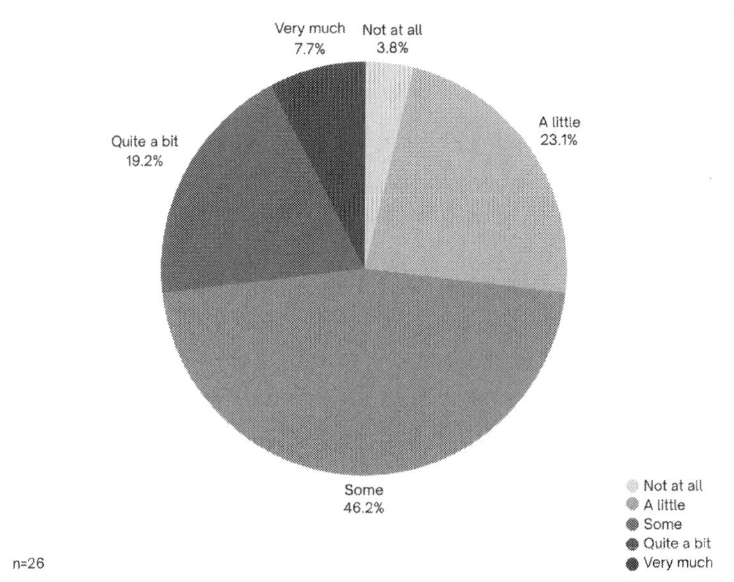

Finding 3. Biblical approaches to conflict resolution are a crucial but underdeveloped leadership skill.

The data consistently reveal that conflict resolution emerged as a significant leadership challenge that participants believe should be addressed through a Biblical lens. Throughout our interviews, many participants identified this as a specific area where they felt Christian leaders needed more training and practical guidance. The data suggest that while conflict is inevitable in workplace settings, many leaders lack the skills and Biblical framework to address it effectively. Participants emphasized that theoretical knowledge about conflict resolution is insufficient; they desire practical, real-world examples of how Biblical principles can guide difficult conversations and workplace disagreements. This finding highlights an important area for leadership development that connects directly to applying faith in professional settings.

Key Themes from Qualitative Interviews

- Participants repeatedly identified conflict resolution as one of the most important and challenging aspects of leadership that requires specific Biblical guidance and training.
- Leaders expressed a strong desire for practical, real-life examples of Biblical conflict resolution in workplace settings, rather than just theoretical policies or general principles.
- Participants see conflict resolution not just as a management skill but as an opportunity to demonstrate Biblical principles of unity, reconciliation, and healthy communication in professional environments.
- Many participants noted that poor conflict resolution skills can undermine a leader's effectiveness and create cascading problems throughout an organization.

Interview Quotes

"I think people miss in their training some of the basic skills, such as giving/setting expectations, giving feedback and handling conflict. This is something that comes up so often in my work. People just don't know how to handle it, and they're actually afraid of it."

"Knowing how to resolve conflict in the workplace is important to me as a necessary component of leadership training. God is very direct and straightforward in how He lays out dealing with conflict in Scripture, and I think that's a challenge for a lot of leaders to do it that way."

"Conflict resolution in the workplace should be one of the topics covered. Not being able to deal with it well really sets you up for a dozen other problems down the road."

Quantitative Insights & Charts

- 65.4% of survey respondents reported the symposium helped them identify which leadership skills they most need to develop "quite a bit" or "some" (see Figure 3).

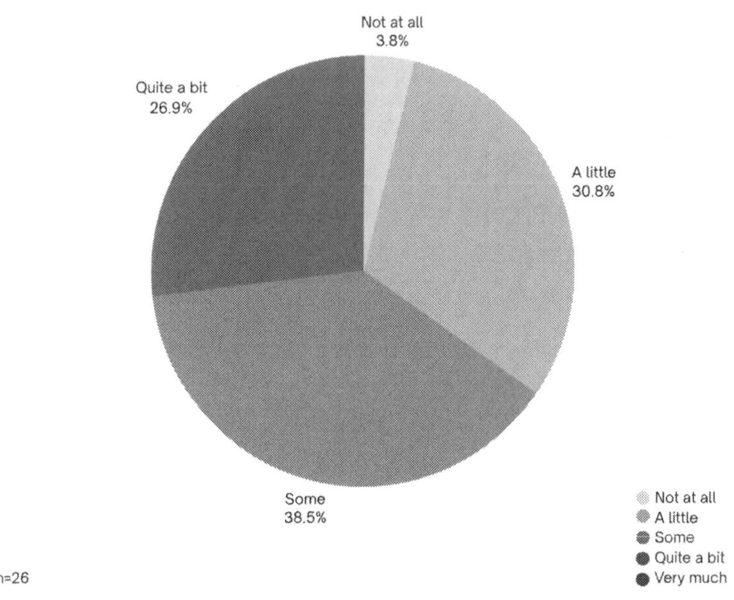

Responses

- Design a dedicated workshop on Biblical conflict resolution with role-playing exercises and real workplace scenarios.
- Invite experienced leaders to share case studies of successful Biblical conflict resolution in professional settings.

Finding 4. Christian leaders consistently value servant leadership qualities in the workplace.

The data reveal a strong consensus among participants regarding the core qualities that Christian leaders should embody in the workplace. Throughout our interviews, participants consistently identified servant leadership qualities—particularly integrity, compassion, empathy, and accountability—as essential for effectively leading from a Biblical perspective. The data suggest that while participants may have struggled to articulate specific Biblical principles in Finding 2, they share a common understanding of how these principles should manifest in leadership behaviors. Participants emphasized that demonstrating these qualities not only reflects Biblical values but also creates more effective and trust-based workplace environments. This finding suggests that leadership development should focus on cultivating and applying these commonly-valued qualities in professional settings.

Key Themes from Qualitative Interviews

- Participants consistently identified specific servant leadership qualities—including integrity, honesty, empathy, and accountability—as essential expressions of Biblical principles in professional leadership roles.
- Leaders particularly emphasized the importance of listening well and truly hearing employees, reflecting the Biblical value of respecting each person's inherent worth and dignity.
- Participants noted that Christian leadership involves "loving people where they are" while maintaining high professional standards and clear expectations.
- The data reveal that participants believe these leadership qualities can transform workplace culture even in secular organizations, without requiring overtly religious language or approaches.

Interview Quotes

> *"High standards in the workplace are a necessity. Integrity and empathy without erosion of standards."*

> *"It's a faith builder when we see like-minded leaders facing the same challenges as I do. Then, I can learn from their experiences."*

> *"You can still share and live your faith in the workplace and not be aggressive."*

> *"A leader who is honest builds trust and credibility with employees and clients, this reflects God's righteousness in the workplace. Honesty builds security in our businesses."*

Quantitative Insights & Charts

- 50.0% of survey respondents reported being "quite a bit" or "very much" more aware of the distinctive qualities of faith-based leadership compared to secular leadership models (see Figure 4).

Figure 4:
How much more aware are you of the distinctive qualities of faith-based leadership compared to secular leadership models?

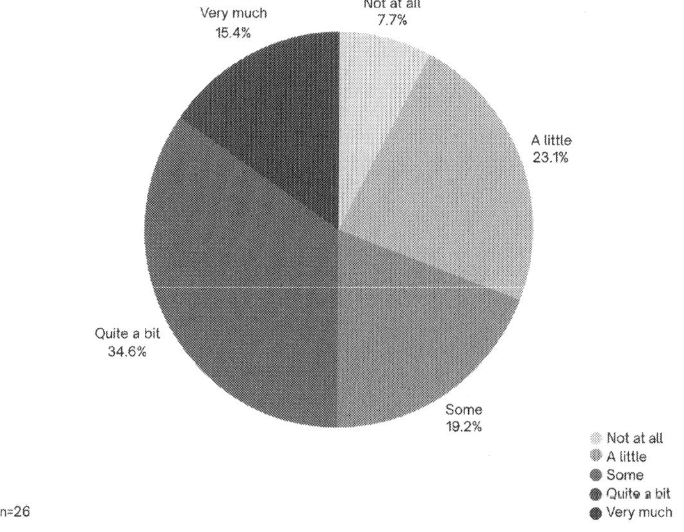

Responses

- Incorporate practical exercises that help participants develop and demonstrate servant leadership qualities in their current roles.
- Create peer learning groups where participants can practice and receive feedback on servant leadership behaviors.

Finding 5. Learning from experienced Christian business leaders' practical examples is highly valued.

The interview data reveals appreciation for hearing from established business leaders who shared concrete examples of how they apply Biblical principles in their workplaces. Throughout our interviews, participants consistently identified the panel discussions as the most valuable component of the program, citing both the practical content and the authentic delivery as meaningful. The sincerity with which panelists shared their experiences—including both successes and challenges—resonated deeply with attendees and created a sense of possibility for their own leadership development. This finding highlights the importance of peer-to-peer learning and storytelling as powerful teaching methods for faith-based leadership development, suggesting that future programs should continue and expand this approach of featuring leaders who can share practical applications of Biblical principles.

Key Themes from Qualitative Interviews

- Participants consistently described learning from experienced Christian business leaders as affirming and encouraging, reinforcing their belief that Biblical principles can be successfully applied in modern workplaces.
- The authenticity and willingness of leaders to share both successes and struggles in applying their faith created a sense of trust and relatability that participants found particularly valuable.
- Many participants expressed a desire for even more concrete examples and stories of how Biblical principles can be practically implemented in various business contexts and situations.
- The panel discussions created a desire for deeper, more comprehensive leadership training that would further develop the concepts and practices that were introduced.

Interview Quotes

"It is a faith-builder when we see like-minded business leaders facing the same challenges I do and being able to learn from their experience."

"As a presenter, it emboldened me even more and I felt affirmed that other business leaders are doing it -- Seeing the sincerity, demeanor, and honesty of their Christian principles, ethics, morals and values and share viewpoints in a public forum was a breath of fresh air."

"Felt the panelists created a desire for more in-depth leadership training."

Quantitative Insights & Charts

- 49.9% of survey respondents reported their awareness of practical ways to implement Biblical principles in business settings increased "quite a bit" or "very much" (see Figure 5).

Figure 5:
How much has your awareness of practical ways to implement Biblical principles in business settings increased?

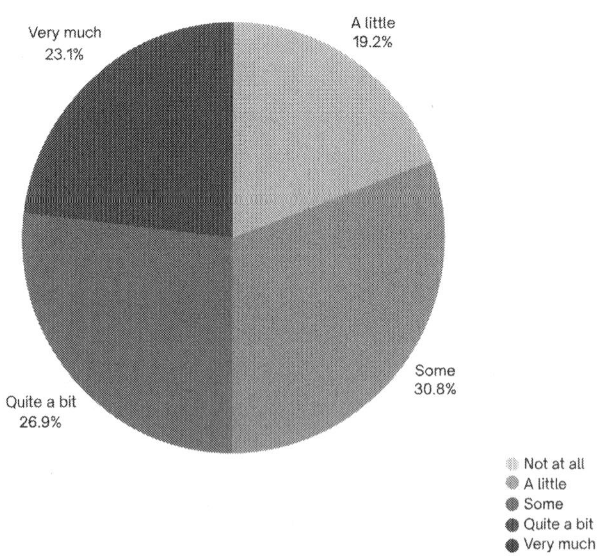

Responses

- Expand the panel discussion format to include more diverse industries and leadership contexts.
- Create a video library of Christian business leaders sharing their stories and practical applications.

Finding 6. Structured mentorship is a desired component of Christian leadership development for women.

The data reveal a strong desire among participants for structured mentoring relationships as part of their professional and spiritual development. Throughout our interviews, many participants emphasized that learning directly from the experiences of others who have successfully integrated faith and business is invaluable. This mentoring need appears to exist at multiple levels, with both younger women seeking guidance from established leaders and experienced women looking for opportunities to share their wisdom. The data suggest that there is a significant gap in Chattanooga for such mentoring relationships, particularly among Christian businesswomen. This finding highlights an important opportunity to create intentional mentoring frameworks that can facilitate the transfer of both practical skills and spiritual wisdom across generations of women leaders.

Key Themes from Qualitative Interviews

- Participants consistently expressed both the desire to be mentored and the willingness to mentor others, suggesting a community ready to engage in reciprocal learning relationships.
- Many interviewees specifically noted the lack of organized Christian mentorship opportunities for businesswomen in the Chattanooga area, identifying a clear gap in professional development resources.
- Participants emphasized that younger women in the workplace particularly need mentorship to navigate the challenges of integrating faith and leadership early in their careers.
- Several interviewees suggested that a well-implemented mentorship program could have transformative effects not just for individuals but for the broader business community in Chattanooga.

Interview Quotes

"I always have a younger and an older mentor to learn from. This is my personal experience."

"Although I am retired, I know I still have a role to play through mentorship."

"Implementing mentorship would change our city."

Quantitative Insights & Charts

- 22.2% of survey respondents reported their ability to mentor others in faith-based leadership improved "quite a bit" or "very much" (see Figure 6).

Figure 6:
How much has your ability to mentor others in faith-based leadership improved?

Very much 7.7%
Not at all 11.5%
Quite a bit 15.4%
A little 30.8%
Some 34.6%

Not at all
A little
Some
Quite a bit
Very much

n=26

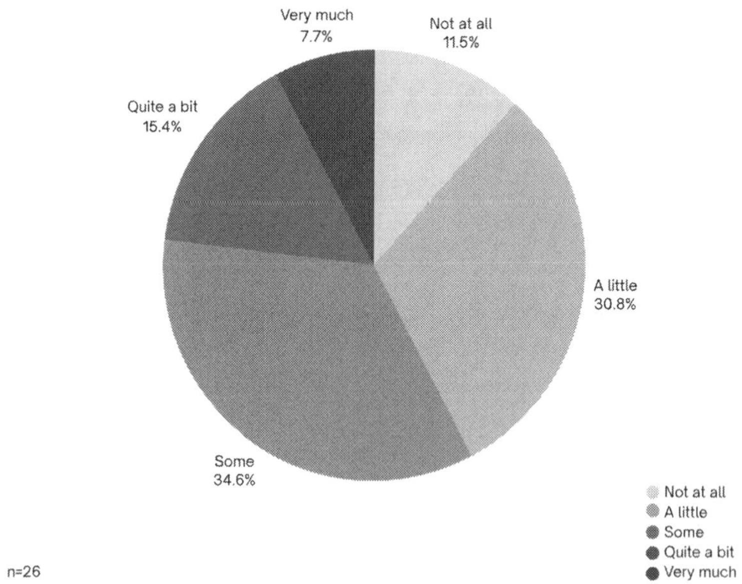

Responses

- Launch a formal mentorship program matching experienced Christian businesswomen with emerging leader.
- Create mentorship guidelines and resources to support effective mentor-mentee relationships.

Finding 7. Legal guidance is needed to confidently express faith within workplace boundaries.

The data reveal significant anxiety and uncertainty among participants regarding the legal boundaries of expressing faith in professional settings. Throughout our interviews, many participants expressed concern about potential negative consequences, including lawsuits, HR conflicts, or harassment claims, that might result from integrating Biblical principles into their leadership. This anxiety appears to create a chilling effect that prevents many leaders from fully expressing their faith-based approach to leadership. Participants consistently expressed a desire for clear, practical guidance from legal and HR professionals who could help them understand exactly what is permissible in different workplace contexts. This finding suggests that addressing legal parameters is not just a practical consideration but a fundamental requirement for enabling Christian leaders to confidently apply Biblical principles in their professional roles.

Key Themes from Qualitative Interviews:

- Many participants expressed uncertainty and anxiety about the legal boundaries of expressing faith in the workplace, which inhibits their willingness to fully integrate Biblical principles into their leadership.
- Participants desire specific guidance from HR/legal specialists who can clearly define what expressions of faith are appropriate and protected in different workplace settings and contexts.
- Leaders recognize the importance of respecting legal requirements and employee choices while still maintaining their faith-based approach to leadership.
- Several participants noted that having established, legally-sound parameters would actually increase their confidence in expressing faith-based leadership rather than restricting it.

Interview Quotes:

> *"The privacy and safety and boldness to speak without stakeholder repercussions or an HR Specialist trying to shut you down is needed."*
>
> *"For Biblical Leadership we will need to minimize fears of lawsuits and harassment."*
>
> *"With established parameters, you become unafraid to say you are a faith-based company and talking in a faith-based way."*
>
> *"Within legal parameters, you can be more bold and comfortable in sharing the things I know to be true."*

Quantitative Insights & Charts

- 34.7% of survey respondents reported feeling "quite a bit" or "very much" less anxious about the challenges of faith-based leadership (see Figure 7).

Figure 7:
How much less anxious do you feel about the challenges of faith-based leadership?

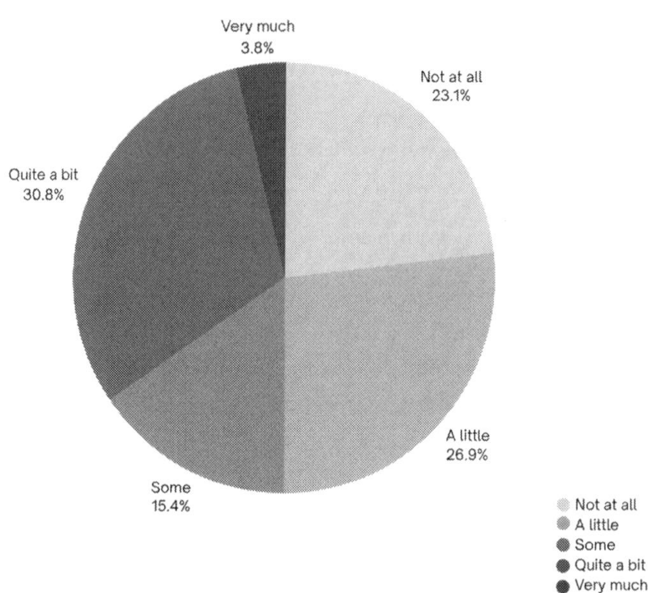

Responses

- Partner with Christian legal professionals to provide clear guidance on faith expression in various workplace contexts.
- Create a resource document outlining legal parameters and best practices for faith-based leadership.
- Host a workshop specifically addressing legal considerations with Q&A opportunities for specific situation.

Finding 8. Leaders need guidance on integrating prayer and spiritual practices in professional settings.

The data reveal that participants consider prayer and personal spiritual practices essential foundations for effective Christian leadership, yet struggle with how to appropriately incorporate these practices in professional settings. Throughout our interviews, participants expressed a desire for practical guidance on establishing personal spiritual rhythms that sustain their leadership and appropriate ways to include prayer and other spiritual practices in their workplaces. Many participants noted that personal spiritual disciplines must be established first, creating a foundation from which workplace applications can naturally flow. This finding highlights the need for leadership development that addresses both personal spiritual formation and its appropriate expression in professional contexts, recognizing that prayer is viewed not simply as a religious practice but as a leadership resource that enhances decision-making and resilience.

Key Themes from Qualitative Interviews

- Participants consistently identified prayer and personal spiritual practices as essential foundations for effective Christian leadership that should be addressed in leadership training.
- Many interviewees expressed uncertainty about how to appropriately incorporate prayer and spiritual practices within different workplace settings while respecting boundaries and diversity.

- Several participants emphasized that developing consistent personal spiritual disciplines must precede attempts to implement faith-based practices in the workplace.
- Leaders noted that when prayer and spiritual practices are thoughtfully integrated into professional settings, they create positive ripple effects throughout organizational culture.

Interview Quotes:

> *"For prayer to be included in the workplace, time and space must be available on a personal level first before implementation into the workplace."*
>
> *"In prepping for meetings, pray first and listen to God."*
>
> *"You need to have certain lifestyle practices that give a clear mind and energy to withstand the trials of being a solid leader.... i.e. The Daniel Principle."*
>
> *"Being focused on Kingdom based culture is energizing once you get over the fear. You know it when someone in the company notices and responds and recognizes the step you made to implement a Kingdom focus."*

Quantitative Insights & Charts

- 50.0% of survey respondents reported their understanding of what makes a Kingdom-focused organizational culture is "quite a bit" or "very much" clearer (see Figure 8).

Responses

- Develop practical guidelines for incorporating prayer and spiritual practices appropriately in different workplace environments.
- Share examples and best practices from organizations that successfully integrate spiritual practices.

Figure 8:
How much clearer is your understanding of what makes a Kingdom-focused organizational culture?

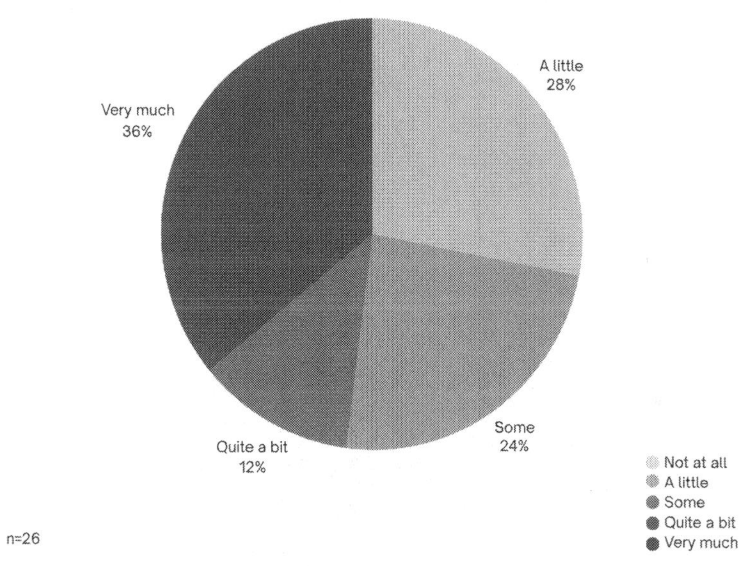

Conclusion

Insights Into Impact

Through this evaluation, we have discovered that our work is successfully addressing a significant and previously unmet need in the Chattanooga community. Our findings confirm that we have identified a genuine gap in leadership development resources for Christian businesswomen, and our symposium format has proven to be an effective starting point for engaging women who are eager to integrate their faith with their professional leadership roles. The overwhelming positive response to our panel discussions and the consistent feedback about the value of learning from experienced Christian business leaders demonstrates that our approach resonates deeply with our target audience. We have successfully created a space for women to explore how Biblical principles can be practically applied in workplace settings, and we have begun building the foundation for a community of like-minded leaders who can support and learn from one another.

Most importantly, our symposium has accomplished its key purpose of helping us understand exactly what our community needs so we can develop effective programming moving forward. The findings provide us with a clear roadmap for curriculum development, revealing that participants need foundational training in identifying and defining Biblical principles before they can effectively apply them in leadership contexts. We now understand that our future programming must address practical challenges like conflict resolution, legal boundaries for faith expression, and the integration of prayer and spiritual practices in professional settings. The strong desire we observed for structured mentorship and ongoing training confirms that there is both demand and readiness for a more comprehensive leadership development program. These insights give us confidence that we can design curriculum and programming that will truly meet the needs of Christian businesswomen in our community, moving beyond awareness-building to provide the systematic training and support that will transform how they lead in their professional settings.

Steps Forward

Based on our findings, we will design a comprehensive faith-based leadership curriculum that builds systematically from foundational concepts to advanced applications. Our curriculum development will begin with creating a foundational module that clearly defines and explains core Biblical principles relevant to workplace leadership, as this emerged as a critical prerequisite that many participants currently lack. We will then develop specialized workshops addressing the specific skill areas our participants identified as priorities, including Biblical approaches to conflict resolution, practical guidelines for integrating prayer and spiritual practices in professional settings, and clear guidance on legal boundaries for faith expression in the workplace. Throughout the curriculum, we will emphasize the servant leadership qualities that participants consistently valued—integrity, empathy, accountability, and compassion—providing practical exercises that help participants develop and demonstrate these qualities in their current roles. To ensure the curriculum maintains the authentic, experiential learning that participants found most valuable in our symposium, we will expand our use of experienced Christian business leaders through case study presentations, mentorship matching, ongoing peer learning opportunities and a resource library.

Opportunities for Future Evaluation

As we move forward with curriculum development, we see value in conducting follow-up evaluations with participants after they complete our training to understand which program elements were most helpful and how effectively they are applyidddng what they learned in their workplaces. We are also interested in evaluating the effectiveness of any mentorship connections we facilitate and gathering feedback on specific workshop topics to help us refine our approach. These focused evaluations will help us improve our programming and ensure we continue meeting the needs we have identified in our community.

EAST LAKE EXPRESSION ENGINE

Student Intern Program

Evelyn Brandes, Rachel Duke, Dj Griffin, Libby O'Neil,
Ashe Sunder, Kyron Walker, Elisa Velasquez

Organization and Program Overview

Introduction to Organization

East Lake Expression Engine's mission is to develop the creativity, discipline, problem-solving skills, social skills, and spiritual maturity of our students through musical instruction and collaboration in a gospel-centered environment. We provide high-quality music education free of charge in a continuous K-12 track, with the opportunity for paid internships in high school. Since 2014, Expression Engine has served 60-100 students annually through our after-school and summer programming, offering instrument group lessons, choir, bucket band, musicianship classes, and various ensembles.

Program Description

The Expression Engine Student Intern Program offers employment to current students aged 14 and up. The program combines continuing musical education with job training for music teaching and arts administration. Interns' duties include teaching younger students, leading workshops alongside staff members, and assisting with daily program logistics and administration. They also have opportunities to provide input on programming decisions. Interns are mentored by our staff and, in turn, serve as mentors to our younger students.

Intended Impacts

Interns become confident, effective leaders. Interns take ownership of responsibilities, make sound decisions, and guide program initiatives effectively.

Interns become skilled, self-assured professionals. Interns develop professional competencies, understand workplace expectations, and gain confidence managing their responsibilities.

Interns become inspiring artist-mentors. Interns progress in their musical craft while developing the ability to effectively teach and inspire others. They gain confidence performing and leading, becoming role models who shape younger students' artistic development.

Interns become vital bridges between youth and adult staff. Interns develop the unique capacity to connect with younger participants while strengthening the program's mentorship structure. They create pathways of trust that enhance the entire program's ability to support youth effectively.

Evaluation Methodology

The aim of our evaluation was to see what kind and quality of impact Expression Engine's Student Intern Program is having on our student interns. To understand this, we explored two broad evaluation questions:

1. What kind and quality of impact are we having on our interns?
2. What aspects of our program are causing this impact?

Over the course of the project, we (a) developed and refined our ideas of intended impact and indicators, (b) designed and implemented a mixed methods outcome evaluation using both qualitative and quantitative means to collect and analyze data, (c) identified themes and findings, and (d) considered the implications to those findings for program improvement and innovation.

This project began by identifying and clarifying the intended impact of Expression Engine's Student Intern Program. Once the ideas of impact had been developed, we used the Heart Triangle™ model to identify qualitative and quantitative indicators of impact on the mental, behavioral, and emotional changes in our interns. We used these indicators to design a qualitative interview protocol and a quantitative questionnaire to evaluate progress toward achieving our intended impact.

Qualitative Data Collection and Analysis

For the qualitative portion of the evaluation, we designed an in-depth interview protocol to gain data about the structural and qualitative changes resulting from our program. The total population size for this evaluation consisted of 24 participants. We used a purposeful stratified sampling technique to select a representative sample from the population we serve. Our sample size was 19, drawn from the following strata of our population:

1. Current Student Interns
2. Past Student Interns

Our interview team consisted of Evelyn Brandes, Rachel Duke, Dj Griffin, Libby O'Neil, Ashe Sunder, Kyron Walker, and Elisa Velasquez. We conducted one-on-one interviews, each lasting 45 minutes to one hour, and collected interview data using typed notes, voice memos, and Otter for transcription.

We then analyzed the data inductively using a modified version of thematic analysis. Each interviewer analyzed the data from their interviews individually to identify initial themes. Together, we developed common themes from all of the interviews collectively. We identified the overarching and inter-interview themes that emerged from the full scope of our data analysis to illuminate the collective insights and discoveries. We mapped these themes visually and examined the dynamics among the themes, causes and catalysts of the themes, new or surprising insights related to the themes, and relationships between the themes that were revealed in the data. We then determined the most significant and meaningful discoveries and brought them forward as findings.

Quantitative Data Collection and Analysis

For the quantitative portion of the evaluation, we designed a questionnaire to collect data on our quantitative indicators of impact. We administered this instrument to 16 and had a response of 11, a 68% response rate. The data were analyzed primarily using measures of central tendency. We identified key insights, patterns, and gaps within the data and incorporated these discoveries into the related findings. The most significant insights from the quantitative data are described in the following narrative.

Limitations

The time period when we were able to administer our quantitative survey was between Expression Engine's Spring term and Summer term, when daily programming was not in session. This resulted in a slightly reduced response rate compared to administering it at the end of a term.

Findings

Finding 1. The internship transforms young people's self-perception from "side person" to confident leader.

The data reveal that many interns enter the program without seeing themselves as leaders, but through their experiences, they develop a strong sense of leadership identity. Participants consistently described how their perception of themselves shifted as they took on more responsibility and successfully navigated challenging situations. The transformation from seeing themselves as followers or "side people" to identifying as capable leaders represents a significant internal change. Several interns expressed surprise at their own abilities to step up when needed, indicating that the program helps reveal leadership potential they didn't know they possessed. This development is particularly meaningful as it represents a shift in how interns see themselves and their capabilities, not just in the specific context of Expression Engine, but in other areas of their lives as well.

Key Themes from Qualitative Interviews

- Interns who initially did not see themselves as leaders develop a leadership identity through the program's opportunities and responsibilities.
- The experience of successfully teaching and managing groups of children builds confidence in leadership abilities.
- Interns learn key leadership principles like empathy, communication, and leading by example.
- Leadership skills developed at Expression Engine transfer to other contexts, including school, church, and family settings.

Interview Quotes

"Before I would not see myself as a leader at all, but now I kind of see that in a way, because now, at my church, I help put up a service where the kids are the ones leading the service and all that."

"What I saw in myself before - I just thought I was gonna be a side person. But then I noticed I will speak up, I will help. I never saw myself as that."

"I did not think of myself of being a leader. If that's one thing that I would avoid, but now I see myself right now, I see myself being a leader."

"That I'm capable. I can do it." (responding to how his view of himself as a leader has changed)

Quantitative Insights & Charts

- Over half (54.6%) of interns surveyed reported that, since becoming an intern at Expression Engine, they felt "Very Much" or "Quite a Bit" more confident stepping into leadership roles (see Figure 1).

Figure 1:
Since becoming an intern at Expression Engine, how much *more* confident do you feel stepping into leadership roles?

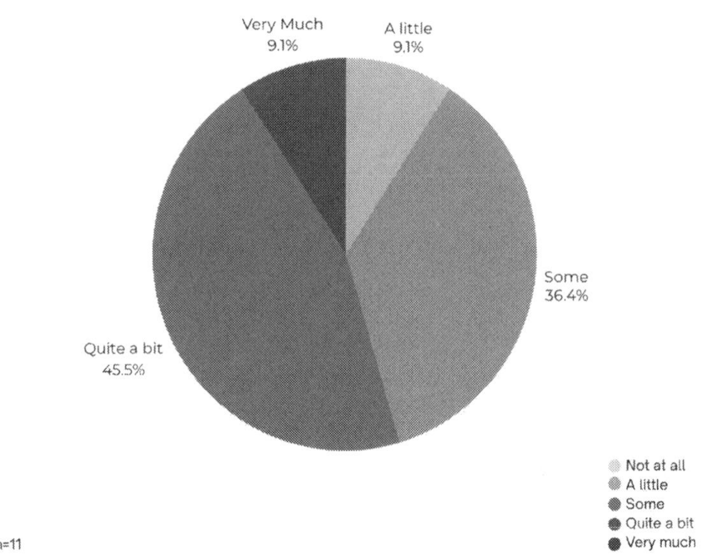

Responses

- Incorporate more reflection sessions where interns can discuss their leadership experiences and receive feedback on their growth.
- Continue to offer a Lead Intern position for a senior intern each year.
- Assign other experienced interns to serve as mentors to newer interns, reinforcing their identity as leaders.

Finding 2 Interns develop essential interpersonal skills, particularly in communication and relationship-building.

Throughout the interviews, participants frequently mentioned growth in their ability to communicate effectively and build relationships with both peers and the children they serve. The data show that many interns initially struggled with social interactions, speaking up, and expressing themselves clearly. However, the program's structure, which requires regular interaction with diverse groups, creates opportunities for significant growth in these areas. Interns described becoming more comfortable talking with people, expressing emotions, and developing the social awareness to "read a room." These skills extend beyond basic communication to include conflict resolution, empathy, and the ability to build meaningful connections. The nurturing environment at Expression Engine appears to provide a safe space for interns to develop these skills through practical experience and supportive relationships.

Key Themes from Qualitative Interviews

- Many interns reported significant growth in their comfort and ability to communicate with both peers and children.
- Social skills developed include conflict resolution, expressing emotions, and building rapport with people of different ages.
- Communication improvements transfer to other contexts, including school and family relationships.
- The development of these skills has increased overall confidence in social situations.

Interview Quotes

"A lot. Empathy. If you can't see yourself in the people you are leading - if you can't see yourself in their shoes - I don't think that's a good leader.

"New skills: Getting comfortable with people, being able to express my emotions more, being able to talk more and learn how to notice small things."

"Public speaking, I've been more confident speaking with my teachers. I don't think I had a group like this where I could express myself."

"I think one skill that has developed is definitely my social skills, like back then, I wouldn't do things that I would be doing now."

Quantitative Insights

- When asked about their most significant change since becoming an intern, survey respondents frequently highlighted improvements in communication and interpersonal abilities, with responses including "leadership and communicating with others," "speaking what's on my mind," and "understanding people with whatever is happening." Multiple interns also cited increased confidence and feeling "more brave," which directly supports the qualitative finding that the program helps interns overcome initial struggles with social interactions and self-expression.

Responses

- Create training for staff members in providing safe, supportive mentorship and listening as part of onboarding.
- Continue to provide relaxed spaces for interns to spend time together on a weekly basis.
- Explore how to add some social outings for interns through our partnerships with local organizations.

Finding 3. The program creates a unique "found family" workplace culture that influences expectations for future employment.

The data reveal that the workplace environment at Expression Engine strongly impacts interns' understanding of what a healthy work environment should be. Participants consistently described the workplace as a "found family" with strong bonds between staff members. This contrasts sharply with many of their previous work experiences or expectations. The support, respect, and camaraderie they experience has created a template for what they now expect and hope for in future workplaces. This family-like atmosphere is characterized by open communication, mutual support, checking in on one another, and having each other's backs. 100% of the interns who responded to the quantitative survey indicated that they felt "Very Much" or "Quite a Bit" like a valued team member at Expression Engine - the top two possible answers. The impact of this experience appears transformative, as many interns expressed that they would actively seek similar environments in their future careers, suggesting that the program is influencing not just their current work experience but their long-term career expectations and values.

Key Themes from Qualitative Interviews

- Interns experience Expression Engine as a family-like community where people genuinely care about each other.
- The workplace culture includes mutual trust, respect, open communication, and supportive relationships.
- This positive work environment contrasts with previous job experiences some interns have had.
- The experience is shaping interns' expectations for future workplaces and careers.

Interview Quotes

"I would describe the people I work with as the closest people in my life. Some of these guys are gonna be in my wedding. It feels good to know I have a support system in and out of work."

"Here people check on you and will help you out. Even if you don't ask, people will help you out. Before I worked at a restaurant: they would ask you to do something and you have to do it no matter how you feel. Here people care about you..."

"Working in a family-like community. It's encouraged me to look into places that value community."

"If everybody gets along, you'd be happy to come to work. It's work and people that love music. It's a pleasant time. If you come to work and someone bothers you, you don't want to leave here and you want to leave faster... Everybody should get along. At the Engine I can pretty much trust anyone. I expect to be able to trust. 'Trust is the main thing for me."

Quantitative Insights

- Survey responses about workplace expectations reveal that interns are internalizing values central to Expression Engine's "found family" culture, with multiple respondents emphasizing relational skills ("being a good team member," "collaboration," "fair treatment of others"), community-oriented values ("you have a strong community," "appropriate conduct"), and personal responsibility ("being responsible in any situation," "being present"). These responses demonstrate that interns are not just experiencing the supportive workplace culture but are actively learning and articulating the specific behaviors and values that create such an environment—suggesting they will carry these expectations into future workplaces.

Responses

- Continue to foster family-like Expression Engine traditions, like sharing thankfulness together at the end of each day.
- Create space each term for interns to reflect on their team dynamic, work on what needs improvement, and celebrate what went well.

Finding 4. Musical growth at Expression Engine is transformative, but extends beyond technical skills to include personal development.

The interview data show that interns experience significant musical growth through the program, but this growth extends far beyond simply acquiring technical skills. While many interns do develop new instrumental abilities or improve existing ones, the more profound impact is in how this musical development shapes their broader identity and capabilities. Many interns described discovering that they had greater musical potential than they previously believed, which then translated to increased confidence in other areas. The experience of teaching music to younger students particularly catalyzes growth, as it requires interns to deepen their own understanding while developing patience and communication skills. For many, the Engine has kept their passion for music alive during challenging periods of their lives, and provided a foundation for continued musical growth and exploration.

Key Themes from Qualitative Interviews

- Interns develop specific musical skills, including learning new instruments and improving their abilities.
- Teaching music to younger students drives interns to deepen their own musical knowledge.
- The program fosters a broader appreciation for music and helps sustain musical passion.
- Musical growth builds confidence that extends to other areas of life.

Interview Quotes

"Without Expression Engine, my love for music would have died."

"I started going back to violin, trying to express myself, trying to come up with melodies on my own."

"They helped forge my talent better. Improvisation was one of the main ones that boosted what I could do. It showed me I was capable of learning multiple instruments."

"I can pretty much teach myself anything and then teach someone else."

"The Engine revolves around improvisation, really."

Quantitative Insights

- Survey responses about musical skill development revealed that interns experienced the most improvement in playing instruments, while also reporting significant growth across multiple other musical areas as a result of their Expression Engine internship.

Responses

- Add intern instrument lessons back into our weekly program schedule.

- Add a music improvisation class specifically for interns.
- Explore how to offer additional opportunities for interns to schedule private lessons with staff or current and former teaching artists outside of program time.

Finding 5. Interns develop patience and flexibility through navigating challenging teaching moments.

The data reveal that many interns develop greater patience and flexibility through the challenges of working with children and teaching music. These qualities emerge as particularly important skills that transfer to many aspects of their lives. Interns frequently mentioned that working with children who learn at different paces or who may be reluctant to engage required them to develop patience they didn't previously possess. The program also places interns in situations where they need to adapt quickly, such as stepping in to lead classes they weren't prepared for or managing unexpected scenarios. These stretching moments, while difficult, have resulted in significant personal growth. The interns' development of patience and adaptability represents a key transformation in how they approach challenges both within and beyond Expression Engine.

Key Themes from Qualitative Interviews

- Working with children who learn at different paces develops patience in interns.
- Unexpected teaching situations require interns to be flexible and adaptable.
- The skills of patience and flexibility transfer to other areas of life, including family relationships and school.
- These qualities help interns manage stress and difficult situations more effectively.

Interview Quotes

"As an intern I learned to stay calm. (this helped with basic training)"

"Patience, actually…sometimes you tell a kid what to do and they don't do it"

"I think patience is one thing I've learned, like how you're being patient with things... especially when teaching. You have to be super patient, because sometimes it won't click the first time, like it will take multiple tries until you get to that point."

"Having to teach classes I know nothing about; like stepping into guitar lessons when the teacher couldn't be there... It teaches you how to improvise."

Quantitative Insights & Charts

- 100% of interns surveyed reported a growth in confidence sharing what they have learned musically, since working at Expression Engine. 9.1% reported "A Little" growth, 54.5% reported "Some" growth, and 36.4% reported "Quite a Bit" of growth (see Figure 2).

Figure 2:
Since working at Expression Engine, how much has your confidence grown in sharing what you have learned musically?

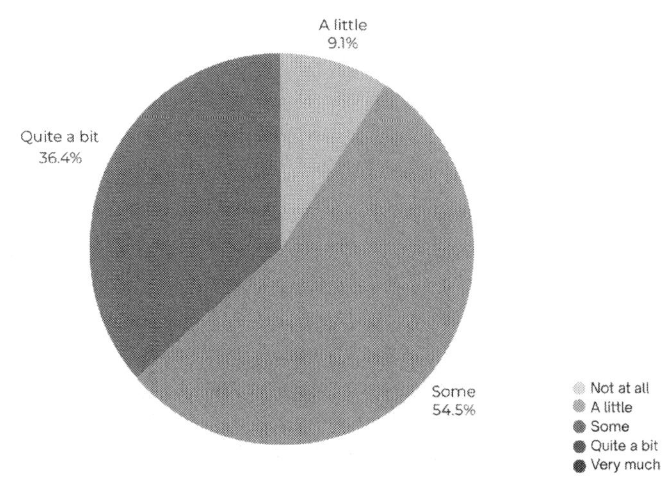

Responses

- Continue to offer interns safe, supportive opportunities to step out of their comfort zone in the classroom.
- Provide a space for interns to study and discuss what it means to lead out of your comfort zone and be a servant leader.

Finding 6. Interns serve as a critical bridge between younger students and adult staff.

The interview data reveal that interns play a unique and essential role by serving as intermediaries between the younger students and adult staff. This bridging function is possible because of the interns' position in the age hierarchy—old enough to be role models for the children but young enough that children often feel more comfortable approaching them than adult staff. Interns described how children will confide in them or seek their guidance in ways they might not with adult staff members. Additionally, interns can interpret and communicate children's needs to adult staff, creating a valuable communication channel. This bridging role appears to be recognized and valued by both the interns themselves and the organization, and it represents an important aspect of the program's effectiveness that extends beyond the personal development of the interns.

Key Themes from Qualitative Interviews

- Interns occupy a unique position between children and adult staff that enables special connections with both groups.
- Children often feel more comfortable approaching interns with questions or concerns.
- Interns can effectively translate between the needs and perspectives of children and adult staff.
- This bridging role helps interns develop communication skills across different age groups.

Interview Quotes

"I could relate to the younger students and I could help the adults understand better."

"The kids, they don't know how to word stuff as an adult should, so... [I'm] listening well to kids, because they don't always word things in the same way as an adult would, but if you really listen, you can kind of understand what they're trying to say."

"The kids sometimes rely on us interns when older staff members are either too busy or don't understand their problems as well as we do."

"There's a kid who during orchestra always looks to me to make sure she's playing her instrument right."

Quantitative Insights & Charts

- 81.8% of interns who responded to the survey reported that younger students share their ideas and questions with them either "Sometimes" or "Often" (see Figure 3).

Figure 3:
How often do younger students share their ideas and questions with you to bring to the adult staff?

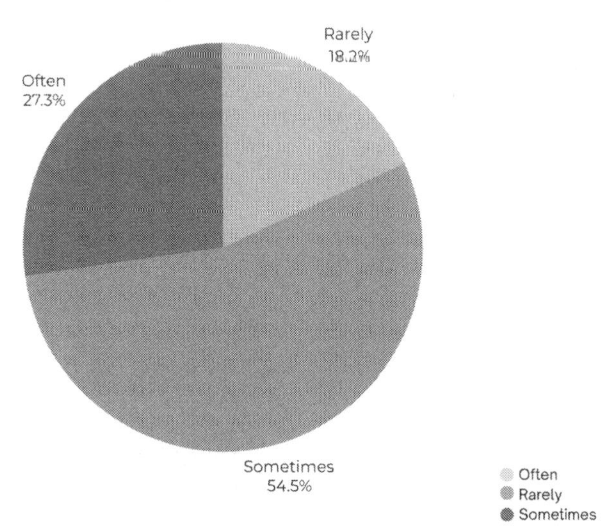

Responses

- Create a training to be held each term, to help interns grow in knowing when to step in and handle something that comes up with younger students, and when to bring in an adult.
- Add instruction about child development levels to our annual pedagogy training.

Finding 7. The program fosters significant growth in confidence and self-efficacy.

Throughout the interviews, a consistent theme emerged of interns developing greater confidence in themselves and their abilities. Many described entering the program feeling shy, insecure, or doubtful about their capabilities, only to experience a transformation in their self-perception. This increased confidence manifests in multiple ways, including greater comfort speaking in public, willingness to take initiative, and belief in their ability to learn new skills. The data suggest that this growth in confidence stems from experiences of successfully navigating challenges, receiving positive feedback, and seeing their positive impact on children. Importantly, this newfound confidence extends beyond the Expression Engine context into other areas of their lives, including school, social relationships, and future aspirations, indicating a fundamental shift in how they view themselves and their potential.

Key Themes from Qualitative Interviews

- Many interns report overcoming shyness and becoming more comfortable in social situations.
- Successfully teaching and leading activities builds confidence in abilities they didn't know they had.
- Growth in confidence extends to other areas of life, including school and family interactions.
- The program helps interns develop a stronger belief in their capability to learn new skills and face challenges.

Interview Quotes

"It's given me a lot more confidence in my abilities as a leader. I feel a lot more sure in any type of setting. I know when to question authority."

"I would say I did have like a hard time trying to speak out, but then having some leadership has given me the confidence just like speak what's on my mind - being more direct."

"I've been getting more open. Getting a lot closer to my parents."

"Before, I was really, really, really insecure, like talking with people, knowing how to talk with them, performing... [Now] I kind of see that in a way [that I'm a leader]."

Quantitative Insights & Charts

- 63.6% of interns who were surveyed reported that they felt more prepared to take brave, uncomfortable steps in their personal lives as a result of their internship (see Figure 4).

Figure 4:
As a result of your internship, how much *more* prepared do you feel to take brave, uncomfortable steps in your personal life?

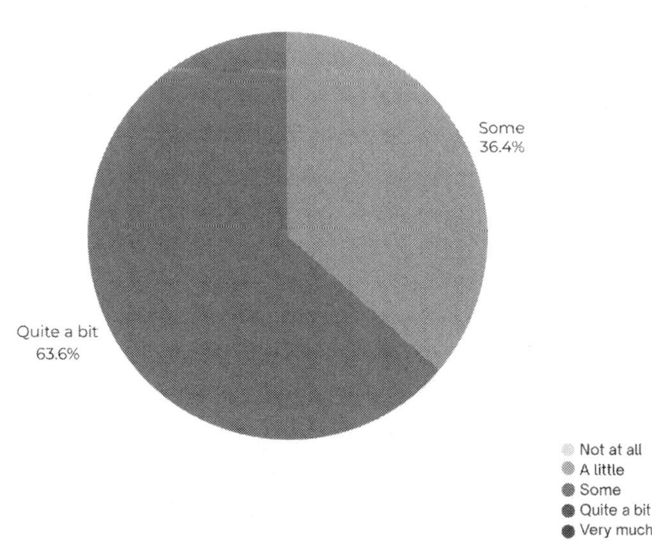

Responses

- Encourage interns to rotate leadership and co-teaching in an ensemble like bucket band, to ensure all interns get some direct experience with teaching a large group.

Finding 8. Classroom management and child development skills become lifelong tools.

The interview data show that interns develop significant skills in classroom management and child development that they view as valuable beyond their time at Expression Engine. Many interns enter the program with limited experience managing groups of children, but through both observation and hands-on practice, they develop effective strategies for engaging children, maintaining order, and promoting learning. These skills include recognizing different learning styles, adapting communication approaches, establishing appropriate boundaries, and creating environments where children feel both supported and challenged. Interns frequently mentioned that these abilities have changed their understanding of how to interact with children and have influenced their future career considerations, with several expressing interest in teaching or other child-focused professions as a result of their experience.

Key Themes from Qualitative Interviews

- Interns develop practical skills in managing groups of children and maintaining order while promoting engagement.
- They learn to recognize and adapt to different learning styles and needs among children.
- These classroom management skills transfer to other contexts where interns interact with children.
- The experience shapes interns' career interests, with several considering teaching or similar professions.

Interview Quotes

"How to manage a classroom. I feel like I know how to do that, and I know how to manage behavior [and] classroom management."

"Since they're young, I'm trying to be a role model so once they grow up to be a better person, and kind and not really not rude."

"I have to have different methods because some kids learn different than others."

"Working here has made me realize that I do want to work with kids in the future. I'd love to be a teacher someday."

Quantitative Insights & Charts

- All the interns surveyed indicated that mentoring students was "Somewhat Important" (9.1%), "Quite Important" (81.8%), or "Very Important" (9.1%) (see Figure 5).

Figure 5:
How important is mentoring younger students to you personally?

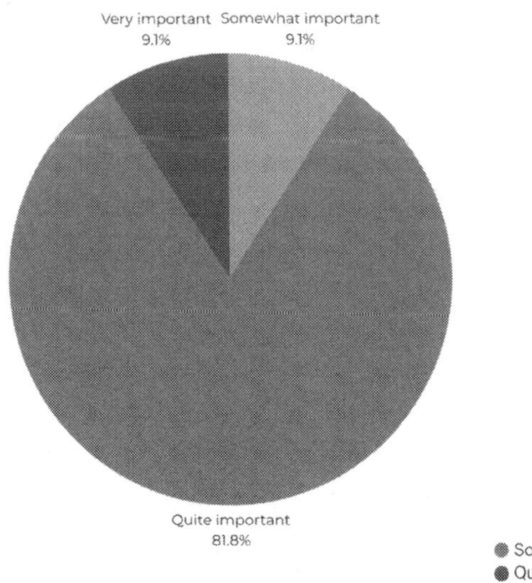

Responses

- Add another opportunity for interns to practice teaching and receive encouragement and critique in it from staff and peers.
- Explore how to partner with other education organizations to allow interns the opportunity to meet and observe different kinds of teachers in other fields besides music.

Finding 9. Interns experience personal growth through taking initiative and responsibility.

The data reveal that taking initiative and assuming responsibility are transformative aspects of the internship experience. Interns consistently described situations where they needed to step up, make decisions, or take action without being explicitly directed to do so. These moments, while sometimes uncomfortable, led to significant personal growth and development of autonomy. The program appears designed to gradually increase interns' level of responsibility, creating opportunities for them to exercise judgment and leadership. Interns described how they learned to identify needs, develop solutions, and implement them independently. This development of initiative extends beyond specific tasks to include a broader sense of ownership over their work and contribution to the organization. Many interns expressed that this aspect of the program has changed how they approach challenges and responsibilities in other areas of their lives.

Key Themes from Qualitative Interviews

- Interns develop the ability to identify needs and take action without being explicitly instructed.
- Taking responsibility for teaching or managing activities builds confidence and autonomy.
- The experience of successfully handling responsibility shapes how interns approach challenges elsewhere.
- Interns develop a greater sense of ownership over their work and contributions.

Interview Quotes

"I guess I could use guitar as an example - instead of me just telling Miss Ashe that this guitar is broken, I took it like a priority and fixed it myself, and made it a lot easier for everybody."

"There were certain times as an intern where I didn't know exactly what I was supposed to be doing, so I had to kind of take initiative myself."

"I take more leadership roles in school now."

"Being put in a leadership role to perform and teach makes me really nervous. Being responsible is the thing that I'm good at."

Quantitative Insights & Charts

- All of the interns surveyed indicated that their leadership skills had grown because of their internships at Expression Engine. Of those, 54.6% indicated that their leadership skills had grown "Quite a Bit" or "Very Much" (see Figure 6).

Figure 6:
Because of your internship at Expression Engine, how much have your leadership skills grown?

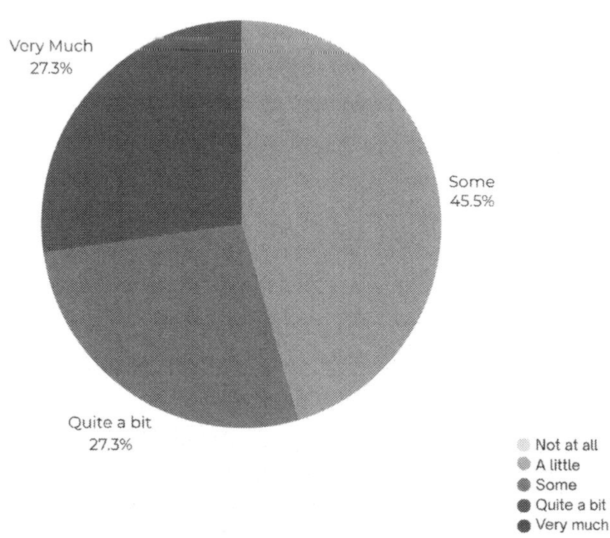

n=11

Responses

- Develop an annual leadership training for interns.
- Widen the number of job types that interns are exposed to, through more field trips and guest speakers.

Finding 10. The internship strengthens external relationships and improves home dynamics.

The interview data reveal an unexpected impact of the internship program: improved relationships outside of Expression Engine, particularly in home and family contexts. Several interns explicitly mentioned how their experience in the program has positively influenced their family dynamics and other external relationships. The skills they develop at Expression Engine—including communication, patience, emotional awareness, and conflict resolution—transfer to their interactions with family members and friends. Some interns described becoming more open with parents, taking on more responsibility at home, or applying their leadership skills in other community contexts like church. This finding suggests that the program's impact extends well beyond the immediate context of Expression Engine into the broader fabric of interns' lives, creating ripple effects that benefit not just the individual interns but also their families and communities.

Key Themes from Qualitative Interviews

- Communication and emotional skills learned at Expression Engine transfer to family relationships.
- Interns report becoming more open, responsible, and engaged in home settings.
- Leadership skills developed in the program are applied in other community contexts.
- The program appears to have a positive impact on interns' overall social integration and community involvement.

Interview Quotes

"It helps out a lot with family. Before I would have gone home and went to bed but now it helps me engage my family more. It helps out a lot recently."

"I've been getting more open. Getting a lot closer to my parents."

"I'm very bad at explaining myself... I don't know how to say it, like, when I say something, it doesn't come out the way that I want it to sound."

"Guess I'm being gentle and caring as we are influenced [by the program]. How I am at home and at school, that's what I learned from here."

Responses

- Provide interns with a personality assessment or survey during their time at Expression Engine.

Conclusion

Insights Into Impact

Based on our evaluation findings, the Student Intern Program is successfully achieving the impacts we set out to create. Our data shows that interns are becoming confident, effective leaders, with many describing a clear transformation from seeing themselves as followers to embracing leadership roles that extend beyond Expression Engine into their schools, churches, and families. The program is also developing skilled, self-assured professionals, though perhaps in ways we didn't fully anticipate. While interns certainly gain workplace competencies, what stands out most is how our "found family" culture creates a template for what they expect from future employers, potentially influencing their career choices for years to come.

The evaluation reveals that interns are becoming inspiring artist-mentors in the fullest sense. Their musical growth goes hand-in-hand with personal development, and the classroom management skills they develop become tools they carry into other areas of life. Several interns mentioned that working at Expression Engine has sparked interest in teaching careers. Additionally, our interns are indeed serving as vital bridges between younger students and adult staff, occupying a unique position that allows them to interpret and connect across age groups in ways that strengthen our entire program.

What makes these impacts particularly meaningful is how they extend beyond our walls. Interns consistently described how skills developed at Expression Engine have improved their family relationships, school performance, and community involvement. This suggests that our program is not simply developing individual leaders, but cultivating young people who carry these transformative qualities into every aspect of their lives, creating ripple effects that benefit their broader communities.

Steps Forward

In light of our findings, we plan to develop more training opportunities for our interns in the growth areas that they have identified as having significant impact in their lives. In some cases, this will simply be a formalization of reflection and conversations that already occur. In other cases, it will require exploring partnership with other organizations to provide external development opportunities for interns.

One focus will be on creating a more robust leadership development curriculum, including an annual leadership training and peer-to-peer intern mentorship opportunities. We believe that additional leadership training will give interns more tools to navigate challenges at work, home, and school.

Another focus will be on intentional investment in the "found family" culture at Expression Engine: staff will be trained in mentorship during onboarding, and we will continue to provide relaxed, social time for interns to form relationships with each other and with staff members. Alongside this, we plan to add more opportunities for interns to reflect together on their team dynamics. We think that providing this space for interns to both celebrate and problem solve together in a supportive environment will continue to strengthen the unique work culture at Expression Engine that interns value.

A third focus will be on increasing the musical training opportunities that are specifically aimed at interns: for example, adding more intern instrument lessons, and rotating leadership opportunities during Expression Engine's weekly classes and ensembles. Since teaching and playing music is such an important catalyst for growth in the lives of our interns, we plan to increase the percentage of interns' time spent in music lessons.

Alongside this, we plan to provide interns with more opportunities to practice hands-on teaching, and learn about child development and classroom management. To support this, we also plan to explore partnerships with other organizations that could allow interns to gain external training about a variety of job types, or shadow teachers outside of Expression Engine. We also hope to add a personality assessment or survey for interns during their time at Expression Engine. Because it is clear that interns' growth is not limited to their time at Expression Engine, we believe that providing both robust pedagogy training and more tools for relational growth will strengthen interns' self-understanding and versatility for whatever jobs they will pursue in the future.

Opportunities for Future Evaluation

Future evaluations could explore several promising areas that emerged from this study. Given the strong evidence that interns serve as vital bridges between younger students and adult staff, it would be valuable to examine the program's impact from the perspective of the younger students, to understand how intern mentorship affects their development and engagement. Additionally, tracking the long-term outcomes of former interns could provide insights into how their Expression Engine experience influences their career paths, leadership development, and community involvement over time. Another area worth exploring is the organizational impact of the intern program on Expression Engine's overall effectiveness, staff development, and program culture. Finally, since several findings revealed unexpected impacts, such as the influence on family relationships and the development of workplace expectations, future evaluations could take a deeper dive into these areas to better understand the mechanisms behind these transformative changes and how they might be intentionally strengthened.

APPENDIX

Qualitative Interview Protocols

Living Free

What have you learned about managing triggers and difficult situations through Living Free? Where do you draw your strength in challenging times? → How has this changed your belief in your ability to handle challenges through godly choices?

After starting Living Free, what spiritual practices are you maintaining regularly? What's been most meaningful? → How are you becoming different through these practices? How has your faith changed or grown?

Since participating in Living Free, when do you feel closest to God in your daily life? What spiritual practices bring you peace? → How has your commitment to strengthening your relationship with Christ grown?

As a result of Living Free's teaching, what have you learned about how choices affect your spiritual growth? What's been most eye-opening? → How has this shaped your understanding of your identity in Christ?

Through your time at Living Free, when do you feel most connected to others in the program? What makes those moments special? → How has your dedication to authentic relationships and community grown? What have you learned about building godly relationships through the Living Free? What aspects make the most sense now? → How has this changed your belief that healthy relationships are possible?

As a result of Living Free, how are you handling relationships with family and friends differently? What changes have been most challenging? → How are you becoming more transparent and invested in these relationships?

Because of your work with Living Free, when do you feel most confident about your future? What gives you hope? → How has your commitment to building a strong foundation for your family grown? Through Living Free, what steps are you taking toward stability in your work and finances? What progress are you most proud of? → How are you becoming more self-sufficient and responsible?

Looking ahead, what is your hope for your future and what do you believe is possible?

Transformation Project

What have you learned that it means to be a child of God through the Transformation Project? How has your outlook on your circumstances changed because of your participation with TP? → How has this understanding transformed the way you see your own worth?

What have you learned about the impact that life-controlling issues have had on your life? → How has your thinking changed about the choices you make because of what you've learned in the TP?

What have you discovered about using the Bible in your daily life? When do you find yourself turning to scripture compared to before? → How has this changed what you believe about God's involvement in your life?

What spiritual practices have you implemented as a result of your participation in the TP? What daily habits have you developed as a result of participating in the TP? → How are you showing up for life differently because of your participation in the TP?

What is the toughest part of applying the principles you've learned in the TP? → How has working on making those a part of your life, even though they have been difficult to do, helped you to grow and you navigate challenges in your life?

What is your most significant accomplishment due to your new understanding of your identity in Christ? What is the most significant change you see? What is the change you still want to see that you haven't yet seen in your life? → How are you applying these skills in other parts of your life and making these habits of life for you?

What do you feel is the most exciting part of what you've learned with TP? → How have those things made you more committed to your faith?

What is the most challenging or frustrating part of walking out your faith? What moments have tested your commitment the most? → How do you stay engaged with your faith when you want to go back to your old life or ways?

What thing or activity are you dedicated to now that you hadn't considered before the TP? → What draws you to continue with this? How has that enhanced your life?

The Knoble

Know → Believe (AWAKEN) Since becoming a member of The Knoble, what have you learned about your role as an FSP in disrupting human crime? What aspects still feel challenging about disrupting Human Crime through your role? → How has this understanding changed what you embrace as important in your work?

Feel → Love (AWAKEN) What has been the most impactful part of being a member of The Knoble? → How has that influenced your dedication to your role?

Do → Become (AWAKEN) Since joining The Knoble, what have you implemented in your life and work to combat Human Crime? What are some barriers to taking actionable steps to combat Human Crime? → How does applying what you have learned from The Knoble enhance your influence at work?

Know → Believe (EQUIP) What have you learned about detecting and reporting human crimes since you've been a member of The Knoble? When do you still struggle to see yourself as capable? → How has this affected your confidence in your ability to create meaningful change in the world?

Do → Become (EQUIP) "What specific actions are you taking to fight exploitation now that you're part of The Knoble? How has becoming an advocate through The Knoble changed who you are as a professional?"

Feel → Love (EQUIP) What do you find most hopeful when you learn about new ways to detect and prevent human crime? What do you find discouraging as you think about the current state of detection and prevention in your financial institution? → How has this growing awareness changed your heart for the work and its importance?'

Know → Believe (MOBILIZE) What have you learned from using your professional skills to fight human crime? → How have these experiences shaped the way you think about taking action to combat human crime?

Do → Become (MOBILIZE) In what ways have you incorporated Human Crime fighting into your daily work since being a member of The Knoble? → How have these efforts stretched you to grow in your effectiveness and influence as a [Job Title]?

Feel → Love (MOBILIZE) Can you share a time when fighting Human Crime felt especially rewarding? How about a time when it was particularly challenging? → How have these feelings/experiences affected your heart for fighting Human Crime?

green | spaces

Through your Build It Green training, what specific green building skills have you gained that you didn't have before? What aspects still challenge you? → How has acquiring these skills changed your belief in your ability to improve people's lives through this work?

What skill was the most difficult to acquire for you during your Build It Green training? How did gaining that skill stretch or enable you to handle other challenges in your life?

What professional skills have you learned through BIG - things like communication, teamwork, or handling conflict? How has the BIG program caused you to take ownership of other areas in your life? What has been your greatest achievement or "win" in your role as a BIG team member? What obstacles did you have to overcome? → How have you been able to apply this achieving mindset at home or in other responsibilities?

How has your self-confidence changed through this program? When do you still struggle with self-doubt? → How has this experience strengthened your commitment to improving your circumstances?

When do you feel most energized or excited by this work? When do you feel most discouraged? → What keeps you passionate and committed to this work even during the challenging times?

What challenges have you faced in staying committed to this program? What aspects of the requirements still test your persistence? → How has overcoming these challenges changed your approach to making and keeping commitments in other areas of your life?

What feels most rewarding about serving your community through Build It Green? What aspects still feel challenging? → How has this connection helped you develop a passion for helping others?

What have you discovered about accessing resources and support through the BIG network? Can you give me a specific example of a resource you've learned about or used? → How has this changed your view of your role in the broader green building community?

Looking ahead for the next year or two, in what ways do you see this program setting you up for success? What changes do you hope to see in your work and family life as a result of BIG?

Chattanooga Room in the Inn

Since being in the program, what have you come to understand about employment and stable income? What still seems confusing or hard to understand? → How has that changed how you see your own potential and opportunity to grow in your career? (Know-Believe)

What knowledge have you been applying from what you've learned in programming that assists in maintaining stable housing? → How have your priorities changed? (Do-Become)

What is the most frustrating aspect of maintaining housing? How has this program helped you remain dedicated to maintaining stability in housing? (Feel-Love)

What have you discovered during your time in this program that helps you understand what it means for your financial future? How has this affected the way you think about spending and saving money? (Know-Believe)

What steps are you taking from the program to improve your financial decision making? → How are you developing habits to maintain financial stability? In what ways are you still struggling to make it a part of your lifestyle? (Do-Become)

What about being in the program has made you feel more excited (or even more comfortable) about financial stability than you used to? What makes you excited about financial stability? → How has this program helped you stay committed to healthy financial practices? (Feel-Love)
Since participating in the program, what have you learned about taking care of your physical and mental health? → How has that made a difference in the way you see the role you play in your own mental and physical health?

What have you been doing differently since the program to uphold your physical and mental well being? What's gone well? What has been really hard to do? → How are you taking ownership and prioritizing your health differently than you used to before the program? (Do-Become)

What do you find more enjoyable now than you used to about being involved in your child's academic success? How has your engagement between school and child changed since being part of this program? (Feel- Love)

How do you hope your experience with Chattanooga Room in the Inn will have made a lasting difference in your life journey? → What strengths and resources have you discovered in yourself through this program that will help you create that future?

CHATT Foundation

(Know → Believe) Through your experience with CHATT Foundation, what have you learned about services like showers, laundry, and mail? What aspects of accessing these services are still unclear? → How has understanding these services changed your belief in your ability to meet your basic needs?

(Do → Become) Because of CHATT Foundation's support, what steps have you taken to build connections with different support services? What challenges have you faced in maintaining these connections? → How have these relationships changed the way you approach getting help?

(Feel → Love) As a result of working with CHATT Foundation, how do you feel about your progress toward stable housing? What fears or worries do you still have about this journey? → How has this process strengthened your commitment to achieving your housing goals?

(Do → Become) Since coming to CHATT Foundation, what new routines have you developed in using services like showers and laundry? What makes it difficult to use these services regularly? → How has having these basic needs met helped you become more stable in your daily life?

(Know → Believe) Through CHATT Foundation's programs, what have you discovered about different support services in our community? What remains confusing about how these services can work together for you? → How has this changed your view about accepting help from others?

(Do → ecome) With CHATT Foundation's assistance, what specific actions have you taken toward finding stable housing or employment? What parts of your stability plan have been hardest to implement? → How has your approach to planning for your future changed?

(Feel → Love) Through your involvement with CHATT Foundation's services, how has having your basic needs met affected your daily stress levels? What situations still make you feel uncertain or anxious? → How has this experience deepened your commitment to caring for yourself?

(Feel → Love) Since engaging with CHATT Foundation, how do you feel about the relationships in your life (family, friends, social programs) now compared to before? What emotions come up when you think about asking for help? → How has this changed your dedication to staying connected with your support system?

(Know → Believe) Through CHATT Foundation's programs, what have you learned about the path to stable housing through our programs? What parts of the housing process still feel overwhelming? → How has this information changed your belief in what's possible for your future?

Scenic City Women's Network

(Know → Believe) What were the key insights about faith-based leadership that stood out to you from the Symposium? What aspects would you like to learn more about? → How did the symposium make a difference in how you think about your own leadership?

(Know → Believe) What do you think is most important for leaders like you to learn about to be better leaders? What do you see as the "miss" in leadership training within the Chattanooga area? → How would filling these gaps change how local Christian leaders view their role?

(Know → Believe) What key principles of Biblical business leadership do you feel are most crucial to understand? What aspects seem most challenging to grasp? → How might developing a deeper understanding of these leadership principles change the mindset or outlook of people who are in leadership?

(Do → Become) What practices or ideas from the Symposium have you tried to implement in your organization? What additional support would help you be more successful? → How do you hope to develop as a leader with more training?

(Do → Become) What specific skills do you feel Christian business leaders in Chattanooga most need to develop? What's currently missing from available training? → In what ways would strengthening these skills transform local leadership?

(Do → Become) Based on your Symposium experience, what practical tools or resources would be most helpful in your leadership journey? → How would having these resources change the kind of leader you're becoming?

(Fee → Love) What aspects of faith-based leadership discussed at the Symposium excited you most? What concerns or anxieties came up for you? → How has this experience deepened your commitment to leading from a Biblical perspective?

(Feel → Love) What about creating a Kingdom-focused organizational culture energizes you most? What feels most daunting? → How has your heart for Biblical leadership grown through this experience? How does the heart of leaders in Chattanooga need to grow and develop to be more committed to the right kinds of things.

(Feel → Love) What areas of Christian leadership do you feel most passionate about developing further? What support would help you grow in these areas? → What keeps you dedicated to this journey even when it's challenging? What do people need to be able to sustain their commitment for the things that matter most?

East Lake Expression Engine

What new skills have you developed as an intern at Expression Engine? When have you surprised yourself by handling situations differently because of your internship experience? What have been the toughest parts of the job for you to do? → In what ways has this role shaped you into a different kind of leader than you initially imagined? (Do → Become)

What key lessons about leadership have you learned as an intern at Expression Engine? → How has what you have learned changed how you see yourself and your potential as a leader? (Know → Believe)

What moments during your internship have stretched you the most as you step into leadership? → How have you grown through these stretching moments at Expression Engine? (Do → Become)

Where do you feel more confident since you have been an intern? Where do you still feel overwhelmed or frustrated as an intern? How has this impacted your heart for the kids over time? (Feel → Love)

What about music or playing an instrument have you learned since becoming an intern? Where do you still lack confidence in your knowledge as a musician? → How has your growth as a musician influenced your beliefs about being both an artist and mentor? (Know → Believe)

What new interests have you discovered as a result of being an intern at the Engine? What are you more passionate about? Have you discovered unexpected struggles as a result of being an intern? What are they? (Feel → Love)

How have you grown in your mentorship and education skills? How does your role as an intern serve as a bridge between younger students and adult staff? How has this changed how you communicate with both kids and adults? (Do → Become)

Since becoming an intern, what have you discovered about what it means to have a healthy workplace environment? → How has this influenced your expectations for your future career? (Know → Believe)

What makes you feel excited or encouraged in your work? How does this keep you engaged in the job? How has this impacted you in other areas of your life? (Feel → Love)

Made in the USA
Columbia, SC
01 July 2025